Ernest George Ravenstein, Arthur Silva White

The Development of Africa

Ernest George Ravenstein, Arthur Silva White

The Development of Africa

ISBN/EAN: 9783744754859

Printed in Europe, USA, Canada, Australia, Japan

Cover: Foto ©Suzi / pixelio.de

More available books at **www.hansebooks.com**

THE
DEVELOPMENT OF AFRICA.

BY

ARTHUR SILVA WHITE,
SECRETARY TO THE ROYAL SCOTTISH GEOGRAPHICAL SOCIETY; EDITOR OF THE
"SCOTTISH GEOGRAPHICAL MAGAZINE;" FELLOW OF THE
ROYAL SOCIETY OF EDINBURGH, ETC.

ILLUSTRATED WITH A SET OF FOURTEEN MAPS
SPECIALLY DESIGNED BY
E. G. RAVENSTEIN, F.R.G.S.

LONDON:
GEORGE PHILIP & SON, 32 FLEET STREET;
LIVERPOOL: 45 TO 51 SOUTH CASTLE STREET.
1890.

PREFACE.

THE awakening of Africa to a new life is one of the most notable events of our times. In consequence of its recognition as a factor in international politics, the continent has assumed a position which, though imperfectly understood, is not the less characteristic and definite.

This result is due to the combined action of Europe. We must assume that the European Powers in Africa have accepted their self-imposed and responsible task of reclaiming the continent with a full knowledge of its extent and difficulty. The development of Africa, however, if it is to be profitable to those who have undertaken it, and not merely a fetish for philanthropic parade, involves far more than blind enthusiasts would have us to believe. It is one of the colonial problems of the next century. The factors that compose it are many and varied, and, it must be confessed, appear to be scarcely known to the majority of those who without hesitation register their vote in favour of unlimited territorial acquisitions. We have been accustomed to enter upon African campaigns with a light heart, neither reckoning the cost nor foreseeing the end; and the experience thereby gained has been dearly bought. Surely, therefore, the time has come when we should take into our councils those whose special knowledge fits them to advise or control?

The African Question is in the main a geographical problem. In its initial stage—the conquest and development of African lands—we have to deal not so much with political as with geographical conditions. It is only after the latter are understood that we can effectually control the former. Although not sufficiently competent myself to treat this geographical problem in a manner that might be regarded as authoritative, I have attempted to define the outlines of an inquiry into the subject.

From an examination of the physical and political phenomena of Africa I have sought to deduce the general laws that should govern its development. Each phase of my subject has been made to illustrate its practical bearing. Thus, from a survey of the mountains, lakes, and rivers of Africa, we discover the lines of least physical resistance to the migrations of men; whilst the consideration of political relations assists us in understanding the movements of commerce. Again, it is necessary for us to know the climatic conditions of the various regions before we are in a position to judge of their suitability for commercial enterprise or as European colonial settlements. Upon the distinctive character and resources of those regions must depend the nature and direction of their political development.

The plan of the book has been to proceed step by step, as far as possible in natural sequence, and to build up Africa under the eyes of the reader, so to speak. Within reasonable limits, and not forgetting the due proportion of their component parts, I have endeavoured to give complete pictures of Africa, by dealing successively with the various aspects under which the continent is known to Europe. I travel again and again over the same ground, but each stage of the survey is undertaken with a different object in view. In the treatment of detail I have proceeded from the general to the particular, every fresh departure being marked by a closer inspection.

The book has been written to meet the requirements of that somewhat mythical and exacting personage, the general reader. Those who are well versed in the geography of Africa may find it deficient in detail, but even to them it may perhaps prove suggestive and profitable.

Mr. E. G. Ravenstein has specially designed a very complete series of maps to accompany the volume; and I am greatly indebted to him, not only for the care he has bestowed on these maps, but also for his assistance in the revision of the text. It is scarcely necessary to add that Mr. Ravenstein's maps, embodying the original researches of a lifetime, are a valuable contribution to the cartography of Africa. By a study of them the reader will not only be assisted in understanding the text, but will also discover a vast amount of detail ignored in my descriptions. Mr. Ravenstein has himself supplied a Note at the end of the volume, discussing the *data* upon which his maps have been constructed.

Finally, it gives me great pleasure to acknowledge the generous co-operation of my publishers.

A. S. W.

EDINBURGH, *October* 1890.

CONTENTS.

CHAPTER I.

A BIRD'S-EYE VIEW.

Preliminary survey of the continent—Its geological and physical structure—Oceanic and inland drainage-basins—Coincidence of political settlement with Oceanic drainage-areas . . . 1

CHAPTER II.

MOUNTAINS, LAKES, AND RIVERS.

Geographical distribution of the chief mountain-systems, and consequent development of the great river-systems, in relation to accessibility from the sea and internal communications . . 17

CHAPTER III.

CLIMATE AND COGNATE PHENOMENA.

Distribution of temperature—Actual temperatures—Distribution of atmospheric pressure, and prevailing winds—Annual rainfall—Distribution of soils—Zones of vegetation—Distribution of animals—Classification of climates—Acclimatisation . . 51

CHAPTER IV.

THE INDIGENOUS POPULATIONS.

General considerations—Linguistic groups and their geographical distribution—Characteristics of Negroes and of native life—Survey of the indigenous populations: their mental, moral, and material culture; their political organisations and social development—Capacity of the Negro for developing higher forms of culture—Non-resistance, from the comparative absence of political cohesion in Bantu Africa, against the European domination—Native rights and European responsibilities . . 85

CHAPTER V.

ISLAM AND CHRISTIANITY.

Historical sketch of the progress of Islam and the extension of Arab influence—The border-land of Islam in the south—Signs of the times—Historical sketch of the progress of Christian missions—Results of missionary enterprise—Methods of Mohammedan propagandism and Arab rule, as compared with those adopted by Christian missions and European rule: in their effect upon the Pagan populations—Conclusions 129

CHAPTER VI.

THE TRAFFIC IN SLAVES.

The sources, conditions, and extent of the Slave Trade—Discussion of remedial measures 161

CHAPTER VII.

PROGRESS OF EXPLORATION.

Historical sketch of the progress of discovery and of exploratory work in Africa—Limits to our present knowledge—The task of the future, its probable direction, and the spirit in which it should be undertaken 183

CHAPTER VIII.

COMMERCIAL RESOURCES.

Progress of exploitation—Commerce, the most important initial factor in African politics—Commercial supremacy rather than empire the underlying motive of European enterprise—The reign of commerce—The value of African lands—Geographical distribution of products, and the movements of commerce—Geographical distribution of ivory—Coincidence of slave-routes with trade-routes, ivory being the principal article of export—The liquor-traffic—The Labour Problem—Colonisation—Chartered companies—"Robber-economy"—Honesty the best policy 217

CHAPTER IX.

THE EUROPEAN DOMINATION.

Relative absence of native political rule—Survey of the European colonies, protectorates, and spheres of influence—The political situation—Comparative absence of effective occupation by the European Powers—Obstacles to European political settlement not necessarily insuperable, but limitations to be observed . 249

CHAPTER X.

POLITICAL PARTITION.

Cause and effect—Methods—Definitions—The Berlin Conference of 1884-85—Territorial boundaries in Africa before the Conference, and those settled at or immediately after the Conference—Progress of the partition of Africa—Diplomatic negotiations, treaties, conventions, &c.—Fixed boundaries—Undefined territorial limits 279

CHAPTER XI.

SUMMARY AND CONCLUSIONS.

General principles underlying the development of Africa along natural lines, derived from an examination of the various aspects under which the continent is known to Europe at the present day 311

NOTES ON THE MAPS, BY E. G. RAVENSTEIN, F.R.G.S. 323

INDEX .   . . 333

LIST OF MAPS

BY

E. G. RAVENSTEIN, F.R.G.S.

—◆◆—

HEIGHT OF LAND (Contoured Map) .	PLATE I.
RIVER-BASINS AND OCEAN CURRENTS	,, II.
MEAN ANNUAL TEMPERATURES . .	,, III.
MEAN ANNUAL RANGE OF TEMPERATURE .	,, IV.
ANNUAL RAINFALL	,, V.
GEOLOGICAL SKETCH .	,, VI.
ZONES OF VEGETATION .	,, VII.
COMMERCIAL PRODUCTS .	,, VIII.
DENSITY OF POPULATION .	,, IX.
LANGUAGES	,, X.
RELIGIONS, AND MISSIONARY STATIONS .	,, XI.
PROGRESS OF EXPLORATION	,, XII.
POLITICAL PARTITION .	,, XIII.
FORMS OF GOVERNMENT	,, XIV.

CHAPTER I.

A BIRD'S-EYE VIEW.

PRELIMINARY SURVEY OF THE CONTINENT—ITS GEOLOGICAL AND PHYSICAL STRUCTURE—OCEANIC AND INLAND DRAINAGE-BASINS—COINCIDENCE OF POLITICAL SETTLEMENT WITH OCEANIC DRAINAGE-AREAS.

MAPS.

CONTOURED MAP .	. *Plate* I.
RIVER-BASINS, &c. .	,, II.
GEOLOGICAL SKETCH .	,, VI.

A

A BIRD'S-EYE VIEW.

AFRICA is the Pariah of Continents. Nature, whilst lavishing on her the most bounteous gifts, has, at the same time, imposed certain barriers and restrictions to their enjoyment which hamper no other continent. Although Egypt and the Mediterranean Littoral saw the dawn of the earliest civilisation, circumstances, chiefly of a geographical character, have been against the development of Africa. Hence it has happened that, at the present day, we have been called upon to re-discover the continent and to exploit its natural resources. *The Pariah Continent.*

We are told that Africa is a continental area of immense antiquity, a large portion of it being built up of rocks belonging to Archaean, Palaeozoic, and early Mesozoic times. These, it is true, are geological terms that may fail to convince the lay reader. Should, however, any further proof of the extreme antiquity of the continent be required, it is afforded by the singular uniformity and simplicity of its coast-line. Therein lies a phenomenon that at once arrests attention. *Its geological antiquity.*

Geologists regard as the continental plateau, not only the great mass of the dry land, but also its extension under the sea to a depth of one thousand fathoms. Now, this so-called continental plateau very closely corresponds in its direction with the present trend of the coast-line on the east, the south, the west, and the north-west. The dry land of Africa, in brief, occupies almost the entire area of the continental plateau. The coast-line shows a general absence of large *Continental plateau.*

Absence of gulfs, &c. estuaries, deep bays, narrow gulfs, firths and fiords, all of which are such characteristic features of the much younger coast-line of North-Western Europe. We miss also the graceful peninsular forms which differentiate the continent of Eurasia. Hence it is that, though Africa is three times greater in area than Europe, its coast-line measures only about 17,700 miles, whilst that of Europe is over 2000 miles longer.

This remarkable absence of bays and gulfs in Africa, or of any large indentations in its coast-line, is explained by the washings of the continent—the immense amount of detritus brought down by the rivers—having, in the course of ages, gradually filled them up. The Gulf of Guinea, so called, is not a true gulf; while the Gulf of Aden and the Red Sea, with which it communicates, belong as much to Asia as to Africa: they simply separate the two continents, and constitute Africa an immense island—for the Suez Canal, 78 miles in length, gives it an *ipso facto* existence as such. Only in the Mediterranean, in the ancient Syrtes, do we recognise something like a true gulf. To the south of this small gulf, and, indeed, at many localities along the shores of the Mediterranean and the Red Sea, are actual depressions below the sea-level, which, at some remote period, must have been the heads of gulfs and straits that have gradually disappeared as the land was elevated: raised beaches, far inland, now mark spots upon which the sea once broke in waves.

Geological systems. Of geological systems in Africa very little need be said. All the greater divisions are represented; but it is to be noted that Archæan, Palæozoic, and Mesozoic strata occupy the major portion of the surface. Rocks of later Mesozoic age extend over large tracts in the northern portion of the continent, while Tertiary deposits are similarly developed across wide regions which drain towards the Mediterranean.

The West Coast—in contradistinction to the North and East Coasts—has shown a remarkable persistency throughout an immense lapse of time, for it seems to have been outlined as far back as in the Palæozoic era; and the general distribution of rocks of this age and of the older Archæan schists throughout the continent would appear to indicate that in Palæozoic times the major portion of what is now land was then under water. Numerous small islands composed of Archæan rocks must in those times have dotted this sea, not only on the West Coast, but also along the main continental axis and elsewhere. In Mesozoic times, the land in the west and in the south and east had considerably increased in extent; but vast areas in the Interior would appear to have been occupied by shallow seas. Within those areas we now find: in Northern Africa, Jurassic and Cretaceous, and in Southern and Central Africa, Triassic strata. The major portion of the continent would thus appear to have been dry land after Mesozoic times. In late Mesozoic times considerable volcanic outpourings took place in Eastern Africa; and it is probable that these volcanic eruptions were connected with the movement that resulted in the intensification of the main continental axis—that large backbone of elevated land which traverses the continent in a N.E.–S.W. direction—and in the accompanying deformations of the earth's crust along the tract within which we now find the great lakes. The only deposits of Quaternary and later age we need refer to here are the enormous alluvial accumulations met with along the courses of the principal rivers and their tributaries, and the drifting sands which overspread such wide regions in the desiccated areas of Northern Africa. *Geological systems.*

In its general configuration, Africa conforms to the continental type. Its highest elevations are found, in accordance with the general law, on that side which faces the deepest *Conformity to continental type.*

sea; next the Indian Ocean. Its land sculpture is due principally to the action of denudation, guided and controlled by the geological character and structure of the rocks.

Characteristic physical features.
We have, then, these characteristic physical features to start with: that the dry land of Africa occupies the greater portion of the continental plateau, and that the shore-line is almost without any great indentations. This absence of spacious bays and protected roadsteads has, it is evident, played an important part in the political development of Africa. The plateau character of the continent has, in like manner, been the means of excluding European enterprise from the interior lands, and has constituted Africa the outcast she now is.

Coastal zone.
From the abysmal depths of the surrounding seas the continent rises by terrace upon terrace. A narrow coastal zone, from 100 to 300 miles in width, and not exceeding, say, 600 feet in elevation, girdles the greater part of the continent. Here the seafaring nations of Europe have timorously planted their colonies, for the expansion of which a coast-line as a base is so absolutely essential. This coastal zone penetrates most deeply into the Mediterranean lands, to the east of the Algerian highlands, into the Western Sahara, and along the valleys of the Lower Niger and of other large rivers.

Inland plateau.
The great inland plateau rises abruptly from the coastal belt, for the most part step-like, in a succession of terraces, its highest elevations being attained in the north-east. As this vast inland plateau, varying between 600 and 3000 feet in elevation above the sea-level, composes the greater part of Africa, and includes very many subsidiary plateaus, it may perhaps be convenient to distinguish it from its component parts by applying to it the term I have already used in its strict geological sense—that of the continental plateau.

It is, however, to be observed that the more we learn of Northern Africa, particularly of the Saharan regions, the less we observe the permanence of the plateau type, though in the southern half of Africa it is well defined.

The main axis of this continental plateau, as we shall henceforth call it, extends like a backbone in a S.W.—N.E. direction from the South-West Coast to the shores of the Red Sea, near which we find its most important nucleus, the volcanic mountain region of Abyssinia. From this main axis three subsidiary axes* strike transversely, like ribs, in a north-westerly direction: one follows the shores of the Red Sea, separating them from the basin of the Nile; another runs parallel to the West Coast, more or less continuously; and the third takes a middle direction, dividing the catchment-basins of the Nile and Congo, and stretching a mighty arm, as it were, across the Sahara to within a comparatively short distance of the Mediterranean.

Continental axis.

The mean altitude of Africa, taken roughly at 2000 feet, conforms very nearly to the mean elevation of the land of the globe. Africa may, therefore, be regarded as a plateau of moderate elevation. Its mean altitude, however, is very greatly exceeded by that of Asia. As far as is known, its highest summits are reached in Kénia, which lies on the Equator, and in Kilima-njaro, a little to the south. The latter is estimated to be 19,680 feet above the sea-level, whilst the former cannot be much under. Mr. Stanley has quite recently (1889) discovered in the Ruwenzori group, situated in the source-region of the Nile, snow-clad peaks which cannot be much under 19,000 feet in elevation. High mountains occur also in South Africa, in Abyssinia, on the Guinea coast, in Morocco, and in the Sahara, the enumeration of which is here unnecessary, because later on we shall

Elevation of land masses.

---

* The contours selected for the map illustrating this chapter may not, however, distinctly bring out these transverse subsidiary axes of the continent.

encounter them again. At present we are concerned only with distributions and generalisations.

General laws of structure.

From this distribution of the great mountain-systems of Africa, it will be seen that they do not exactly follow the law that holds good in regard to other continents: that the main continental axis coincides with its greatest length; although, if we regard the subsidiary axes above referred to, we see in them only a variation of this physical law. There is another general law, which, on the other hand, is well exemplified in Africa: that the chief island masses occur to the south and east of continents. Thus, we find Madagascar—which at one time, however remote, formed part of the mainland—situated, in accordance with this law, to the south and east. Madagascar itself, built up in terraces just like the parent mass, is, it is true, the only African island of any size. In the Gulf of Guinea there are a few small volcanic islands, stretching in a south-westerly direction from Mount Camarons; and small groups of volcanic islands appear off the North-West Coast; but they are comparatively insignificant.

Vast size of Africa.

It is difficult to realise the immense size of Africa. Its simplicity of form imposes upon the mind of the casual observer. Many people, in fact, regard it as a country, and not as a large continent. Yet, if we seek its continental centre, or that point in the Interior which is most remote from all the surrounding coasts, we find that, in order to reach it, we should require to travel a distance of over 1100 miles. Only in Asia, whose continental centre is as remote as 1600 miles, should we require to travel a greater distance; but then Asia is one-third larger than Africa.

Emboss- ment.

The exterior margins of the broad plateaus of Africa will generally be found, as in those of other continents, to be higher than their central portions, thus presenting toward the sea a sort of natural rampart. This peculiar emboss-

ment of the continent, whilst determining its river-systems,
has formed one of the most hostile impediments in regard
to the accessibility of the interior lands. The rivers and   Cataracts.
lakes are, of course, the true natural highways; but all the
large rivers, not only in their upper, but also in their middle
and lower courses, where they break through the margins
of the plateaus, have, in consequence, their beds filled with
all sorts of rocky obstructions; and so great is their inclina-
tion that the accelerated waters become rapids, or break
into cataracts, or fall down sheer heights, in their eager
passage to the sea. And unfortunately, from the fact of the
inland or continental plateau approaching so near to the
coasts, all the great rivers have their navigation obstructed
at relatively short distances from their mouths. Serious
obstacles are thus placed in the way of free commercial
intercourse between Inner Africa and the outside world.

In order better to realise the physical relief of Africa,   Drainage-areas.
let us endeavour to picture the disposition of its oceanic
and inland drainage-basins,* thus illustrating in the most
forcible manner possible the chief slopes of the continent
towards the surrounding seas, or into those enclosed basins
whose drainage-waters never reach the Ocean at all. Of
these catchment-basins, by far the most important is that
draining into the Atlantic Ocean. In this respect Africa
agrees with Europe and the Americas: about half of the
land of the globe drains into the Atlantic.

The following are the drainage-areas of Africa:—

  1. Atlantic Ocean.
  2. Mediterranean Sea.
  3. Indian Ocean.
     (*a.*) Madagascar.

---

* By drainage-basins I refer to *surface* drainage only,—more correctly speaking, catchment-basins.

4. Three Inland drainage-areas:—
   (*a.*) Sahara Desert.
   (*b.*) Kalahari Desert.
   (*c.*) Eastern Abyssinia.

Oceanic drainage basins.

By consulting the map, it will be seen at a glance how greatly the Atlantic Ocean drainage-area is in excess of the other drainage-areas of the African continent. It includes, of course, the mighty river-systems of the Niger and Congo, besides all the river-basins of the West Coast. The Congo alone discharges as great a volume of water as probably all the rivers of Africa taken together, the Niger in this respect coming next, and the dissipated Nile taking only a fourth place. The Nile, originating below the Equator, is the only river of importance in the Mediterranean drainage-basin, its magnificent system extending like a tongue far into the interior of Africa. The Indian Ocean drainage-basin includes, besides Madagascar, all the rivers of the East Coast, of which the Zambezi and Limpopo are the chief, from the Cape up to the Eastern Horn.

Enclosed basins.

Of the enclosed basins, or those basins having a self-contained hydrographical system, by far the most extensive is that of the Sahara, which in the south impinges on the Sûdan. Lake Tsad lies in a trough, but not by any means, as was at one time supposed, in the lowest part of the Saharan plateau. Besides the small enclosed basin between the Abyssinian highlands and the sea, in which there are restricted areas of absolute depression, there is a third, surrounding the Kalahari desert and holding Lake N'gami. These are all more or less desert or riverless regions, in which the annual rainfall is under five or ten inches; and the explanation of their origin, though partly due to the configuration of the land, will be given when we come to consider the meteorological conditions of Africa.

If we compare the chief rivers of Africa with the great

rivers of the world, the Congo will be found to rank second River-systems. only to the Amazons in those respects which constitute an important river, namely, in point of drainage-area and annual discharge of water. The fact of their mouths being situated on or near the Equator, and their catchment-basins receiving in consequence an excessive rainfall, sufficiently accounts for their abnormal volumes of discharge. But in regard to mere length, the Congo is exceeded by six of the great rivers of the world. Of these, the Mississippi-Missouri heads the list with a course of 4192 miles, and the Nile comes next with 4018 miles (though some day it may establish even a closer contest). In its lengthy course through desert lands the Nile, however, loses more water by evaporation than any other river of the same or of much lesser importance; hence the comparatively small volume of its discharge.

The discharge of a river may, roughly speaking, be said Discharge of rivers. to equal the excess of rainfall over evaporation in its basin. The usual discharge of Tropical or sub-Tropical rivers is calculated by Dr. John Murray to be about one-fifth of the rainfall on the river's basin; but the Nile discharges only about one-thirty-seventh. European rivers discharge between one-third and one-fourth of the rainfall on their catchment-basins.

The lakes of Africa, which play so important a part in Lakes. the accessibility of the continent, conform to the general law as regards the salinity or freshness of their waters; that is to say, those not provided with outlets have, for the most part, salt or brackish water, unless submarine outlets carry off the salts held in solution. Lakes thus fall under two comprehensive divisions.

All the great lakes of Africa, except Tsad, are situated along the continental axis, in areas of relative depression, or along the line of great faults or fractures in the earth's crust.

Lakes. Though most of them fluctuate in level, they are all very different in character to lakes like Tsad and N'gami, which, being situated in low, swampy ground, expand and contract enormously, in accordance with the seasons. Another class of lake is to be found in those expansions of a river's course in low or "spongy" ground, such as are common in the basin of the Congo. But all of these lakes are formed in areas of relative depression, and are, therefore, to be again differentiated from the lakelets or marshes bordering the shores of the Mediterranean and Red Seas, where there are small areas of absolute depression—that is to say, localities lying below the sea-level. One might go on multiplying instances of dissimilarity in the characteristics of the various lakes of Africa, but our present purpose has been served in what has already been said in regard to them.

Coincidence of political settlement with drainage-areas. We have completed our preliminary survey of the continent in its orographical and hydrographical relations—sketched, it is true, in broad outlines; but before proceeding in the next chapter to fill in details, attention should be directed to a very striking fact. It will be found, on comparing the maps, that what may be called political settlement in Africa has coincided very closely with the oceanic drainage-areas, while the inland drainage-areas have been practically deserted by man, as they have been paralysed by Nature.

Physical obstacles against political expansion. This phenomenon illustrates in a very lucid manner how political settlement is controlled by physical obstacles. In Africa it has, in fact, after first finding a footing on the coasts, endeavoured to penetrate into the Interior by the most natural highways—those afforded by the great river-systems. Bearing this parallel in mind, we have at once some explanation of the fact that, for instance, the Mediterranean Littoral has from time immemorial been European rather than African. The Sahara desert has proved an impassable barrier against any considerable political expansion southwards.

In practical politics, therefore, Africa may be said to be limited on the north by the Sahara-Mediterranean waterparting. Elsewhere we shall show how, in a far greater degree, physical obstacles of one kind or another have controlled or limited the expansion of political power in Africa, which, in its natural course, by following the lines of least resistance, would endeavour to proceed along the fluvial highways of the continent.

CHAPTER II.

MOUNTAINS, LAKES, AND RIVERS.

GEOGRAPHICAL DISTRIBUTION OF THE CHIEF MOUNTAIN-SYSTEMS, AND CONSEQUENT DEVELOPMENT OF THE GREAT RIVER-SYSTEMS, IN RELATION TO ACCESSIBILITY FROM THE SEA AND INTERNAL COMMUNICATIONS.

MAPS.

Contoured Map	*Plate* I.
River-Basins, &c.	,, II.

MOUNTAINS, LAKES, AND RIVERS.

IN the present chapter we shall examine in detail the oceanic and inland drainage-basins of Africa.

The most prominent physical features of the Mediterranean seaboard are concentrated in and around the highland region extending eastwards from the Atlas Mountains to the Gulf of Gabes. The Atlas range in the east sinks towards the highlands of Algeria. The uplands of Algeria and Tunis rise in terraces at a short distance from the coast, but on their south side they fall rapidly to those remarkable depressions called *shotts*, which extend inland westwards from the Gulf of Gabes for a distance of about 235 miles. As these *shotts* are probably the vestiges of what was once an inland sea, and some of them at least could be connected by canals, efforts have not been wanting on the part of the French Government to turn them to account as fluvial highways into the Interior. The maritime lowlands are continued almost uninterruptedly eastwards to the Nile delta, and have a breadth of 100 miles or less in most places. They are backed in the south by stony desert lands, called *hammadas* and *serirs*—of which the latter are relatively the higher; and the uniform flatness along the coast is broken by the bold and picturesque promontory of Barka (the ancient Cyrenaica), which advances its steep and rugged sides far into the sea. At one part of the Gulf of the Syrtes the *hammadas*, or stony plateaus, impinge upon the coast, and attain elevations of over 2500 feet.

Mediterranean seaboard.

In no part of the Mediterranean Littoral are large rivers

Absence of large rivers.

possible. Even in Algeria the river-beds are filled with water only in the rainy season. Along the remainder of the coast the conditions are still less favourable to the formation of large streams, though in past ages the deep channels leading into the Gulf of the Syrtes must have held considerable rivers.

Atlas Mountains.

Before entering the Sahara, it will be more convenient to continue our survey of North Africa westwards to the Ocean, where we enter the northern portion of the Atlantic drainage-basin. This corner of Africa is occupied by the imposing range of the Atlas Mountains, which runs as a backbone along it. Into its Alpine fastnesses few travellers have penetrated, but those few have returned with the most inspiring accounts. Peaks reaching from 11,000 to 12,000 feet and more, to the south of Morocco city, have been reported as common. The highest summit of which we have any precise knowledge appears to be Tizi-n-Tamjurt, which Mr. Joseph Thomson estimated at about 15,500 feet. Fine valleys and gorges penetrate the mountains in all directions, and there are several practicable passes. The range, which is of no great geological antiquity, is built up in long terraces. Archaean rocks occur, but they have been ridged up by subsequent movements. In the west the mountain range breaks into a plateau at about sixty miles distant from the Atlantic coast. The coast-line itself, opposite the Canary Islands, is low, and is everywhere cut up by wadis, which only contain any considerable amount of water in the season when the snows of the Atlas are melting.

Sahara region.

We now enter the domain of the Sahara. There is sufficient evidence to show that this great sandstone plateau at one time, not very remote in geological history, was to a large extent submerged; though this is a contention disputed by some authorities. Fossil remains have been discovered in many places, and there are still several minor depressions and lakes left. By depressions we do not mean all the *hofra* of the Arabs, who sometimes apply this term in a relative sense, but those small enclosed areas which are actually below the sea-level. Of these, reference has already been made to the *shotts* on the northern border-land of the Sahara, into which wide and lengthy channels conduct the scanty water-supply of the inland plateau. Others of smaller area are found in the northern portion of the Libyan Desert, west of the Lower Nile, in Siwah and elsewhere, upon which have grown up flourishing oases.

Over one-half of the Sahara is occupied by plateaus and mountains; the remainder is steppe-land and desert, dotted with oases. The transition areas bordering on the cultivated zones are more extensive in the extreme south than in the north. Not more than one-ninth is covered by the endless sands which popular tradition formerly ascribed to the whole area of the Sahara.

Physical features.

The highest elevations occupy the middle regions, along the central axis of the Saharan plateau, running in a N.W.—S.E. direction, and culminating in the mountains of Tibesti—an imposing nucleus, with summits of nearly 8000 feet. Its extension in the plateau to the N.W. contains summits of over 5000 feet. This highland region, built up of limestone and sandstone, though falling under the mean elevation of the chief European ranges, rivals them both in length and extent; it is, in fact, about 1000 miles long. Between it and Tripoli another highland region occurs in the border-range; and outlying groups of mountains, containing heights of 5000 feet, are found elsewhere within the Sahara, as in the Azben plateau. In the east the Sahara plateau adjoins the watershed of the Nile; in the south it meets that of the Congo, and in the west that of the Niger-Benué. The Ahaggar highlands drain by wadis into the

Niger basin; but some of the streams flow north, and others are lost in the inland basin of the desert.

Enclosed areas of relative depression occur more especially in the Western Sahara; and others are found near the borders of the highest mountains, as, for instance, that lying under the Borku plateau—the Bodeli, which receives the overflow waters of Lake Tsad by the Bahr-el-Ghazal channel.

<small>Water-supply.</small>

The Sahara is furrowed in many directions by river-beds, none of which contain water the whole year round; but in the length and width of their channels they rival the great rivers of Europe, thus pointing to a time when, under more favourable climatic conditions, this region was traversed by magnificent waterways. The underground supply of water at the present day is, on the other hand, remarkably great. In most places, especially near high land, water is easily reached by sinking for it. This subterranean water-supply, when brought to the surface by artesian wells, and when naturally flowing near the surface or into areas of relative depression, creates, as if by magic, those refreshing oases on the caravan routes between the Mediterranean States and the Súdan, which serve as so many stepping-stones across the inhospitable wastes. Upon the nature of the water-supply depend, of course, the character and extent of the oasis. In general terms it may be stated that, other conditions being favourable, wherever the water reaches the surface, at that spot an oasis is formed. When the water lies as much as fifteen to thirty feet below, artesian wells are required to reach it. At other spots it percolates to the surface in the form of springs, or wells up as surface-drainage, or by other direct means of infiltration. Water, in fact, is the life-blood of Africa, more especially in the rainless regions such as we are now considering, and it is more precious than "much fine gold."

The Wadi Draa, the length of whose channel exceeds that of the Rhine, is the best example of a true desert stream under the most favourable conditions. Its upper course, draining from the southern slopes of the Atlas, carries a certain amount of water all the year round; but only when the snows of the Atlas are melting does the river ever reach the sea, owing to the immense amount of evaporation and absorption it undergoes in passing through the arid regions of its middle and lower courses. Farther to the east we find another large river-bed, that of the Igharghar, which in places is as much as fifteen miles wide. This remarkable river-channel, coming from the south and pursuing a course of 700 miles, receives from the S.W. a tributary arm of almost equal size, and eventually leads into the Shott Mehrihr. There are, moreover, many other wadis conducting their scanty water-supply into the sandy wastes, which greedily absorb what little water is left after the abnormal evaporation, or into areas of relative depression, where marshes are formed in the season of rains. In the latter case, if the waters have held solutions of saline matter, large areas are left during the dry season over which the salt lies stretched out like a crystal sea. The Sahara in this way offers a valuable commercial commodity to any who may take the trouble to gather it. *Desert streams.*

The Tsad basin, situated in a trough lying between the watersheds of the three chief rivers of Africa, the Nile, the Congo, and the Niger, is an immense self-contained hydrographical system situated in the very heart of Africa. The elevation of the lake above the sea-level is about 800 feet. In the dry season it resembles a marsh, occupied by a cluster of large islands, but a marsh greater in area than the island of Sicily. In the season of rains its waters rise from twenty to thirty feet, and then the Tsad becomes an inland sea of imposing proportions. It occasionally overflows by its outlet, the *Tsad basin.*

Bahr-el-Ghazal, whose channel conducts in a N.E. direction for a distance of about 300 miles into the Bodeli depression. Lake Tsad receives many important tributary streams—one from the west equalling the Rhine in length; and its chief feeder, the Shari, is the largest river in Africa not reaching the sea. The Shari and its tributaries drain the high watershed country to the south-east of the lake. Whether the Tsad basin is hydrographically connected with that of the Benué-Niger in the season of rains is a point not yet sufficiently elucidated; but there is strong evidence, such as that furnished by Barth and Vogel, in favour of some such connection between the Shari and the Benué.

Means of communication.

It is obvious, from what has been said in our survey of the Sahara as an inland drainage-basin, that the desert possesses no natural means of communication. Although there are no insurmountable physical obstacles, as far as the lie of the land is concerned, conditions of climate, which we shall subsequently consider, have condemned the greater portion of this region as one of peril. Into it none may thoughtlessly enter. To cross it, utilising the oases as stepping-stones, requires the resources of a large caravan, and necessitates an immense waste of time, some three or four months being required for the overland journey. We have seen, too, how politically isolated it has been in the past; and farther on we shall find that, as regards commercial intercourse with the chief centres of population within its basin, more advantageous highways are offered than those by the overland caravan routes.

The Tsad region, on the other hand, though technically belonging to the Sahara drainage-basin, is climatically and in other respects an integral portion of the great Súdan, stretching from ocean to ocean. Access to its basin is afforded by other routes, from the east, west, and south; and, given the trade to attract, there need be no obstacles

in the way of permanent commercial highways converging
from those directions upon the important regions bordering
the Lake, but more especially the densely populated countries
to the south of it.

The valley of the Nile, in its entire length from the *Nile valley.*
Equator to the Mediterranean, to which drainage-basin it
consequently belongs, is the next area we have to consider.
The mighty river, issuing from its lake-reservoirs, drains
nearly the whole of North-Eastern Africa, receiving its
chief affluents west and east of its lower middle course,
and finally empties its waters into the Mediterranean. The
Victoria Nyanza, its highest source-reservoir, is situated
at about 4000 feet above the level of the sea; and, as the
Nile is about 4000 miles in length, its average fall to the
sea is consequently one foot per mile. The watershed
enclosing its basin approaches very close upon the source-
country, but widens out enormously in the middle region,
both east and west; it then closes in gradually upon the
banks of the Lower Nile, until it merges in the Deltaic lands.

The highest source-stream of the Nile will be found in *Source-*
one of the large feeders entering the Victoria Nyanza from *streams and lake-*
the south. This lake, receiving tributary streams from all *reservoirs.*
sides, is the largest in Africa: it is estimated to exceed
the area of Scotland. The Nile, issuing from the head of
this immense reservoir, breaks through the mountainous
country on its northern border by cataracts and falls, forming by the way many enlargements of its channel, and joins
the Albert Nyanza. Lake Albert, situated some 1600 feet
below the level of the Victoria, is probably nothing more
than the eroded valley of a once mighty affluent of the Nile,
for the rocks on either side, rising in corresponding terraces,
are of the same geological formation. It now acts as the
second reservoir of the Nile, and is itself connected in the
S.W. with the third reservoir, the Albert Edward Nyanza,

3307 feet above sea-level, by a newly discovered river called the Semliki. These two lakes, therefore, with the Semliki River, form the south-western arm of the Upper Nile. The Albert Edward Nyanza and its outlet, the Semliki, receive innumerable tributary streams from the high mountain mass of Ruwenzori.

Source-country. The source-country of the Nile is, in brief, situated within an immense irregular triangle, the apex of which is formed by the confluence of its S.E. and S.W. branches, and the base of which is represented by the Congo watershed.

Nile system. We can now trace the Nile as it issues out of the head of Lake Albert, a majestic stream, bound on its long journey to the Mediterranean. Passing through a valley flanked on either side by mountains which recede as the river flows north—eventually leaving only a few sentinel groups to mark its banks—the Nile soon leaves the plateau-country finally behind, and enters the steppe-land, where its banks are lost in extensive swamps. Its first important accession is where it is joined, from the west, by the Bahr-el-Ghazal. This affluent, striking the Nile almost at right angles to its course, contributes the large supply of water which its tributaries gather from the northern slopes of the Congo-Nile watershed. The united stream, a little lower down, receives through its right bank the tributary waters of the Sobat, draining from the southern extension of the Abyssinian highlands. With this accession to its strength, the Nile takes up a definite northern course and flows as a bold stream. At Khartúm it receives its chief right-hand tributary, the Blue Nile. Up to this junction, the main stream is known under several designations, but it may be exclusively regarded by us as the White Nile.

Blue and White Niles. The Blue Nile, originating in the Alpine heights of Abyssinia, is an important river-system in itself. It too, like the White Nile, has its lake-reservoir, the Tsana, situated 5760 feet above the sea-level. Out of this lake the Blue Nile issues from the south. As if in mere exaltation of spirit, the river at first describes a magnificent bend, and finally, leaving its home of high birth, enters lower country. Here, it must be confessed, it pursues an irregular course until its union with the White Nile at Khartúm.

We observe, therefore, two highly important confluences in the upper reaches of the Nile: the one where all the source-streams of the White Nile are united in Lake Albert; and the other at Khartúm, where the White and Blue Niles mingle their waters. Confluences.

From Khartúm, the Nile, as a sober and respectable river that has abandoned the frolics of its youth, enters a new phase, and one which is often experienced by man in the middle course of life: serious troubles come. It has to contend against a hostile environment and to struggle for mere existence. It soon receives, it is true, a small accession of strength in the tributary waters of the Atbara, from Abyssinia; but from thence its onward course is an unaided and a very weary one indeed. It has to traverse 1200 miles, for the most part through arid deserts, which constantly sap its strength, before it can relinquish the burden of its existence on the shores of the Mediterranean. The united Nile.

Before singing the requiem of the Nile, however, a passing reference is due to Abyssinia. These picturesquely sculptured highlands, rising at least on two sides from a forbidding steppe-country, form a sanatorium in that part of Africa, the possession of or control over which should some day prove highly advantageous to Italy. In the north, the country falls in gentle declivities and in low hills to the desert country between the Nile and Red Sea; and in the south it is in a sense united by isolated groups of mountains and high-lying valleys with the main axis of the continent. In the east, the mountains are abrupt and precipitous, and Abyssinia.

practically no drainage-waters find their way in that direction; but in the west the slopes are more gradual, and on that side they send tributary waters to the Nile. The highest peaks of Abyssinia are evenly distributed, several of them attaining altitudes little under 15,000 feet. But, owing to the highly mountainous character of the country, its rivers are torrents and they pursue very tortuous courses. In regard to the Atbara, one interesting fact may be recorded. It is this river that brings to the Nile the fertile alluvium which, in the course of ages, has contributed to the formation of its delta.

Means of communication. Regarding the Nile as a means of communication, we can readily understand how its immense fluvial system must have appealed in the past to those who had only an imperfect knowledge of its hydrography as a magnificent highway into Central Africa. Unhappily, the Nile valley, so tempting in its apparent directness of communication with the Interior, is obstructed by obstacles that, even apart from the utterly hostile conditions of climate, impose limits which up to the present day have never been passed. Some of these obstacles may be referred to in this place.

It is only natural that in the source-country of the Nile the river's bed should be obstructed so as to defy navigation; but between Khartûm and Assuan there are six cataracts, which more or less hinder navigation. Although at Assuan and elsewhere safe passages may be found in the season of rains, this, the First Cataract, may be regarded as the natural southern frontier of Lower Egypt. Above this point no firm hold can be kept upon the riverain population for any considerable distance. Of course, the Nile valley can again be easily reached much farther south,—for instance, at Berber, by a line of rails laid from Sawákin (Suakin); but that would be practically introducing a new

highway, although not a fluvial one, and at once removing
the political base of operations from the shores of the
Mediterranean to those of the Red Sea. The country
within the loop of the Nile occupied by the Nubian Desert
has in the past, and will doubtless in the future, set a limit
to any effective administration originating from Lower
Egypt; and this for reasons which will more fittingly be
given in the next chapter.

The Red Sea drainage-area, with its short wadis, may *Red Sea drainage-basin.*
be regarded as relatively of no hydrographical importance.
The water-parting between the Nile and the Red Sea passes
over desert country, for the most part occupied by barren
hills, although mountains reaching over 6000 feet are found,
and, near Abyssinia, even as high as 8000 feet.

The enclosed hydrographical basin between Abyssinia and *Enclosed basin.*
the sea is a triangular region of considerable extent. The
south-west coast of the Gulf of Aden has undergone certain modifications of level; behind it lies a broad zone of
flooded land, containing depressions below the sea-level, and
the land rises inland in terraces. Except the Hawash, flowing from Abyssinia, and losing itself in the thirsty soil,
there are no permanent streams within this enclosed basin,
its deeply eroded valleys carrying water only in the rainy
season.

We now come to the most important drainage-basin of *Atlantic drainage-basin.*
Africa, that of the Atlantic, the extreme northern corner of
which has already been referred to.

The great bend which the coast makes, forming in its *Gulf of Guinea*
innermost recess what is known as the Gulf of Guinea,
claims our chief attention, because into this sheltered sea—
taking its widest limits—about three-fourths of the total
drainage-waters of the continent ultimately find their way.
In no other part of the world, Mr. J. Y. Buchanan affirms,
does the influence of the coast make itself felt so far out at

sea. The Niger and the Congo are, of course, the chief of the many important rivers of that portion of Africa; and the enormous deposits of dark mud which they bring down to the ocean have contributed in a remarkable degree to the filling up of the coast-line. The soft muds off the mouth of the Congo have, in fact, been traced out at sea as far as 600 miles, at depths of 3000 fathoms.

Atlantic drainage-area defined.

The Atlantic Ocean drainage-basin includes all the river-systems from the Senegal, opposite the Cape Verde Islands, in the north to near the Cape of Good Hope in the south. In the Equatorial regions the Congo and its affluents carry the interior watershed, in the neighbourhood of Tanganika, almost to the East Coast. The Niger, also, in the north encroaches boldly upon the Sahara regions. The outstanding topographical features of the Atlantic drainage-basin are the almost uninterrupted coastal ranges, situated at no very great distance inland, behind which the rivers are developed, and through which they ultimately force their way in their journey to the ocean. There are detached groups of mountains, such as Mount Camarons and others to the south of it, from whose valleys issue large rivers, but none larger than the Ogowé. We then approach the Congo as it breaks through the outer rim of the inland plateau. South of the Congo, again, the coastal highlands unite with the main continental axis.

Senegal and Gambia Rivers.

The Upper Guinea Coast is, for the most part, flat and cut up into numerous lagoons, into which the smaller rivers find their way. The Futa Jallon highlands give birth not only to the large rivers Senegal and Gambia, but also to several tributaries of the Upper Niger. The Senegal and the Gambia are navigable for long distances from their mouths, especially in the season of rains,—the former up to the rapids near Mediné, and the latter up to the rapids of Barrakunda.

The Niger, rising also in the Futa Jallon highlands, at River Niger.
first flows in a northerly direction to its enlargement in
Lake Diebo, from whence its course is more sinuous to
Timbuktu, at first north-east, and then almost due east to
the meridian of Greenwich. In the neighbourhood of this
locality the slope of the land is shown by several wadis
which join the Niger from the north and north-east, whilst
the river's course is deflected to the south-east. After pursuing this direction for some distance, the Niger begins to
break through the edge of the inland plateau in its descent
to the coast; and, with the help of some tributaries, it forces
its way through rocky ground as far as Rabba, above which
spot, or at about 600 miles from its mouth, rapids occur
which obstruct navigation. From thence to the sea, however, navigation is possible for at least seven months in the
year, as the river flows in an ever-widening channel, and
the highlands recede from its banks, leaving a fine open
valley. Near Lokoja the Niger receives its chief affluent,
the Benué. The Benué is navigable for another 600 miles; River Benué
so that, if there be any truth in the hypothesis before
alluded to in regard to the Shari and Benué being connected in the rainy season, a navigable highway of nearly
1000 miles would thus lead into the Central Súdan. The
Niger-Benué, as a united stream, then breaks through the
last obstacles of the inland plateau and enters the lowlying coastal zone. The Deltaic lands, and for miles behind
them, are a dead flat; and the Niger empties into the sea
by over twenty mouths.

Passing the Old Calabar River we skirt the slopes of Physical features between the Niger and Congo.
Mount Camarons. This is the landward peak of a chain of
volcanic mountains stretching away from it in a S.W.
direction, the summits of which appear above the ocean
waters in the islands of Fernando Po, Principé, São Thomé,
&c. A narrow coastal zone extends south, gradually widen-

ing into the valleys occupied by the large estuary of the Gabún and by the Ogowé, the chief river of this part of Africa. The Ogowé has a very extensive delta: it empties its waters into the sea by two branches, fifty miles apart, the low-lying intervening country being cut up in all directions by interlacing channels. The coast-line itself for some distance south is broken by lagoons. The Upper Ogowé rises behind the coastal range, in the plateau country that forms the watershed between the Congo and the Atlantic. This coastal region of highlands sends some smaller rivers direct to the sea; and a little farther south it is entirely broken through by the impetuous rush of water which the mighty Congo gathers for its final assault in order to reach the ocean.

Congo basin.

When we consider that the Congo and its tributaries drain an area over thirty-three times that of the little State of Belgium, which controls its political destinies, we can readily grasp the full significance of what such a magnificent fluvial system implies. Were the basin of the Congo cut up by mountain ranges, we should not have such an infinite number of large tributaries; but the greater part of its catchment-area is occupied by what at one time, however remote, must have been a vast lake or inland sea. One proof of this is afforded by the fact that its important tributaries join the main stream in its upper course, while portions of their banks are only slightly elevated above the river-bed, and in the rainy season are inundated. The basin of the Congo is therefore comparable to the dry bed of an inland sea, in the furrows of which its drainage-waters are constantly flowing down the general slope of the continent towards the Atlantic Ocean. Its ancient shores are now represented by the high land or rim of the basin, which surrounds it on all sides. The process of wearing away the coastal range must have been the work of ages; it must have begun at a time when the waters of the ancient lake or sea were of sufficient height to use its outlet or drain as a channel, in the same way as the Lukuga has periodically conducted the overflow waters of Tanganika into the basin of the Upper Congo.

From what has been said, it is evident that, where the upper courses of the Congo and its tributaries break through the plateau-country in order to reach the lower basin, there must be rocky obstructions in their beds, forming rapids, cataracts, and waterfalls. This is illustrated very strikingly by the southern tributaries, which, flowing almost parallel to each other in a northerly direction, in order to unite with the Kasaï and Sankuru, all have their beds obstructed by cataracts beyond the parallel of 5° south latitude.

Obstructions in river-bed.

Following our usual plan of first tracing and defining broad features and subsequently filling in details, we now observe that the main stream of the Congo, rising in the high-plateau country to the south-west of Tanganika, issues out of Lake Bangweolo as the Luapula. It then joins Lake Moëro in the south. Flowing out of this lake again in the north, as the Luapula still, it strikes a more westerly course, until it joins a chain of lakelets that are united together by its tributary, the Lualaba, a river which is fed by numerous affluents rising in the same source-country as, though more to the west of, the parent stream. The Lualaba and Luapula then drain into a small depression, which their united waters fill up as a small lake, and they issue forth again as the Congo proper. Receiving several streams by the way, the Congo, ever increasing in volume, pursues a bold and decisive course to Stanley Falls, after passing over which it receives some more important tributaries through both banks, but especially through its right, from whence the drainage-waters of the high-plateau join it, deflecting it more and more to the west. The

Bird's-eye view of Congo basin.

<small>Congo: tributary systems.</small>

magnificent sweep which the Congo makes in its middle course has often been commented upon. As it turns and flows to the south-west, it gathers in some considerable streams from its left, but receives a still more important tributary system through its right bank, where the M'bangi joins it as one large river. The M'bangi, the upper course of which is known as the Wellé-Makwa, drains all the north-eastern region of the Congo basin, and is one of its two chief feeders or arms. The other, which at no great distance from the M'bangi confluence joins the Congo on its left bank, is a still more important one: it receives innumerable tributary streams through the Kasaï and Sankuru, and falls into the Congo at Kwamouth. With this enormous influx to its waters the Congo carries everything before it in its final onrush to the sea.

Broadly defined, then, we may regard the main stream or chief artery of the Congo system of waterways as issuing out of Lake Bangweolo, and being joined north and south by two other arteries. In the numerous tributaries we recognise so many veins. Such a highly-developed system as that which the Congo possesses entitles it to rank as a peer among the rivers of the world, and has earned for it, as our explorers have laid it bare, the consideration it deserves.

<small>Orographical features.</small>

To retrace our steps. Between the continental axis of elevation and the plains of the Congo is an intervening region of middle heights, through which most of the tributaries must flow in their upper courses. The continental axis forms in the south and east a right-angled triangle, and this middle region occupies the enclosed area, the hypothenuse of which is well defined. The source-streams of the Congo, as we have seen, are found in the high-level lake-country which gives rise to three of the four chief rivers of Africa: the Congo, the Nile, and the Zambezi. The Congo, like the Nile, has its source-reservoirs, and at very much the same elevation. Lakes Bangweolo and Moëro are situated at altitudes above the sea-level of 4100 feet and 3000 feet respectively. It is instructive in this respect to note that Lake Nyassa, lying to the east of Bangweolo, is situated about 2500 feet below the level of the latter. Lake Tanganika, on the other hand, situated nearly 2700 feet above the sea, belongs to the basin of the Congo, though its outlet by the Lukuga can only fulfil its drainage functions when, at rare periods, the lake overflows.

The mountains surrounding Tanganika rise 2000 to 3000 feet above its waters, whilst the lake itself lies in a deep trough, receiving tributary streams from all sides. Southeast of the Tanganika is a small lake, called the Hikwa. Captain Storms considers that this lake at one time overflowed into the Tanganika, the waters of which were thereby raised so as to drain out by the Lukuga into the Lualaba basin of the Congo: the soft rocks at the break in the western ramparts of Tanganika were thus gradually eroded into a channel in the rainy season, though in the dry season it may have formed a watershed. *Lake Tanganika.*

The Wellé-Makwa-M'bangi arm of the Congo receives its head-waters from the mountainous region to the northwest of the Albert Lake. Its numerous northern tributaries are considerable streams, but those which join the river from the south have, in consequence of the proximity of the main arm of the Congo, no great scope for development. The M'bangi, shortly before its confluence with the Congo, in piercing a mountain chain which lies athwart its course, forms at Zongo six rapids. For twenty-four miles the river is greatly contracted, and at places the rocky ground divides the stream into several channels. *Congo: northern arm.*

The tributaries of the Kasaï-Sankuru arm of the Congo, flowing parallel to each other, drain the northern slopes of the South-Central African plateau. This tributary system *Congo: southern arm.*

rivals in importance the main arm of the Congo itself. Between it and the Congo are situated two lakes, which, as far as has been ascertained, have no hydrographical connection with one another.

Lower Congo.

The Lower Congo extends from its mouth for 120 miles to Matadi, from whence cataracts obstruct the river as far as the neighbourhood of Stanley Pool. Below Matadi, however, the river rushes past the bases of steep mountains, and then expands to three times its former breadth,—to about twelve miles across; and it is studded with islands, which are of constant occurrence in the bed of the Congo. Between Stanley Pool and Kwamouth, at the confluence of the Kasaï, the river passes between rocky heights of from 600 to 1000 feet.

Congo estuary.

We thus see how, according to the nature of the country through which it passes, the Congo varies so greatly in width. But at its estuary, between Banana and Shark Point, it is only eight miles across, with depths of sixty fathoms. The current at this point runs at about three knots an hour; and, as the Congo is estimated to discharge over one million tons of water per second, we can realise its in-

Submarine cañon.

fluence on the coast-line. The sediment which its heavily charged waters carry out to sea is deposited, for a distance of over 300 miles, on either side of its ocean course, in submarine mountains of detritus and slime raised as high as 5000 feet. The soundings made by the *Buccaneer* demonstrated that the walls of this submarine cañon are raised to within 100 fathoms of the surface of the sea, whilst between them the sounding-line had to travel ten times that distance in order to reach the bed of the ocean. As, for reasons which have already been mentioned, the waters of the Gulf of Guinea are slowly receding, we may confidently point to the formation in the course of ages of a delta of enormous extent at the mouth of the Congo. It must not, however,

be supposed that this submarine cañon is in any way due <small>Its origin.</small>
to erosion by the river, the effect of which in this respect
cannot be felt for any great distance from shore, because
the river current itself, as Mr. J. Y. Buchanan has pointed
out, does not prevail below the surface of the sea for more
than twenty fathoms, and gradually thins out in its onward
course. For many miles from shore the colour of this ocean
river is of a darkish yellow, tinged with red; and at more
remote places this layer of fresh water is so thin that the
screw of a steamer will churn it up and disclose the deep-
sea water below. Mr. Buchanan has, in fact, demonstrated
that the cañon has not been hollowed out, but that it has
been built up by the sediment deposited through the agency
of the circulation of the sea water.

We may now regard the Congo river-system as a means <small>Means of communi-</small>
of communication between the sea and the interior lands <small>cation.</small>
which it drains. For this purpose we may regard the
intricate network of waterways above Stanley Pool as belonging to the Upper Congo. From Stanley Falls to Stanley
Pool the main arm of the Congo traverses a distance of
nearly 1000 miles, and is navigable throughout the entire
distance. It is very broad all the way, measuring in
places as much as fifteen or even twenty-one miles across.
According to the latest estimates by Belgian officers, which
may possibly prove to be too sanguine, the Kasaï and
Sankuru have about an equal extent of navigable waters;
and the third great affluent of the Congo, the M'bangi,
has about 600 miles. Moreover, we are told that, taking
all the tributaries into account, there are over 7000 miles
of continuous waterways accessible from Stanley Pool. We
must, therefore, at once recognise the importance of this
centre, situated, as it is, so near to the West Coast. If
we accept the Belgian estimates as accurate, the aggregate
length of the banks of the navigable waterways of the

Upper Congo must be 14,000 miles, or about that of the coast-line of Europe from the North Cape to Constantinople. One can understand the enthusiasm of Mr. Stanley in regarding such a length of navigable rivers, with people on their shores waiting to be supplied with the manufactures of Europe! The recent discovery that the Lomami is navigable for 600 miles from its confluence with the Congo to a point a little beyond the latitude of Nyangwé, which lies only a short distance to the east, carries our fluvial communications into the very heart of Africa. As regards the Lower Congo, ocean-going steamers stop at the port of Boma, though there is water enough to float them up to Matadi: the depths, however, are constantly changing, owing to the shifting sandbanks. Between Matadi and Stanley Pool, past the cataracts, a railway is in progress of construction; so that these insuperable obstacles to transport by water will eventually be overcome by the enterprise of man.

Between the Congo and Orange Rivers.

Proceeding south, from the mouth of the Congo, we enter upon an extensive region draining into the Atlantic. The western slopes of the continental axis, extending between the Congo and Orange Rivers, send several important streams to the ocean. Chief among them are the Kwanza and Kunéné, which rise from opposite sides of a watershed in the South-Central plateau country, their source-streams being in proximity to one another and not far removed—say, about 100 miles—from the coast.

Geographical features.

The country south of the Lower Congo, although gradually ascending from the coast into the Interior, does not at first rise in terraces. It will be seen that the highest land is not at first far removed from the coast, and that it gradually draws closer as we proceed south. There are districts in the Interior lying at an average elevation of 5000 feet, and enjoying a Temperate climate, which are as well watered as any other parts of Africa. The Kwanza is navigable for 250 miles from its mouth. The Kunéné, on the other hand, is shallow, even in its lower course, and is not navigable.

South of the Kunéné, as far as the Orange River, there extends a dreary coastal region, which, as it rises gradually into the Interior, is said to improve in quality; but it sends no permanent streams to the sea. Along this coast there are no harbours, though Walvisch Bay affords a secure roadstead. Behind this British possession there are tracks into the Interior, but along the rest of the coast, to the north and to the south, there are practically none. *Absence of harbours.*

The Orange River and its tributaries are comprised under a self-contained system, resembling in many hydrographical respects that of the great Congo itself. We here leave, it is true, the important region of the continental axis of elevation, but we find its counterpart in the south, bearing a very close resemblance in miniature, and trending also in a S.W.—N.E. direction. The Orange River rises at no great distance from the East Coast, in the high border-range of the Draken Berge—one peak towering over its source at an elevation of over 10,000 feet; and it receives fine tributaries from the north and from the south. As a river-system it occupies the whole Atlantic drainage-area of South Africa proper. The watershed between it and the Indian Ocean drainage-basin culminates towards the east in the *massifs* of the Draken Berge. This mountain-range falls in steep terraces towards the Natal coast, but its inland slope, towards the Transvaal plateau, is more gentle. Situated between the Vaal and Molopo tributaries of the Orange River is the fine plateau of Southern Bechuana-land, which in parts reaches 5000 feet, but sinks towards the enclosed area around Lake N'gami to some 2000 feet. *Orange River.*

Communications.

The Orange River, on account of the numerous cataracts formed in the country through which it flows, is practically unnavigable. It is, in consequence, of little or no use as a means of communication. Moreover, with the exception of Saldanha Bay, situated some sixty miles to the north of Cape Town and providing a good natural harbour, there are no places on this coast where ships can find safe anchorage.

Lake N'gami.

In the large enclosed hydrographical basin holding Lake N'gami we have a reproduction on a small scale of that of Lake Tsad. The former lies to the north of the Orange River and the latter to the north of the Congo: hence we have another remarkable bathyhypsographical feature in which these two river-systems resemble one another. The N'gami, however, though fluctuating in size like its prototype, is a comparatively insignificant lake. It, too, like the Tsad, lies on the border of a desert zone—that of the Kalahari. In its neighbourhood are numerous depressions, in which salt-pans are formed; and there exist also many large river-beds with little or no water in them. The N'gami has its outlet in the Zuga channel, which carries off its overflow waters into the salt-pans.

This concludes our survey of the whole Atlantic drainage-area. The Indian Ocean drainage-basin is the last we shall have to consider.

Indian Ocean drainage-basin.

That portion of South Africa the mountain torrents of which drain into the Indian Ocean is comprised under the southern slopes of the high border-range which, starting from the Cape of Good Hope, runs parallel to the coast in a north-easterly direction to the Draken Berge. The land rises in regular terraces from the sea, and there is a middle coastal range between it and the Orange River watershed. We are, consequently, not surprised to find the submarine bank off Cape Agulhas—the most southerly point of Africa —continuing the same physical formation far into the ocean.

Between the coastal-range and the border-range there is a large plateau, the Great Karoo, from sixty to ninety miles wide, and situated between two and three thousand feet above the sea. In this desert region of sand and clay we do not expect to find permanent rivers. The rivers of the Cape generally are mostly mountain torrents, flowing through deep gorges, though as we proceed east they have a more permanent water-supply. Happily, however, the Cape is not dependent on its waterways for access into the Interior. *Cape rivers.*

It is not until we reach the Limpopo that we discover any river of consequence in this part of Africa. The Limpopo, which is navigable for sixty miles from its mouth for vessels of 200 tons, rises in the South African plateau, from which it receives several large tributaries, and, after describing a wide bend by the north, falls into the sea near the finest harbour in South-East Africa—Delagoa Bay. The valley of the Limpopo is, it is evident, of some consequence as a means of communication. *Limpopo River.*

North of the Limpopo the coastal zone begins to broaden out, until it merges in the valley of the Zambezi. The watershed between these rivers and the Sofala coast is considerably cut up, and sends no important streams to the sea.

The Zambezi River and its magnificent system of accessible waterways is the "Congo" of the East Coast. The catchment-basin of the river itself is equal to three times the area of France. Indeed, as a means of communication with the interior parts of Africa, and especially with the most healthy parts, it may be questioned whether the Zambezi, or the Congo, or the Nile is the most valuable as a commercial highway. Affording, as it does, ready access to what has been called the high-level lake-region of Africa—the region most suited to European settlement—the Zambezi may be *Zambezi River: comparison with the Congo.*

regarded as second to none. Curiously enough, too, its source-streams are quite close to those of the Congo, the watershed between the two river-systems running across the South-Central plateau and then striking north-east, between Lakes Nyassa and Tanganika. The slopes in the South-Central plateau are scarcely perceptible, and, as far as the inequalities of the land are concerned, there is easy access between the two basins.

Course of the Zambezi.

But, to begin at the beginning. The Upper Zambezi, draining the southern slopes of the South-Central plateau, derives its highest source-streams from the country to the west of Bangweolo, at a romantic spot called Border Craig by Mr. Arnot, because on the other side of the watershed probably the highest source-stream of the Congo takes its rise. The Zambezi does not originate, as formerly supposed, in Lake Dilolo, but passes through it. In its upper course it receives through its right bank several large tributaries from the far west. After entering the valley which it traverses in its middle course, it skirts the southern border of the South-Central plateau, receiving tributaries through either bank, until it is joined by the Loangwa, which rises in the highland country to the west of Lake Nyassa. Between the upper course of the Loangwa and the Congo basin there is a range of mountains over 6000 feet high, which ultimately merges in the plateau country between Lakes Nyassa and Tanganika. The Zambezi, after its confluence with the Loangwa, begins to work its way into the coastal zone, and its bed consequently becomes obstructed at the rim of the interior plateau. When, finally, it gets fairly away into the lowlands it becomes a fine, bold stream.

Zambezi Delta.

Shortly before entering the low-lying country, in which, ninety miles from the coast, it begins to form a delta, the Zambezi receives through its left bank the tributary waters of the Shiré. The entire delta of the Zambezi, comprising an area of 2500 square miles, is only slightly elevated above the level of the sea, with which it imperceptibly merges. Of the innumerable channels only seven may be regarded as the actual mouths of the river, and of these the Madredane is the channel most used for navigation. Unfortunately, all the mouths of the Zambezi are barred, as they are constantly silting up, and the river-beds consequently undergo changes of level, which present serious obstacles to navigation. The Madredane itself is frequently choked with vegetation. Mr. D. J. Rankin claims to have discovered in the Chindé (Shindé) mouth an alternative passage from the sea into the Zambezi, which ultimately may prove to be of value; and, of course, there are others not mentioned here, which are practicable; but, as a general rule, it may be stated that the mouths of the Zambezi are all so liable to be silted up that only costly measures, effectively maintained, can ever preserve them as permanent, navigable highways for steamers. *Navigable channels.*

It is the Kwakwa or Kilimani River by which, up to the present, the best access to the Zambezi has been available for commerce. But between the upper course of the Kwakwa and the Zambezi Rivers a portage of five miles is necessary; so that, for international and commercial purposes, the use of the Kwakwa River, passing through Portuguese territory, has its disadvantages. The Zambezi, on the other hand, being a free river, is the best, as it is the most natural, highway into the interior lands; and, as there are no insuperable obstacles to the navigation of its available channels, we may be sure that, when the proper time comes, adequate and effective measures will be taken for the safety of vessels using them. *Kwakwa River.*

As Lake Nyassa is situated 1570 feet above the level of the sea, it follows that its outlet, the Shiré, in order to travel the short distance to join the Zambezi, must fall very rapidly, *Shiré River.*

especially where it breaks away from the inland plateau. At this locality the Murchison cataracts are formed, and prevail for some fifty miles. Here, in proceeding up the Shiré from the Zambezi to Lake Nyassa, a portage is necessary.

Means of communication. Regarding the Zambezi as a means of communication with the Interior, we see at a glance, from what has been said, that there are really no insuperable obstacles to uninterrupted navigation from the sea until we reach the *Karoa basa* rapids above Tete. Farther up, its bed is again and again interrupted by the inequalities of the land through which the river flows. In the Victoria Falls, for example, we witness a phenomenon the grandeur of which is unsurpassed even by the Falls of Niagara; for here the Zambezi, 1000 yards broad, drops 100 feet into a fissure of the earth's surface, which stretches right across its bed and is continued past its left bank for over thirty miles.

But the Zambezi also offers access from the sea to another water-and-land route, which, conducting over the high-level Lake country, ultimately connects in the north with the Congo and Nile basins, thus affording a practicable highway across the continent of Africa. Let us briefly examine this route in detail.

A highway across Africa. In the initial stage of our journey we enter either the Zambezi itself, by one of its mouths, or the Kwakwa River. In the former case we can navigate vessels right up to the Murchison cataracts on the Shiré, but in the latter case a five-mile portage between the Kwakwa and Zambezi is necessary. Past the Murchison cataracts another portage, of sixty miles, is essential; but from thence to the Nyassa we have free access by water. Between Lakes Nyassa and Tanganika the so-called Stevenson Road stretches for 250 miles; whilst the Victoria Nyanza, according to Stanley's latest discovery of its south-westerly extension, is only 155 miles distant from the Tanganika. Such a route as this, by far the greater portion of which is by water, cannot fail to be of immense value to those who, by opening up the continent and introducing legitimate commerce, hope to impose a higher civilisation upon its native inhabitants.

A glance at Lake Nyassa, and we have done with the Zambezi catchment-basin. Lakes Nyassa and Tanganika closely resemble one another in their hydrographical relations: as Tanganika is to the Congo, so is Nyassa to the Zambezi. It is a striking fact that the three great river-systems of Africa—the Nile, the Congo, and the Zambezi—should all be provided with large lake-reservoirs. Though the Congo now receives no overflow waters from Tanganika, owing to the subsidence of the lake, it must have done so in former times, and might possibly do so again. Lake Nyassa, like Tanganika, has in the south its satellite lake, that of Shirwa, which, like Hikwa, is a self-contained hydrographical basin. Shirwa lies 400 feet above the level of Nyassa, and was for a time supposed to be connected with the river Lujenda, from which it is separated by an elevated ridge of sandy soil. Whether, as native report has it, the lake may still have some subterranean connection, is a moot-point. At least, it does not overflow into the Nyassa, but belongs rather to the Lujenda system, though its mention in this place is more convenient. {Lake Nyassa: comparative view.}

Lake Nyassa, in fact, receives no tributaries of any size. It is 350 miles in length, and averages nearly forty miles in breadth, its mean depth being about 100 fathoms. The highest elevations on its shores are those in the north-east, where the Livingstone mountains average as much as 10,000 feet, and extend for 100 miles.

We now enter the domain properly regarded as the East Coast of Africa, stretching from the delta of the Zambezi northwards to the Gulf of Aden. Throughout the length of {East Coast.}

East Coast.

this coast, and its interior region draining into the Indian Ocean, there are no navigable rivers, properly so regarded: all of them, as they break through the terrace-like formations of the inland plateau, form rapids. The watershed, starting from the south, coincides with the high country that separates the hydrographical systems of the great Lakes, and ultimately unites with the Abyssinian highlands in the north. From south to north, within this drainage-area, the inland plateau recedes more and more from the shores of the Indian Ocean; but, in the extreme north, the high-level country, starting from the nucleus of Abyssinia, takes a direct easterly trend, so as to form the backbone of the great Horn of Africa. Dipping under the surface of the sea at Cape Guardafui, it plainly indicates its submarine extension in the direction of the island of Sokotra, which, like a sentinel, raises its summit above the ocean waters. The coastal zone of East Africa maintains a corresponding increase in its average breadth; and there is a well-defined intermediate zone of elevation between the lowland and the highland regions.

Rovuma River.

Between Lake Nyassa and the Indian Ocean the only river of prime importance is the Rovuma, which rises in the high country near the eastern shores of the lake. The Rovuma forms a cataract forty miles above its confluence with the Lujenda, and its bed is elsewhere obstructed; so that, as a means of communication with the East Coast—which Livingstone had ardently wished to discover in it—the river is of no special value. The Lujenda, rising to the north of Lake Shirwa, issues out of two small lakes, and then breaks away through the rough country that divides it from the upper course of the Rovuma, receiving tributary waters through both banks. The united streams, near their confluence, are as broad as 700 feet.

Opposite Zanzibar, and between the Rufiji and Ruvu

(Pangani)—the former coming from the highlands on the north-east of Nyassa, the latter from the slopes of Kilima-njaro—there is an interesting region, broken up by mountains, and sending only small unnavigable streams to the sea. We have, first, the coastal zone, stretching inland to the uplands of Usagara, behind which the continent rises and expands into plateaus and tablelands. The immense plateau lying to the east of Tanganika averages over 4000 feet in elevation above the sea-level. Mounts Kilima-njaro and Kénia, farther north, are the southerly outposts and culminating elevations of a volcanic region in which large isolated mountain-masses occur among the plateaus. How far north this region extends it would be difficult to define, but its characteristics are more or less apparent in all the highland country up to Abyssinia. Numerous small lakes occur, some fresh, some salt, but none of them provided with an outlet. There is a long chain of these lakelets in an apparent cleft of the earth's surface situated to the east of the Victoria Nyanza, and extending north and south for a distance of over 600 miles. Of these, the Naivasha Lake, 6000 feet above the sea, is the highest in elevation. From this central point, in the watershed country between Kénia and the Victoria Nyanza, the valley slopes north- and south-wards.

<small>Zanzibar mainland.</small>

The chief river of this part of the East Coast, the Tana, derives its head-waters from the slopes of Mount Kénia and beyond. It is a permanent stream, and conveniently overflows when the snows of Mount Kénia are melting under a summer sun.

<small>Tana River.</small>

To the north of the region we have been surveying lie the Somáli- and Galla-lands. What little we know of this extensive tract of country is that it slopes from the north southwards, and, of course, from the west eastwards, thus giving a general S.E. slope towards the Indian Ocean, in

<small>Somáli- and Galla-lands.</small>

which direction it falls in successive, long, flat terraces. The whole of the country is scored by wide, but for the most part dry, river-beds, only two of which carry permanent streams.

Remarks. We have now finished our hasty survey of the mountains, lakes, and rivers of Africa. Unconscionably long and wearisome as it may have appeared to those who have had the courage to accompany me so far, step by step, it fills me with remorse to think how much I have necessarily omitted: really large and important districts, which, in order to preserve some sort of balance, have been entirely overlooked on account only of their relative insignificance. For the same reason, that of proportion, some regions have had but slight notice. Only general terms have been employed in describing what it were possible to have seen, say, from the car of a balloon; if, on the other hand, we came to the earth and examined it more closely, our descriptions would require considerable modifications.

The points I have endeavoured to bring out in strong relief are—(1.) The distribution of the great land-masses, resulting in the formation of the chief drainage-systems; and (2.) the general configuration of the land, as indicated by the courses of the arterial rivers and their tributary systems.

As in the early stages of drawing a picture, we have first dashed in the broad outlines and then filled in the salient details, leaving a great deal unrecorded, owing to the limitation of our view. But our picture of Africa is, up to the present, only a black-and-white sketch, more white than black; and we can only hope to convey a semblance of realism when we resort to colours, when we clothe the mountains and the plains with vegetation.

We have regarded our subject-matter in the present

chapter from one point of view only: accessibility. In how far is the continent, by the natural disposition of its mountain barriers, favourable or otherwise to the migratory movements of men? In how far do the rivers of Africa, from their facility for navigation, offer highways into the interior lands?

Accessibility of African lands.

Well, if we have seen anything at all, we must have recognised how the great river-systems of Africa give free access into the Interior at least up to the points where, as cataracts and rapids, they break through the rim of the continental plateau. Railways could be built to obviate such hindrances to internal communications, such as at the cataracts of the Lower Congo, where the upper reaches of the river are sufficiently valuable and attractive as highways. As far as roads are concerned, it is well known that native tracks lead from every village to every other village; and then there are the caravan routes, to which we shall refer subsequently. Highways, like the Stevenson Road between Lakes Nyassa and Tanganika, will be built when the proper time arrives: that is to say, when trade prospects warrant their construction. Across the unhealthy coastal zone, from the depôts of commerce, also, railways will in time run inland to the chief commercial centres. Though we are told it is unwise to prophecy until we are sure, I venture to remark that, in the end, it will be found impossible for Europeans to colonise Africa without the rapid means, such as railways afford, to reach the high-lying and relatively healthier regions of the Interior. It is all a question of time and of experience. At present we have the most elementary notions as to the proper manner of "opening up" Africa. Elsewhere will be explained some of the difficulties we shall have to face and the problems to be solved.

It is evident that the physical embossment of Africa, although providing splendid waterways throughout the inland plateau, does not afford steamers uninterrupted access from the sea, except in most cases for comparatively short distances. And this is one of the reasons, though not the chief, why at the present day we see the coasts occupied by Europeans and Inner Africa by unregenerate Natives.

CHAPTER III.

CLIMATE AND COGNATE PHENOMENA.

DISTRIBUTION OF TEMPERATURE—ACTUAL TEMPERATURES—DISTRIBUTION OF ATMOSPHERIC PRESSURE, AND PREVAILING WINDS—ANNUAL RAINFALL—DISTRIBUTION OF SOILS—ZONES OF VEGETATION—DISTRIBUTION OF ANIMALS—CLASSIFICATION OF CLIMATES—ACCLIMATISATION.

MAPS.

MEAN ANNUAL TEMPERATURES (ACTUAL)	Plate III.
MEAN ANNUAL RANGE OF TEMPERATURE	,, IV.
ANNUAL RAINFALL	,, V.
GEOLOGICAL SKETCH	,, VI.
ZONES OF VEGETATION	,, VII.

CLIMATE AND COGNATE PHENOMENA.

THE phenomena of climate are so manifold and complex, **Phenomena of climate.** and our *data* in Africa are, moreover, so limited and imperfect, that we can refer to them here only in very general terms, and in so far as their practical application is concerned. They necessarily include atmospheric pressure, temperature, humidity, and the resulting aërial circulation or prevailing winds, which in the main determine rainfall. Vegetation, in its turn, depends partly on rainfall; the geographical distribution of animals is largely controlled by vegetation; and upon both of these depends in a great measure the distribution of the populations. In working up to this final result, therefore, we shall be following the natural sequence of physical phenomena, or of cause and effect, by first considering the meteorological conditions of Africa.

First, then, as regards temperature.* As the greater **Mean annual temperature.** portion of Africa lies within the Tropics, we are prepared to find there a very high mean annual temperature. From the Northern Tropic (Cancer) southwards to the Orange River, and excepting only the western seaboard and a small portion of the South-East Coast, which are cooled by their proximity to the ocean, there is a zone with a mean annual

---

* The *data* in regard to temperature and atmospheric pressure are derived mainly from Dr. Alexander Buchan's monumental maps of the world illustrating the *Challenger* volume on the subject. These maps are the most recent and authoritative we possess. They do not give *actual* temperatures, of course, but temperatures reduced to sea-level. The former we shall consider apart, in connection with Mr. Ravenstein's map (Plate III.).

temperature of 80° Fahr. This zone encloses a corresponding inner zone of 85° Fahr. To the north, the Sahara and Libyan deserts lie within the zone of 70° to 80° Fahr.; and to the south we find a corresponding zone of mean annual temperature along the West Coast and in the high-plateau country of South Africa. The Mediterranean seaboard, the South-West Coast, and the southern-most part of Cape Colony enjoy the mean annual temperature of Southern Europe: from 60° to 70° Fahr.

Mean temperatures: February. Bearing in mind these zones of mean annual temperature, it will be instructive to compare them with the mean temperatures of the two extreme months, February and August, when the juxtaposition and interchange of seasons between the northern and southern Hemispheres is well exemplified in Africa. In February—the winter of the northern, and the summer of the southern, Hemisphere—the zone of 80° Fahr. lies more to the south and west, whilst the zone of 85° Fahr. is immensely increased in size, and encloses two large patches or areas indicating as high a temperature as 90° Fahr. These two patches are situated, the one—and the smaller one—to the north of the Equator, in the source-country of the Upper Nile; the other, south of the Equator, in the high-plateau country between Lake Tanganika and the Orange River. The zone of 70° to 80° Fahr. includes part of the West Coast and the south coast of Cape Colony, in the southern Hemisphere; while, in the northern Hemisphere, the Saharan regions experience a mean temperature of from 60 to 80° Fahr. The Mediterranean seaboard has, however, a mean temperature of from 50° to 60° Fahr.

Mean temperatures: August. We naturally find very nearly the reverse of these conditions in August, when the northern Hemisphere enjoys its summer. Then the zone of 80° Fahr., though prevailing as far south as Lake Nyassa, reaches the shores of the Mediterranean, and leaves only a portion of North-West Africa "out in the (comparative) cold" of from 70° to 80° Fahr. Within this zone of 80° Fahr. we find, well to the north of the Equator, interior zones of 85°, 90°, and even 95° Fahr., their axes lying, roughly, N.W. and S.E. The innermost zone of 95° Fahr. is situated in the heart of the Sahara. South of the isothermal line of 80° Fahr. are zones of 70°, 60°, and 55° Fahr., extending to the Cape.

All of these isothermal lines, enclosing the zones above referred to, are, of course, more and more deflected as the neighbourhood of the sea is approached, and therefore assume approximately the curvature of the coasts. *Influence the ocean upon temperature.*

So far we have discussed temperatures reduced to sea-level; but Mr. Ravenstein's map (Plate III.) illustrating this chapter will convey to the reader a far more realistic idea of this dry subject, for there only *actual* temperatures have been given. It will be seen how relatively few places there are in Tropical Africa where temperatures favourable to Europeans can be found. A mean annual temperature of from 72° to 80° Fahr. prevails almost everywhere, and in the East Coastal zone it rises to and above 80° Fahr. Only in the very highest regions do we find temperatures of from 64° to 72° Fahr. When, however, we enter the more Temperate regions of Africa, in the north and in the south, we there find temperatures congenial to Europeans. But, of course, temperature is not everything: it is modified in many ways by local conditions, and more especially by the relative humidity of the atmosphere. *Actual temperatures.*

Having glanced at mean temperatures in Africa, we may briefly consider the prevailing winds.

The sun, which is the source of all life, is the prime cause of the movements of the atmosphere. Without its beneficent action there would be stagnation above and death below. In its apparent path through the Tropics, the sun gives rise to those variations of atmospheric pressure known in meteor- *Atmospheric pressure.*

ological science as areas of low and of high pressure.* But the distribution of atmospheric pressure is further determined by the geographical distribution of land and water. Hence we have those phenomena which lead to diversity of climate.

Prevailing winds.
It is not my intention here to exhibit the working of the machinery, so to speak, but simply the manufactured result. Upon the varying relative distribution of atmospheric pressure depends the prevailing winds, or, as Dr. Buchan lucidly expresses it: "the flow of the air from a region of higher towards a region of lower pressure, or from where there is a surplus to where there is a deficiency of air."

Land and sea breezes.
We have not space even to glance at diurnal phenomena, of which the land and sea breezes are the most notable examples. Of the prevailing winds in the interior of Africa we know next to nothing; and, indeed, we can speak only very approximately of those in other parts of the continent, except perhaps in Algeria, in South Africa, and on the Red Sea.

In discussing the prevailing winds of Africa, the most

---

* Areas of *low pressure* follow approximately the path of the sun, but are ultimately determined by the chief land-masses; and for the following reasons. In the summer months the land is much warmer than the ocean in the same latitudes; hence pressure is lower, owing to the ascending heated currents carrying away a portion of the atmosphere, whose place is then taken by relatively colder, and therefore heavier, air. Also, in higher latitudes over the ocean in the winter the temperature is higher than over the land in the same latitude; hence ascending currents of air set in, and pressure is lower.

These physical phenomena are simply reversed in areas of *high pressure*. In the winter months temperature over the land is lower than over the ocean in the same latitudes, consequently the air is denser or heavier, and pressure is high; hence it is that pressure is high over all the continents during the winter months of those continents.

Furthermore, it is essential to bear in mind that, on the eastern sides of all the great oceans, between about latitudes 20° to 40° north and south, pressure is *high at all seasons*, but highest in the summer months of the respective oceans.

These remarks are introduced in order to assist lay readers the better to understand the meteorological phenomena with which we are dealing.

important factor to take into account is that of the Trade-winds, which, though shifting with the apparent path of the sun, blow more or less constantly, unless locally affected, from the N.E. in the northern Hemisphere and from the S.E. in the southern Hemisphere. The intervening region is a belt of calms. In the southern Hemisphere the S.E. Trades prevail more or less regularly off the West and South-East Coasts; but in the northern Hemisphere the N.E. Trades are only constant off the Atlantic shores of Africa. *Trade-winds.*

In the northern Equatorial regions of Africa, both on the West and East Coasts, there are monsoon winds. Off the West Coast the S.W. monsoon blows into the Gulf of Guinea as the prevailing wind throughout the year, though this is a region which is comparatively calm. On the East Coast, on the other hand, the monsoons are controlled by the disturbing element of a large continental mass in proximity—Asia. These winds prevail in Southern Asia more or less from the S.W., by S., to the S.E. from April to October, and from N.E. during the other months of the year; and their influence is felt over the whole of the great Horn of Africa as well as off the coasts. Along the Red Sea the wind is almost always northerly; and on the Mediterranean seaboard the winds vary from S.W., N.W., and N.E. throughout the year. *Monsoon winds.*

How far these winds are likely to prevail in the Interior can only be approximately determined by a careful examination of isobaric charts, showing atmospheric pressure, and, inferentially, the prevailing winds, month by month. We have, however, said enough to assist us in making the application we are about to consider—the rainfall of Africa.*

The heaviest rainfall occurs in the Equatorial regions. Enclosed longitudinal zones of from 50 to 100 inches of annual rainfall are found at several places within those *Rainfall: Equatorial zone.*

* See map (Plate V.) illustrating this subject.

limits. In the heart of Africa—the Congo forest region—a zone of over 50 inches extends as far south as the Zambezi watershed. Within this Equatorial belt there are, moreover, two districts which receive an even heavier annual rainfall —over 100 inches. The S.W. monsoon winds carry from the region of calms in the Gulf of Guinea an abnormal amount of moisture, which is precipitated on coming in contact with the cooling influence of the coastal uplands; and a similar patch of heavy rainfall occurs near Sierra Leone. Curiously enough, in the extreme north-west of Madagascar there is also a heavy annual rainfall of over 100 inches.

<small>Rainfall: Tropical and sub-Tropical zones.</small>

Outside this rainy Equatorial zone we find in the north two zones, of from 25 to 50 inches, and of from 10 to 25 inches of annual rainfall, respectively, extending up to the southern borders of the Sahara; and in the south there are corresponding zones, but, instead of their axes lying east and west, they extend, roughly, N.N.W. and S.S.E., making a deep inland curve on the South-West Coast.

<small>Desert regions.</small>

The greater portion of the Sahara receives under 5 inches of annual rainfall: hence its desert character. For the winds coming from Europe and blowing from a colder to a warmer region, the air thereby gradually increases its capacity for absorbing and retaining moisture, very little of which is precipitated over the thirsty desert lands. But in the transitional regions north and south of the Sahara, as well as in the mountain districts, an annual rainfall of from 5 to 10 inches is found. Much the same conditions prevail in the domain of the Kalahari Desert, whence, however, the winds blow outwards to the sea. The Atlas Mountains, on the other hand, arrest the rainfall, and enjoy as much as from 10 to 50 inches during the year.

<small>Sources of great river-systems.</small>

We have now some explanation of why the great river-systems of Africa are situated where they are found: their source-streams originate in the regions of relatively the highest annual rainfall.

As regards the seasons of rain, we may thus broadly define them. The Mediterranean seaboard receives its rains in the winter months; so also do the extra-Tropical coasts of South Africa. Where the abnormal rainfall on the northern shores of the Gulf of Guinea occurs, there is a double rainy season; the same conditions prevail also on the coast of Angóla, south of the Congo, where the rainfall is small. The eastern Horn of Africa, enjoying only a light rainfall, is under the influence of the monsoon rains, which extend far inland—between the Red Sea, on the latitude of Sawákin, in the north and Zanzibar in the south. The Sahara and Libyan desert (excepting the mountain regions), the Kalahari, a portion of the South-West Coast, and other smaller districts in Africa, are rainless regions. But the remainder of the continent, and by far the larger portion, has a single rainy season. The seasons at which rain falls in this inter-Tropical zone vary with the position of the sun. In the belt of calms along the Equator, however, as might be expected, there is rain all the year round: for there the light airs meet and discharge their moisture, which otherwise would be carried away.

<small>Rainy seasons.</small>

The Equatorial limit of snowfall reaches the African shores of the Mediterranean in the northern Hemisphere, and the highlands of the Cape in the southern Hemisphere; whilst in the most elevated districts of both of these regions snow may fall in the middle of every winter. Snow falls also on the very highest mountains of Africa wherever they may rise above a certain altitude, even at the Equator; but this vertical limit of snowfall is too uncertain for us to consider it in any detail. Suffice it to say that Mounts Kilima-njaro, Kénia, Ruwenzori, and probably also the mountains of Abyssinia, thrust their crests above the line of perennial snow.

<small>Snow-line.</small>

Distribution of soils. From the consideration of meteorological conditions we pass by a natural transition to the question of soils, which have a reflex action upon climate. In regard to the distribution of soils in Africa, which, from the agricultural standpoint as well as from that of political settlement, is of prime importance, very little can be said with certainty: our *data* in this respect are of the most imperfect and limited kind. On referring to our geological map (Plate VI.), however, we can broadly distinguish the soils which must be more or less developed in the great geological divisions.

Soils: Archæan rocks. The Archæan rocks, for instance, frequently yield soils not unlike those of granitic tracts; that is to say, where the slope of the ground is considerable, the soil is necessarily thin and gravelly, and is not cultivable; but, in the lower-lying tracts where such rocks prevail, clay-like soils are occasionally well developed. Such soils, with proper treatment, are often fertile.

Soils: Palæozoic division. Of rocks belonging to the great Palæozoic division, it may be said in general terms that the soils most likely to be encountered will be argillaceous or clay-like in character, though many are more or less arenaceous or sandy. And as regards the fertility of the soils overlying these rocks, much depends on the configuration of the ground. On moderate slopes and gently undulating ground the soils and subsoils are often of considerable depth. All gradations of character are met with, from more or less loose sandy soils to very heavy soils consisting largely of clay. The fertility of all these soils is, of course, largely influenced by the amount of organic matter which they may happen to contain.

Soils: Mesozoic strata. The Mesozoic strata of Central and South Africa have a prevalent arenaceous or sandy character, and the soils yielded by them on sloping ground and uplands are somewhat open and light. In the north of Africa, where the later Mesozoic strata are well developed, limestones and calcareous sandstones are tolerably abundant, and the overlying soils, in places where the slope of the ground allows of their accumulation, are usually fertile. In Abyssinia enormous areas are occupied by volcanic rocks, which are believed to be of Mesozoic age, and the soils formed from the disintegration of these rocks is almost invariably fertile; but, unfortunately, owing to the configuration of the country, the loose soils are continuously swept down from the plateaus and terraces into the great river valleys. We have already observed how the River Atbara carries away the sediment which goes to form the Nile Delta.

Tertiary rocks are developed chiefly along the Mediterranean seaboard, and consist largely of limestones and calcareous strata. The soils yielded by these, under normal climatic conditions, are frequently highly fertile; but, unfortunately,* the regions in Africa over which Tertiary strata are principally developed are characterised by an extremely dry climate, so that wide areas are practically desert. On the other hand, where water is plentiful, the abundant growth of vegetation indicates the natural fertility of the land; and, doubtless, irrigation on an extended scale would reclaim many broad tracts of desert lands which in former times appear to have been cultivated with success. Enormous regions in Northern Africa have become desiccated even within historical times. Abundant facts tend to show that, in the flourishing days of Egypt and Carthage, for instance, Northern Africa was much better watered than it is now, and sustained a very large population; the land, which was also irrigated, was, in fact, under extensive cultivation.

<small>Soils: Tertiary rocks.</small>

The Quaternary and Recent deposits consist in North Africa chiefly of moving sands and of the gravel and grit that strew the courses of rivers which have either ceased to

<small>Soils: Quaternary and Recent deposits.</small>

---

* In African affairs this term is a qualification that necessarily occurs again and again.

exist or are greatly diminished in volume; and in Central and South Africa these deposits are represented by the alluvial accumulations of the great rivers and their tributaries.

Best soils for agricultural purposes.

Looked at broadly, therefore, it is obvious that the soils most readily available for agricultural purposes are those great flats which border the streams and rivers. But there must be enormous tracts in the Mesozoic and Palæozoic areas readily capable of being brought under cultivation; while, with judicious disforesting, large regions of uplands might be converted into rich pasture-lands. Nor can it be doubted that if the forests, which in the times of the Romans and Carthaginians clothed large districts of North Africa, were in part restored, and good systems of irrigation adopted, the soils of these regions would soon cease to be regarded as barren. The influence of forests in regulating the rain-supply is undoubted, for they prevent the rain from being rapidly absorbed underground, besides keeping the soils from being washed away and inducing a more humid climate generally.

Effect of forests on rain-supply.

Before leaving this question of the distribution of soils in Africa and their fertility, the attention of the reader should be specially directed to the maps illustrating this chapter, which may be studied for the elucidation of details into which space forbids us to enter. And, as a rough and ready guidance to the subject, it may be added that the best agricultural regions of England have from twenty-five to twenty-eight inches of annual rainfall.

Distribution of vegetation.

The vegetation of Africa naturally falls to be described under latitudinal zones.

According to Dr. Behm,* the area of Africa may be thus distinguished:—

---

* *Die Bevölkerung der Erde*, vi. 1880. *Ergänzungsheft, Petermanns Mitteilungen*, No. 62, p. 59.

36.4 per cent. is occupied by deserts.
14.6 „   „   „   „   steppes.
5.3   „   „   „   „   scrub.
21.3 „   „   „   „   savannas.
21.8 „   „   „   „   forests* and cultivated land.
.6   „   „   „   „   the larger lakes.

Roughly speaking, therefore, about half the continent is occupied by deserts and steppes, and of the other half the moiety is an area of savannas. We have left less than a quarter of the area of Africa in which fairly fertile land is found, and a large portion of that, especially in the Equatorial regions, is covered with forests. Almost the whole of the northern Hemisphere is desert or steppe country, and the most fertile lands are in the southern Hemisphere, chiefly distributed along the continental axis and in the river valleys.

The typical zones of vegetation in Africa are thus broadly distinguishable:—(1.) The Mediterranean zone; (2.) Sahara desert zone; (3.) Equatorial zone of Tropical vegetation; and (4.) Savannas of South-Central and South Africa. {Vegetation: typical zones.}

This being the general distribution of vegetation in Africa, we may proceed to view it in somewhat greater detail. What we want to arrive at is the outward aspect of the continent in its characteristic features, upon which only we can afford to dwell.

The Mediterranean lands, with the exception of the desert tracts on the eastern Littoral, sustain a vegetation similar to that of Southern Europe, if somewhat more Tropical. In the highly mountainous regions of Morocco there are fine forests and pasture-lands with rich soils capable of yielding any growth, according to altitude; but this development of vegetation applies only to the northern slopes; for, as we {Mediterranean zone.}

* The above estimate was, of course, antecedent to Stanley's discoveries.

cross the watershed and enter the domain of the Sahara, we abruptly emerge upon the broad steppes. The finest soils are found in the *Tell* lands, of moderate elevation, which intervene between the coast and the "Middle Atlas;" and there a climate, with seasonal changes not unlike those of England, is found. The farther we penetrate south, vegetation in Algeria becomes scantier; and we eventually pass over a rocky steppe-country into the Algerian Sahara. This border-land of desert is dotted with oases, in which the date-palm is the typical growth. Much the same conditions prevail in Tunis. But in Tripoli, along the remainder of the Mediterranean coast up to the Nile Delta, except in the peninsula of Barka and the narrow coastal zone in its neighbourhood, we encounter a soil of almost universal barrenness, favourable for little else but the growth of marketable grasses, vegetables, and Tropical fruits. The steppes and deserts extend in many places right up to the sea, and are backed, at a very short distance inland, by stony plateaus. The terrible Libyan Desert itself advances to the coast-line and encroaches upon the Nile Delta. The luxuriant vegetation of the Mediterranean basin is, therefore, limited to the highland region in the north-west, and is thereby carried still farther, to the Atlantic.

Desert zone.   South of this zone is the pitiless desert plateau, stretching from shore to shore across the immense breadth of North Africa, and continuing its characteristic features eastwards into Asia, thus raising a most effectual barrier between the two largest centres of population in the world, the inconvenience of which for purposes of inter-communication has only partially been obviated by the fortunate coincidence of the Isthmus of Suez and by the genius of De Lesseps. The desert zone is supreme, then, between the Atlantic and the Red Sea. The Lower Nile, which traverses the Libyan, Nubian, and Arabian deserts, carries only a thin thread of vegetation, practically limited to its narrow valley, through the thirsty land of the Pharaohs; whilst the Upper Nile flows through a savanna and steppe region. Where, however, the mountains of the Sahara reach a superior elevation, or where the water comes to the surface and forms oases, a corresponding desert vegetation is encouraged. Let us try to realise what the Sahara is really like. It is not by any means as yellow as it is painted.

The desert of the Sahara is popularly regarded as a level expanse of sand of indefinite extent, resembling an ocean. But regions of this character within its domain are rare and comparatively restricted. The Libyan desert, it is true, is an immense district in itself (not much smaller than European Russia), and resembles very closely an ocean of sand, the high dunes formed by the prevailing N.E. wind counterfeiting "Atlantic rollers;" but the Libyan Desert, where organic life is scarcely possible, is the most desolate region in the whole of this zone, though some consider the bare rocky plateaus of certain portions of the Sahara are infinitely more depressing, for they have so gloomy and sombre a hue. The true desert is where, in this vast plateau, the dunes lie heaped up and murmur like the waves of the sea;* where animal life, if it exist at all, assumes the protective colour of the sand; where there are no birds, no trees, no flowers: "the sky without clouds, the sands without shadow:" "the region of blind forces of heat and wind."

A picture of the Sahara desert

Only about one-ninth of the Sahara is covered with sand; the remainder consists of mountains and rocks, steppes and oases. In the high-lying districts, the valleys are covered with trees and are fairly habitable; and in the

* In the regions of dunes the sand emits a sound like a clarion, whether by the rubbing together of the molecules it is not possible to say (Reclus).

Arabian desert, to the east, a luxuriant vegetation exists in the river valleys. The Western Sahara is somewhat different in character: there are extensive plains, with mountains, hills, and valleys, and dry wadis; and the land is not so desolate but that life can be supported almost anywhere within its borders. Of the oases little need be said, they are so familiar to all of us: their luxuriant vegetation standing out, in our imagination, as in a sea of fire,—safe ports for the exhausted convoy of dusty and parched travellers.

This is what the Sahara is not unlike in fine weather, but when a sandstorm occurs, or when the suffocating hot winds blow, then it is a region unfit for man or beast.

Transition region. Between latitudes 13° and 15° north, we emerge almost imperceptibly on the transitional region of pastoral steppe-country, which grows grasses and sometimes edible corn, and heralds a land of plenty beyond. Between this intermediate region and the Tropical forest zone extends, almost continuously between the oceans, a fine park-like country, with antelopes and giraffes a-hiding, and mimosa trees casting shadows over the grassy tracts, or congregating into open forests.

Kalahari desert zone. The desert zone of the northern Hemisphere has its counterpart in the much more restricted desert zone of the South-West Coast, which, increasing in depth from Ambriz to Mossâmedes, eventually penetrates into the Kalahari domain, and, farther east, merges gradually in the fine grass-country of the Transvaal and Orange Free State. Patches of desert land occur also in the *karoos* of South Africa and in the steppe-districts of other portions of Africa. In these stony and sandy places there is a desert vegetation, which, after a heavy rainfall, is remarkably developed; the soils are alternately drenched and baked, and the plants strike their roots deep underground, some storing up their moisture-supply in bulbs, like the "kengwe" (water-melon). Where iron occurs, the sandy or clay soils obtain a reddish tinge. Salt-pans are formed in many places. In the river-beds which carry off the surface-drainage there is always a certain amount of vegetation apparent. The origin and general characteristics of these desert zones have already been commented upon; it is sufficient for our present purpose to remember that they mostly afford a precarious subsistence to a hardy, half-savage, indigenous population.

The regions of Tropical vegetation are more or less co-incident with those enjoying the highest mean annual temperature and heaviest rainfall: that is to say, they border the Gulf of Guinea and prevail inland, up to the great Lakes in the east, and in the Congo basin. South and west of the Congo the dry coast-lands effectually limit this Tropical zone of vegetation; and patches of savannas occur elsewhere within its domain. Zone of Tropical vegetation.

The mangrove swamps and alluvial plains of the Lower Niger give place, as we penetrate into the inland plateau and leave the primeval forest behind, to the hardier vegetation of a drier soil and climate: in room of the palm-oil tree we find the shea-butter tree, and instead of yams we meet with native corn and maize. From the low, sandy coasts of Upper Guinea we may have to pass over grassy plains, or perhaps steppes, before gaining the primeval forest; but once this region is reached, we encounter a dense and tangled growth of Tropical vegetation, the luxuriance of which is extraordinary. Nor is this vegetable *abandon* peculiar to the coast inland from the Gulf of Guinea: it is also widely distributed in the Central Súdan and in the Congo basin.

Mr. Stanley, in lucid and picturesque language, thus describes the dense forest region which he recently discovered and traversed between the Congo and Lake Albert: The great Congo Forest

Mr. Stanley's description of the great Congo Forest.

"The mornings generally were stern and sombre, the sky covered with lowering and heavy clouds; at other times a thick mist buried everything, clearing off about 9 A.M., sometimes not till 11 A.M. Nothing stirs then: the insect life is still asleep; the forest is still as death; the dark river (Ituri), darkened by lofty walls of thick forest and vegetation, is silent as a grave; our heart-throbs seem almost clamorous, and our inmost thoughts loud. If no rain follows this darkness, the sun appears from behind the cloudy masses; the mist disappears; life wakens up before its brilliancy; butterflies skurry through the air; a solitary ibis croaks an alarm; a diver flies across the stream; the forest is full of a strange murmur; and somewhere up-river booms the alarm-drum—the quick-sighted natives have seen us; voices vociferate challenges; there is a flash of spears, and hostile passions are aroused." *

This short passage gives a very vivid impression of the primeval forest. In the same paper Mr. Stanley speaks of the impediments that arrested the progress of his expedition: "These consisted of creepers, varying from one-eighth of an inch to fifteen inches in diameter, swinging across the path in bowlines or loops, sometimes massed and twisted together; also of a low, dense bush occupying the sites of old clearings, which had to be carved through before a passage was possible. Where years had elapsed since the clearings had been abandoned, we found a young forest, and the spaces between the trees choked with climbing plants, vegetable creepers, and tall plants. This kind had to be tunnelled through before an inch of progress could be made. The primeval forest offered least obstruction; but the atmosphere was close, stagnant, impure; and an eternal gloom reigned there, intensified every other day by the thick black clouds charged with rain,—so characteristic of this forest region."

* *Scottish Geographical Magazine*, vol. v., p. 228.

We may take Mr. Stanley's descriptions, quoted above, as illustrative of other and similar regions in Africa.

The zone of primeval forest and dense Tropical vegetation finds an irregular northern limit in about the tenth parallel of north latitude. It includes, besides the Guinea Coast and Lower Niger, some interior parts beyond the coastal range and a considerable portion of the Congo basin, the southern tributaries of which, however, flow through prairie country of unsurpassed fertility. Though this rich Tropical growth finds its easterly limit on the approach to the high-plateau country, in which the Upper Nile and Upper Congo have their origin and where the great Lakes are situated, large patches of Tropical or sub-Tropical vegetation and forests are found within the confines of Abyssinia, up to an altitude of nearly 10,000 feet, around the western sources of the Nile, along the East Coast, up the great river-valleys, and elsewhere. *Limits of zone of primeval forest and Tropical vegetation.*

South of the Equator vegetation is much richer and more widely distributed than in the corresponding regions of the northern Hemisphere; and it is relatively more developed towards the East Coast: for there we encounter a plateau-country with a higher mean annual temperature and heavier rainfall. Moreover, on the East Coast, south of the Equator, the transition areas between one zone of vegetation and another are more gradual than on the West Coast, not only on account of the prevailing winds and heavier rainfall, but because the East Coast is washed by relatively warm ocean-currents, whilst the West Coast is washed by relatively cold ocean-currents. The effect on vegetation is therefore well marked. To take an example: the southern limit of the occurrence of the palm is, on that account, advanced some sixteen degrees farther down the shores of the Indian Ocean than on the Atlantic seaboard. *Zones of vegetation compared.*

Savannas.

The entire area coloured on our map (Plate VII.) as a region of savannas is in reality very diversified, and may be said to include all the vegetations of Africa. It is consequently very representative, not in regard to vegetation only, but also in the distribution of animals and in other respects.

Vegetation: latitudinal and longitudinal developments.

We have thus not only a latitudinal, but also a longitudinal, development of vegetation south of the Equator. Vegetation is richer as we proceed from south to north and also from west to east. On the East Coast, again, north of the Equator, vegetation is less rich, although the climate is healthier, than in the corresponding region to the south.

These general remarks on the distribution of vegetation in Africa may serve as a running commentary on the maps. Later on, in dealing with natural products, we shall gain more detailed information in regard to the character and fertility of the respective districts.

Distribution of fauna.

The distribution of the fauna of any continent being controlled by the distribution of vegetation, which, in its turn, depends largely on climate, we naturally expect to find in Africa a fauna strictly Tropical. The faunas of Africa are, in fact, remarkably homogeneous, and the most representative of the Tropics. Animals, far more than plants, possess the power of migration; and in the Equatorial regions of Africa this movement is probably from north to south. Owing to the difference in the seasons of rain in the verdant uplands north and south of the Equator, the greater number of African animals desert the dry tracts and migrate in search of sustenance to more favoured districts. This migratory movement cannot be determined with any certainty, for we know very little about the subject; but the N. to S. direction seems to hold true in respect of birds of passage in Equatorial

Africa.* Wallace's classification of zoological provinces in Africa may be still regarded as acceptable in all essential particulars.

The continent of Africa preserves faunal types of a very remote period of creation, which exist nowhere else: these are the hippopotamus and the giraffe. It seems only fitting that this vast, antique continent should be the last resting-place of the largest animals; although they are everywhere retiring or are being exterminated along the paths of European invasion—I mean progress. Unique faunal types.

We may recall some of the benefits we owe to African products. Of such, Elisée Reclus specially mentions durrah, the date, the banana; certain species of dogs, the guinea-fowl, the cat, and the patient ass; possibly also the goat, the sheep, and the ox. African legacies.

Of the zoo-geographical regions of the world, the Ethiopian or African realm is one of the richest. As we have noted elsewhere in regard to geology and climate, the Mediterranean region and an adjoining portion of the Sahara constitute an area of transition, the faunal development of which is more or less uniform with that of Southern Europe, the deserts of Arabia, Asia Minor, and beyond. This exception gives emphasis to the obvious fact that it is the deserts, and not the mountains, which separate faunal regions. Fauna: African realm.

Professor Heilprin, in his *Distribution of Animals*, to which I am indebted for most of my facts in this section, thus divides the faunal sub-regions of Africa:—(1.) The vast pasture-lands of East Central Africa, which are the most representative of all; (2.) the forest zone of West Africa; and (3.) the Sahara Desert. The latter contains a comparatively limited fauna, merging almost imperceptibly in Faunal sub-regions.

* Compare *Emin Pacha in Central Africa*, p. 391 *et seq.* London: George Philip & Son.

that of the Mediterranean. The islands comprise an independent sub-region of their own.

Mammalian fauna. Of the mammalian fauna, the carnivorous and hoofed animals exist in exceptional and many other varieties. They have unique representatives, as we have said, in the hippopotamus and giraffe. The former is found in all the larger rivers south of the Sahara; the latter ranges almost everywhere over the open country, and sometimes enters the forests. The elephant is widely distributed throughout Equatorial Africa south of the Sahara.* There is an extraordinary number of species of antelope; some frequent the desert regions, some are confined to the forests, some are found in mountain fastnesses, and some range over the open plains. The last mentioned comprise the greatest number of species, and are met with in herds of many hundreds. The Cape buffalo is found in most parts of South, Central, and West Africa. There are zebras and quaggas; and there is the patriarchal wild ass of Abyssinia, from which country our present domesticated variety is supposed to have sprung. Of beasts of prey, there are the lion, leopard, panther, hyena, and jackal; but the tiger is entirely absent. An important group is represented by the Ethiopian apes, the anthropoid apes, chimpanzees and gorillas. Chimpanzees and gorillas have been found more especially on the West Coast; but possibly they roam far inland towards the Nile watershed, in the Equatorial zone of forest. Of monkeys there are many of a large and savage kind, widely distributed over the continent.

Other faunas. The bird fauna of Africa is not so rich; but the reptile fauna is largely developed. Vipers of the most deadly kind, such as the puff-adder, are encountered. Crocodiles abound in all the larger rivers.

---

* In discussing, under Products, the various kinds of ivory, we shall refer at some length to the distribution of the elephant in Africa.

Of the extraordinary abundance of insect life much **Insect pests.** might be said, for it is largely due to this cause that travelling in the continent becomes so painful and difficult for Europeans. We must, however, pass over this subject merely with a reference to the locusts, which are a veritable plague in some parts, and to the tsétsé fly (*Glossina morsitans*). The tsétsé fly, especially, is a most deadly enemy. It is common enough in some parts of South and Central Africa, but does not appear to pass beyond the Bahr-el-Ghazal and Sennar, and it is quite unknown in the north-west of the continent. Its bite causes the death of horses, oxen, camels, sheep, and dogs; but, curiously enough, it is innocuous to man, to buffaloes, zebras, goats, jackals, hyenas, and several wild animals. Why this is so no one appears to know. As the country is cleared, however, the tsétsé fly becomes rarer; and, considering the importance of destroying this deadly pest, no efforts should be spared to protect domesticated and draught animals against attack.

We may now apply our meteorological *data* to what it is **Climatology.** one purpose of this chapter to illustrate—the habitability of Africa and the acclimatisation of Europeans.

We have referred to the distribution of temperature, the **Factors of climate.** prevailing winds, the rainfall, and the vegetation. These, taken together, practically determine climate. The most important factor of climate is, of course, distance from the Equator; but other factors, which profoundly modify climate, have to be taken into account. What is gained by horizontal distance is also obtained in part by vertical height: that is to say, distance from the Equator has, other things being equal, the same effect as height above sea-level—a lowering of temperature. Now, the decrease of temperature with height, though varying according to local conditions, may be stated to be, roughly, 1° Fahr. for every 300 feet

Hence it is that mountains of such great height as Kilimanjaro, Kénia, and perhaps Ruwenzori, though lying on or near the Equator, have their summits covered with snow all the year round; consequently, in passing from their base upwards, one passes through zones of vegetation which are characteristic of almost every class of climate. Vegetation and soil also react upon climate. Loose and sandy soils, for instance, are bad conductors of heat: the temperature, instead of penetrating to considerable depths, like in close, loamy, or clayey soils, is concentrated on the surface, and is more rapidly radiated at night,—thus giving rise to extreme and rapid fluctuations of temperature in the superincumbent atmosphere. On the other hand, where the ground is covered by thick vegetation, especially by dense forests, the sun's rays do not reach the earth at all, or only indirectly: the temperature is therefore more equally distributed, and humidity is increased.

Modifications of climate.

Owing to the unequal conducting powers of land and water—water being the very worst conductor of heat, absorbing it slowly and releasing it slowly—we have important modifications of climate where land and sea are in proximity. And, finally, there is always the factor of the surface-currents of the ocean to take into account. These currents follow, in the main, the prevailing winds, and profoundly affect the climate of the shores they wash.

The climates of the world range between what are comprehensively known as oceanic, insular, and continental; but it is only with the latter class that we shall have to concern ourselves.

Comparison between climates.

Since the greater part of Africa lies within the Tropics, it follows that its climate must be, in the main, Tropical, except in so far as it is subject to local modifications. Thus, along the great axis of the continent, with elevations of over

6000 feet, though solar radiation is very great, the temperature of the air is not felt to be so oppressive as in the lower-lying and more humid lands. In proximity to large sheets of water, like the great Lakes, the climate is moister and more equable than at a distance from them; whilst proximity to the ocean ensures still greater uniformity in climatic phenomena. In highly mountainous regions the climate varies in accordance with the configuration of the land: thus, if a mountain range lie athwart the path of the prevailing wind, the leeward side will get little or nothing of the rainfall, which is nearly all precipitated on the windward side. As a general rule, the leeward slopes of mountain ranges thus situated have relatively colder winters and hotter summers than the windward slopes.

Hence it is that the South-West Coast of Africa, stretching inland to the Kalahari, receives little or no rainfall from the Indian Ocean, and is consequently a desert. Moreover, the South East Trades of the Atlantic, though they originate off this coast, blow outwards to sea. The Sahara Desert, and, in fact, the whole of North Africa except the Atlas regions, owes its sterile character chiefly to the fact that the prevailing winds, carrying moisture from the Mediterranean, proceed from a colder to a warmer zone: the atmosphere thus gains progressively in its capacity for absorbing and retaining moisture; and there is consequently no rainfall, unless, as in the case of the Atlas, great mountains intervene to throw the winds into higher regions, and thereby cool the air, bringing about a precipitation. *Application of known laws.*

The chief qualities of desert climates are the intense heat by day and the severe cold by night. We have, therefore, in the Sahara and Kalahari regions and on the South-West Coast, not to mention lesser areas, well-marked characteristics of climate. Compared to the other climates of Africa, they are relatively healthy. *Desert climates.*

Climate of coastal zone.

The low-lying coastal zone of Equatorial Africa has a distinct climate of its own, which prevails in some cases along the lower courses of the great rivers. This region, for reasons which we shall learn later on, is by far the most humid and pestiferous.

Sub-Tropical climates.

The sub-Tropical northern seaboard enjoys more or less a Mediterranean climate, and the sub-Tropical region of the Cape one equally favourable.

Taken as a whole, it seems evident that for Europeans Africa is by far the least habitable of any of the continents, and, speaking generally, it is the malarial fevers that render it so unfitted for European settlement. It is true we do not know very much about Tropical diseases,* their distribution, and the causes of their inception and propagation; but of Tropical diseases generally we shall have little to say: it is malarial fevers that must chiefly concern us.

Malarial fevers.

Malarial fevers are of two kinds, intermittent and remittent, and there are many degrees of intensity and virulence between them. They are endemic and epidemic. The intermittent varieties are the most widely distributed in Africa, as elsewhere; indeed, no continent is free from them. But Africa is subject to intermittent malarial fevers in an extraordinary degree; and the reason of this is not hidden: the mean annual temperature and rainfall, being the predisposing and exciting causes of the disease, are excessive in the habitable parts of the continent.

Malarial poisons.

Malarial poisons are generated in marshy ground, and the denser the soil, if impregnated with vegetable matter, the more virulent is the disease. Thus, the malarial poisons are most easily generated and retained in clay or close soils;

---

* My *data* in this respect are partly derived from Dr. R. W. Felkin's *Tropical Diseases*, republished from the *Proceedings of the Royal Society of Edinburgh*.

but in sandy or porous soils, unless the subsoils lie near to the surface, the morbific agents have a better chance of escape.

Temperature, humidity, and the character of soil are, therefore, the main factors with which we have to reckon. As regards temperature, which is lowered in inverse ratio to vertical height, it has been stated that in Equatorial Africa malaria scarcely occurs above 3000 or 5000 feet in altitude; but this is a doubtful point. Malaria is certainly most virulent on the coasts. In the latter case it has been observed that a height of 500 feet or more will perceptibly modify its intensity, especially in places where the winds disperse the poisonous exhalations of the soil. The fevers have their maxima at certain seasons, and are most dangerous at the time of seasonal changes, especially after prolonged drought or succeeding rainfall. *Other factors.*

Humidity and soil may be considered in conjunction. The soils most favourable to the propagation of malaria are naturally those along the coasts and up the middle and lower valleys of the great rivers; and these regions of Equatorial Africa lie in the zones of the highest mean annual temperature and rainfall. Here we find malarial fevers in their worst or remittent forms: they are endemic. This pernicious variety prevails also in low-lying, marshy districts under a certain altitude. To turn up the virgin soil in such districts is to release the poisonous messengers of death: hence no European, however seasoned, should be employed in such work. *Humidity and soil.*

According to Mr. W. North,* malaria in its highest degree of intensity is met with in Senegal, on the coasts of the Gulf of Guinea, the West Coast down to the twentieth degree of south latitude, Madagascar, Nubia, parts of Abyssinia and the Súdan, the East Coast, and Egypt. In a milder form it is met with in Tripoli, Algeria, *Distribution of malaria.*

* *Nineteenth Century*, June 1889.

Morocco, the Cape de Verde Islands, and the oases of the Sahara.

Remedial measures. Other things being equal, malaria prevails in its worst form where the amount of rotting vegetation or organic matter is greatest. Obviously, therefore, it would be checked or palliated by either flooding or draining marshy lands. Plantations of *Eucalyptus* are also recommended as a remedial measure.

Other Tropical diseases. Of other Tropical diseases only a few need be referred to. Asiatic cholera has touched the Mediterranean and East coasts of Africa, but apparently it has not penetrated into the Interior. Yellow fever is known on the Guinea Coast. Tropical dysentery is widely diffused: all along the Guinea Coast and southwards to the Congo, between this coastal region and the Nile, on the Mediterranean seaboard, in Egypt, Mozambique, Madagascar, and in Cape Colony.

Guinea Coast. I will not depress the reader by mentioning more. One thing is notable: all Tropical diseases appear to find a congenial home on the Coast of Guinea.

Acclimatisation. The question naturally arises, to what extent can Europeans become fever-proof: acclimatised, in short? When it is remembered that the Natives themselves, in migrating from one district to another, are subject to the malaria of strange localities, though proof against that prevailing in their own, it at once becomes evident that acclimatisation is only in a measure possible. The acclimatisation of man, like that of animals, is a process of time, of generations, and not of months only. Months! Why, European travellers, traders, and missionaries, in their eager haste to reach the goal of their ambition, dash recklessly into the fever-beds of Africa without the slightest hesitation or precaution. And few escape the fever. Some die after an attack or two; some drag on, with the poison degenerating their blood and tissues, for years. Those who are wisest return periodically to Europe or go to some sanatorium, of which there are many even in Africa. But either the grim fascination which the Dark Continent exercises over all who have business therein or other personal interests draw them back again, to expend the new lease of life they have elsewhere gained, to become bankrupt of which is to wilfully arraign oneself at the Highest Court before which man can be tried.

Some of my personal acquaintances have passed many years of their lives in the most fever-stricken parts of Africa, the Guinea Coast, where all the elements of malarial fever are rifest; and they tell me that, though none escape the fever, those with sound constitutions may, with due care and precautions, prolong life indefinitely at the most pestiferous places. The main precautions appear to be to avoid alcoholic liquors, to lead a regular, careful, and quiet life, and to take plenty of exercise. Well, in a climate like that of Africa, especially in the moist heat of the coast-lands, to lead a life of this kind is not so easy as it might appear to be; for men are human, and there are relatively few distractions "on the Coast" to nourish their higher aspirations. My impression is that Europeans, by long residence there, lose so much of their moral as well as of their vital powers, that they are only able to combat the subversive elements of life in an ever-lessening degree: they succumb to the climate in the first generation, though in the second and subsequent generations their descendants may become more and more acclimatised, and may develop a mind and body better suited to existence under such conditions. And even then, whatever his development and however complete his acclimatisation, the European cannot compare his hybrid constitution with that of the Negro, to whom must be intrusted all hard manual labour or work requiring constant outdoor exposure.

DEVELOPMENT OF AFRICA.

Habitability of Africa.

We will now attempt to focus the information brought together in this chapter on the point it is designed to illustrate: the habitability of Africa. By habitability I refer, of course, to the favourable conditions of climate and soil for settlement by Europeans. Such an essay must, at best, be a tentative one, and I venture on it with diffidence, because we really know so little of Africa, when all has been said.

Unsettleable lands.

First, then, we can eliminate the three inland-drainage areas as desert lands quite unfitted for European settlement.

We have left, in something like a natural order:—

Settleable lands.

(1.) The Mediterranean seaboard and Lower Egypt, (2.) North-West Africa, (3.) Upper Guinea, (4.) the Súdan, (5.) Red Sea Littoral, (6.) Abyssinia, (7.) Lower Guinea, (8.) Congo basin, (9.) Portuguese West Africa, (10.) South Africa, (11.) South-East Africa (Zambezi basin), (12.) East Coast, and (13.) the high-plateau countries.

Regions north of Equator.

Of these regions, the Mediterranean seaboard has been shown to belong, both climatically and politically, more to Europe than to Africa, from the continental portions of which it is cut off by the Sahara Desert. Lower Egypt falls very much under the same category, for the Nubian Desert acts in precisely the same manner as the Sahara, though in a more limited degree. Climatic phenomena, therefore, relegate this region outside of Continental Africa.

The late lamented Egyptian Súdan, on the other hand, is accessible in the north from the Red Sea, and in the south from the lost Equatorial Province, which in its turn can be reached from the East Coast. But this region is at present closed to us by as deadly, if not so unconquerable, a foe as climate—the Mahdists and Arab patriots.

North-West Africa would appear to be habitable enough;

but the Upper Guinea Coast has been demonstrated as the unhealthiest region of the continent. Of the Red Sea Littoral the less said the better; we know how our troops suffered at Sawákin. Abyssinia, on the other hand, is for the most part a sanatorium in itself, and offers one of the best routes into Africa, *viâ* Kassála, from the Red Sea.

This almost disposes of the whole of the continent north of the Equator. In the greater part of that region we see now how the factor of climate is hostile to European enterprise, and how in the past it has been the most effective bulwark for the preservation of native independence. Protected by the deserts in the north, with only two fairly accessible highways * from the east, is it to be wondered at that, these two feasible routes having been entirely neglected so far—they are infamously bad in any case—the Mahdists and their adherents should have proved such formidable foes? By the loss of Khartúm and of Emin's province we have been deprived of the only two, or at least the best, points of vantage from whence effective political control could be exercised. As regards the approach from the west, south of the Equator, Stanley's recent expedition demonstrated the almost superhuman difficulties of opening up a route from the Congo to the Lakes, to maintain which for effective political action appears next to impossible, at least in the near future.

Effects of climate.

We perceive, therefore, that on the Upper Nile we have a region which, climatically, is an *enclave* most difficult to penetrate from any side. It is closed to us now; and to enter it again will tax all the resources of civilisation. Alas! for the fall of Emin Pacha, who so nobly maintained for fifteen years our most advanced stronghold in Mohammedan Africa. Abyssinia, perhaps, may in the future be

Upper Nile region.

---

* From the Red Sea and from the East Coast.

a factor of importance to us; but at present, in spite of Italy's political ascendancy, we are very far from making any use of this pseudo-Christian kingdom. It is too early as yet to reckon on Uganda.

Central Sudan.
We still have left the great Mohammedan States of the Súdan; but they are accessible only from the unhealthy Guinea Coast. Access to these States is practicable enough: and, when once the plateau is gained, the climate of the higher-lying regions is sufficiently favourable to Europeans. Behind the Coast, too, at a certain altitude above sea-level, healthy districts may be found—Mount Camarons, for instance, is a sanatorium in itself; and the perfect climate of the Canaries might be enjoyed periodically without necessitating too long a sea-voyage for Europeans.

Regions south of Equator.
Of the regions lying to the south of the Equator, in the strictly Tropical parts of Africa, we have three distinct classes of climates—the coastal, the highlands, and the intermediate zones. The coastal belt and the river valleys have already been spoken of as in the main unhealthy, though fairly habitable for Europeans, provided certain protective measures are not neglected, such as great care of health, draining of swamps, &c. It will be noticeable, in fact, that, along the coasts of Africa, European settlements are mostly situated on islands near the shore or on peninsular lands; and it cannot be doubted that this measure of precaution has been adopted more from hygienic considerations than from reasons of safety against attack.

Intermediate and highland regions.
The regions of moderate elevation intervening between the coasts and the high-plateau country necessarily contain districts in which European settlements are possible. But it is to the highland countries along the main axis of the continent that we must look for the most favourable districts of Equatorial Africa; it is there that, for climatic

as well as for political reasons, we have our best chance
of personally and effectually controlling the destinies of
Africa. The magnificent water communications and the
relatively healthy climate are factors in our hands which
compensate for their absence north of the Equator.

It seems as if Africa had been thus delimitated by Nature, <small>Cross and Crescent.</small>
in the north for the sphere of inaccessible and unchange-
able Islam, and in the south for the impressionable Bantu,
who has been taken under the ægis of Christian Europe.
Therein lies our hope and our responsibility. The development of Africa is, in the end, a contest between Cross
and Crescent, for the benefit not only of the cause itself,
but also of Pagan Africa. Whether the struggle be undertaken for commercial profit or political aggrandisement,
the issue must be very much the same.

Now, we have seen that, for the effective administration <small>Essentials of effective occupation.</small>
of European political power, a base on the coast is absolutely
essential. Hence it happens that the possession of our
South African Empire, extending practically from the Cape
to the banks of the Zambezi, and embracing the finest
climates and the richest lands in Africa, places us in a
peculiarly advantageous position for influencing and eventually controlling the countries lying to the north. It is
almost unnecessary to point out the obvious conclusion,
that on the power and cohesion of our forces in South
Africa must depend not merely the welfare of the colony,
but also the success of our mission in Africa and the welfare of its indigenous populations. European interests and
native African interests are so far inseparable and identical.
The natives must be either our allies or our foes: to use
them only as instruments were a crime.

CHAPTER IV.

THE INDIGENOUS POPULATIONS.

GENERAL CONSIDERATIONS—LINGUISTIC GROUPS AND THEIR GEOGRAPHICAL DISTRIBUTION—CHARACTERISTICS OF NEGROES AND OF NATIVE LIFE—SURVEY OF THE INDIGENOUS POPULATIONS: THEIR MENTAL, MORAL, AND MATERIAL CULTURE; THEIR POLITICAL ORGANISATIONS AND SOCIAL DEVELOPMENT—CAPACITY OF THE NEGRO FOR DEVELOPING HIGHER FORMS OF CULTURE—NON-RESISTANCE, FROM THE COMPARATIVE ABSENCE OF POLITICAL COHESION IN BANTU AFRICA, AGAINST THE EUROPEAN DOMINATION—NATIVE RIGHTS AND EUROPEAN RESPONSIBILITIES.

MAPS.

LANGUAGES	*Plate* X.
FORMS OF GOVERNMENT .	„ XIV.
DENSITY OF POPULATION .	„ IX.

THE INDIGENOUS POPULATIONS.

IN former chapters we have endeavoured to elucidate physical phenomena in Africa by reference to the laws governing them, and to deduce practical hints for our guidance in "opening up" the continent. In dealing with the political aspects of our subject, we shall see in how far they have been controlled by physical causes. It is only by understanding this interaction between physical and political phenomena that we can hope to lay the foundation of a rational policy in Africa: for violation of Nature's laws brings the inevitable Nemesis.

Interaction between physical and political phenomena.

We have now to deal with the distribution of the native populations. Our knowledge of the innumerable tribes inhabiting Africa and of their languages—in the examination of which the best classification may be sought—is, it is true, not much more extensive and complete than our knowledge of the geological structure of the continent: that is to say, we know a good deal of the coastal tribes and of those in direct contact with them, but of the remainder and greater number we have only a specimen here and there, so to speak, to guide us. A rough and general classification can, however, be made.

Distribution of the native populations.

Dr. Cust, writing * in 1887, informs us that there are 438 languages and 153 dialects spoken in Africa: say, therefore, there are 600 languages and dialects, and we shall not be very far wrong. But over and above this wealth of linguistic material, the difficulty of classifying the indigenous tribes on the basis of language is, in

Languages and dialects.

---
* *Languages of Africa* (Linguistic and Oriental Essays. Trübner & Co.).

the present state of our knowledge, very great. As an example, Professor Keane points out * that the pure Negro race—a very large and important section of the African Family—" presents apparent ethnological unity with obvious linguistic diversity." Moreover, many of the tribes, the names only of which we know, have been shifted from group to group in accordance with the genius and ingenuity of the operator; frequent migratory movements have also occurred: thus, tribes taking their distinctive names from their chiefs have undergone kaleidoscopic changes on the map. Whilst, therefore, making language the basis of a classification, our inquiry may be modified or amplified in various directions as the occasion demands.

Population of Africa. The total population of Africa, which has been variously estimated, is usually regarded as being upwards of two hundred millions. But quite recently Mr. E. G. Ravenstein has made a careful calculation, independent of all others: and he has very kindly placed his figures at my disposal. The result is surprising. Mr. Ravenstein estimates the total population of Africa at only 127,038,370, distributed as follows:—

	Area. English sq. miles.	Population.
Morocco and Tuat	314,027	6,076,000
Algeria	257,600	3,870,000
Tunis	44,800	1,500,000
Tripoli	400,000	1,010,000
Sahara	2,386,000	1,400,000
Egypt Proper	436,000	6,970,000
„ Old Dependencies	685,000	7,162,000
Abyssinia	128,000	3,000,000
Galla- and Somâli-lands	732,100	3,190,000
Central Sûdan	662,200	31,880,000
West Sûdan and Upper Guinea	770,000	14,266,000
Equatorial and South Africa	4,458,700	41,818,170
Islands	239,880	4,896,200
	11,514,307	127,038,370 †

* Appendix to Stanford's *Africa* (Keith Johnston), p. 523.
† Density of population, 11 per sq. mile: rate of increase per decade, 10 per cent.

Mr. Ravenstein further calculates the areas of Africa, and the populations they support, to be divided as under:— *Population: Territorial divisions.*

	Area. English sq. miles.	Population.
Under Turkish rule :—		
Egypt . .	436,000	6,970,000
Tripoli . .	400,000	1,010,000
	836,000	7,980,000
European Possessions, &c. :—		
British . .	2,351,936	39,289,500
French . .	2,783,948	21,947,600
German . .	832,750	5,105,000
Italian . .	315,070	5,369,000
Portuguese .	909,820	5,513,900
Spanish . .	246,760	444,000
Belgian . .	827,000	15,000,000
	8,267,284	92,669,000
Liberia	37,000	1,050,000
Boer States . . .	173,350	744,000
Independent . . .	2,120,323	24,595,370
Great Lakes . . .	80,350	... ...
Grand totals .	11,514,307	127,038,370

The indigenous races of Africa may be classified in many different ways. Two instances may be given. First, in respect of the character of hair: the Semites, Hamites, and Fulah have curly hair; the Negroes and Bantu have woolly or fleecy hair; and the Hottentots also have woolly hair, but growing in tufts. Second, as regards the colour of skin: it ranges through every diversity from yellow to brown and from brown to black, or what appears to be black,—for dark-brown would be a more accurate definition. The light-coloured races, as one might expect from the phenomena of climate, are found in the north and extreme south-west, and the dark-coloured races in the intermediate Tropical regions. The former division includes the Mediterranean seaboard, Lower Egypt, and the greater part of the Sahara in the north, and the countries of the Hottentots and Bushmen (Bojesmans) in the south-west; *Classification of races.*

Vagaries of ethnographic distributions.

whilst the latter, embracing the remainder of the continent, is subdivisible into the Súdan and Bantu Africa. It must not, however, be supposed that this distribution according to colour is at all restrictive, for light-coloured peoples are found in other regions than those ascribed to them in the above classification. The Monbuttu, for example, who live to the south of the Niam-Niam cannibals, have remarkably light complexions, and some even have fair hair; they have also beards and aquiline noses. Dr. Schweinfurth estimated that one in every twenty of the Monbuttu cannibals is fair. Some think that this is due to a meat diet, as against a vegetable diet. M. Antoine d'Abbadie's hypothesis, that among the Ethiopians the flesh-eating tribes have the fairest complexions, has been corroborated by others—not, I believe, on account of their diet, but because they more readily obtain the flesh of animals in the higher plateau-countries, where herds and flocks are reared. They thus enjoy a relatively cooler climate. As in the distribution of temperature, distance from the Equator is in a measure balanced by vertical height, as far as the colour of skin is concerned. It is a curious fact, upon which several explorers have commented, that the cannibal tribes are relatively of higher mental endowment and of better physique than their more prosaic neighbours. But then, again, are not these cannibals flesh-eating tribes, living in the high plateau-countries?

Climatic conditions.

While climatic conditions are in a measure responsible for the colour of the peoples and the character of their hair, it is also to these phenomena we must look in reference to their occupations and to their general distribution over the land. It will be found that the populations follow approximately the systems of climate in proportion to the abundance of rain and vegetation. We do not, of course, expect to find a dense population in the Sahara;

but, as soon as we enter the fertile Súdan, we encounter, in
the basins of the Tsad and Niger, and in Nigritia generally,
the densest populations of Africa. And in other parts—
as, for example, in the Congo basin, parts of the Lakes
district, and along the valley of the Lower Nile—the
populations are also very dense. In such regions Nature
herself has largely provided the means of support.

Then, as regards the occupations of the natives, it is obvious that our remarks on the vegetation of the continent must afford the best key to a classification. Thus, shepherds, herdsmen, and agriculturists are found in all the favourable regions of North and South-West Africa; agriculturists in the rich Equatorial countries; and shepherds, dominating agriculturists, in the lands lying immediately to the north, including the Súdan and the whole of the Eastern Horn; while purely agricultural tribes and herdsmen are encountered in the South-Central plateaus, Abyssinia, the Upper Nile territories, and Morocco. The nomad Bushmen and some of the other dwarfish tribes are, most naturally, found in the barren or isolated districts—but chiefly south of the Equator—whither they have fled for protection from aggressive neighbours.

Occupations of the natives.

In Egypt and along the Mediterranean shores of Africa there are archaeological remains dating back to the earliest historical times. Of the rest of Africa, almost without exception, it may be said that races of men may have come and gone, but neither we nor their representatives at the present day are apparently the better for them: not a monument, not a vestige of culture and civilisation have been left behind. The Bushmen, it is true, were artists in their way, and have left rude mural decorations, portraying exciting scenes of the chase and of battle, much in the style of a precocious child's "first attempt." This entire absence of monuments, to say nothing of a written language,

Archæology.

throughout the greater part of Africa renders a satisfactory systematic investigation into the ethnic affinities of the peoples extremely difficult, if not for the present impossible.

Distinct races.

Six distinct races are distinguishable: the Negroes proper, the Fulah, the Bantu, the Hottentots, the Semites, and the Hamites. The last two races are restricted almost exclusively to the north and north-east; the Negroes proper and the Fulah occupy the vast Central zone between the Atlantic and the Upper Nile region; and the Bantu overspread the whole of the continent in the south, with the exception of the barren coastal enclave in the south-west, where the Hottentots eke out a precarious livelihood. At present we shall not concern ourselves with European residents, excursionists, and incursionists.

Linguistic groups: Distribution.

From these general considerations we may proceed to particulars. We boldly adopt the classification of Dr. F. Müller,* who recognised the following seven distinct linguistic groups:—

1. The Semitic Family, along the North Coast and in Abyssinia.

2. The Hamitic Family, mainly in the Sahara, Egypt, Galla- and Somál-lands, Morocco, and Algeria.

3. The Fulah and Nuba groups, in the Western, Central, and Eastern Súdan.

4. The Negro systems, in the Western and Central Súdan, Upper Guinea, and the Upper Nile region.

5. The Bantu Family, everywhere south of about 4° N. latitude, except in the Hottentot domain.

6. The Hottentot group, in the extreme south-western corner, from the Tropic of Capricorn to the Cape.

7. The Malayo-Polynesian Family, in Madagascar.

* *Allgemeine Ethnographie.* From Appendix to Stanford's *Africa.* p. 526.

In the coastal lands and in the smaller African islands the languages of European or foreign dominations largely prevail, while other *linguæ francæ* are in current use elsewhere—such as Swahéli on the East Coast and Arabic and Hausa in the Súdan. *Alien languages.*

The whole of North Africa is occupied by the descendants of the Hamites and Semites. The former is the most ancient race of which we have any knowledge in Africa. The Hamitic peoples (Egyptians, Libyans, and Numidians) at one time occupied the whole of North Africa and a large part of the East Coast north of the Equator, and the basis of the present stock still hold their ground over wide areas. They are purest in type in the Central Sahara, where the Tuareg tribes constitute a nucleus. The isolated Tibesti highlands appear to have been the cradle of the Tibu, who occupy a dual ethnographic position. *Hamites and Semites.*

Between the Middle Nile and the Red Sea, in Galla- and Somál-lands, in parts of the Western Sahara, and in Morocco, Algeria, and Tunis, Hamitic peoples either predominate or form the basis of the populations. The Semites, on the other hand, have dispossessed the Hamites in various regions. Their oldest representatives appear to be in Abyssinia; but the Arabs, who at present form the bulk of their numbers, are the descendants of the Mohammedan incursionists of the seventh century, and are widely distributed in the basin of the Upper Nile westwards to Lake Tsad, and in North Africa.

The basis of the populations of Morocco, Algeria, and Tunis is composed of Hamitic Berbers. They are a pastoral people, and do not mix with the dominant race, the Arabs (Moors), who out-number them in the large towns. The constant immigration of Negroes from across the Sahara, and the presence in the towns of Jews, a *Diverse ethnical elements.*

despised and maltreated race in those parts, add to these diverse ethnical elements, which evince no sign of assimilation. The Berbers appear to be the most hopeful stock to encourage; but their want of unity renders difficult any plan that might be undertaken for their support. The wild tribes of the Sahara, at constant feud among themselves, are quite beyond control.

Arabs. In the Nile basin the races are very mixed, but Semitic or Arab influences are in the ascendant. The Bedwins are of pure Arab blood and are nomadic in their mode of life; while the Fellahin half-castes constitute the sedentary Arab populations. In Morocco and Algeria the Moors compose the sedentary Arab population, chiefly in the towns, and the nomad Arabs or Bedwins are to them a constant terror. The patriarchal Somal and Galla tribes are also nomadic and warlike; but they are not fused together, and are equally inimical to foreign influence.

Negro systems. Between these regions and the uncertain boundary of Bantu Africa we find the true home of the Negro. The Nuba and Fulah groups, usually classed together, and the great and diverse Negro systems, evince a remarkable degree of development. It will be safer to consider them as a whole.

The Fulah, or Fellata, or Fillani, as they are variously styled, though the dominant race in many parts of Nigritia, form only a fragment of the Negro populations under their sway, of which the Hausa are deservedly prominent. Sokoto is the chief of the Fulah States. From being simple herdsmen at the commencement of the nineteenth century, they have gradually become, by their prowess in war, their intelligence, and their proselytising zeal, the ruling people between Timbuktu and Bornu.

The Negro peoples are too numerous and diverse to

admit of classification. They extend right across the continent, from the northern shores of the Gulf of Guinea to the Upper Nile, in the neighbourhood of which we find some of the purest Negro tribes, such as the Bongo, Bari, and Shillúk.

In sharp contrast to the multitudinous Negro systems, the Bantu Family shows striking linguistic unity over a third of the continent. Of the innumerable Bantu tribes,* the Lunda peoples occupy the central and the Zulu peoples the eastern regions. {Bantu Family.}

In the south-western corner, as we have seen, is the Hottentot group. {Hottentots.}

The island of Madagascar, belonging linguistically to the Malayo-Polynesian Family of languages, has the Hova as the ruling class in the central plateau-districts, and the Sakalava on the western seaboard. {Malayo-Polynesians.}

Having alluded to the geographical distribution of the native races on the basis of language, we may now regard the various tribes at closer quarters.

Of the light-coloured peoples of South-West Africa, the two chief groups, the Hottentots and Bushmen (Bojesmans), appear to be the remnants of a primeval race that formerly ranged over the greater part of South Africa. By the incursion of stronger Kafir tribes they were expelled from the more fertile lands on the east, and for self-protection took refuge in the barren districts now occupied by them. Here, too, as a nomadic and hunting people, divisions among themselves took place. In bodily appearance they still resemble one another, but in language they are differentiated. The Bushmen have remained a more primitive {Hottentots and Bushmen compared.}

* In reading off the map the names of Bantu peoples, it is necessary to remember the force of the various tribal or collective prefixes: such as *ama-*, *ma-*, *m'-*, *aba-*, *ba-*, *be-*, *wa-*, *o-va-*. Throughout East Africa the following prefixes are used for special designations: *m-* or *mu-* implies an individual of the tribe; *u-*, the country; and *ki-*, the language of the country.

people, while the Hottentots have become assimilated with their conquerors. The Bushmen have persistently refused to be enslaved; they love freedom, and, in their search for it, they have penetrated farther and farther into the wilderness. The Hottentots, on the other hand, unlike their wilder brethren, have mixed freely with the European colonists: but from their unhappy union has sprung up a breed of half-castes, who have inherited the vices and none of the virtues of the parents on either side.

Bushmen.

The Bushman, by the necessities of his lot, has evolved those instincts which, as a hunted creature, are most serviceable to him. In spite of his dwarf stature—the average Bushman being about 4 ft. 6 in. in height—and meagre muscular development, he is remarkably enduring; moreover, he is swift as a deer on foot, and his animal faculties are preternaturally keen. His courage is great, but his cruelty is greater. Being an inveterate nomad, he requires no hut; he roams the country in quest of food, and takes shelter in caves and holes. The women, being physically weaker than their lords, are oppressed; and they are employed in all inferior capacities. The Bushmen roam about in small bands, and are found in considerable numbers on the Orange River only. The colour of their skin is of a reddish, inclining to a coppery, hue; fat is freely used as a protection against the cold; and a small hide is the only covering to their bodies. Yet, though so low in the scale of humanity, they believe not only in a spirit-world but also in a future life: they have a proverb, "Death is only sleep." The curious practice of mutilating the fingers, chiefly of the left hand, by occasionally taking off a joint, may be regarded either as a propitiation to "the gods" or as a surgical remedy; for the Bushmen believe in blood-letting.

The Hottentots, like the Bushmen, have delicately formed

limbs and are of slight muscular development, but they are Hottentots.
of greater stature, being of the medium height of man.
In the tawny-yellow colour of their skin they outwardly
resemble the Mongolian races. Prior to contact with the
European colonists, the Hottentots were simple herdsmen
and comparatively well off; about a century afterwards, Dispersal of Hottentot tribes.
however, they were driven from their pasture grounds;
and by 1810 they were all dispersed. The Griqua half-
breeds are now the most Europeanised of the Hottentot
tribes. The Namaqua, on the other hand, migrated north,
roaming far over the inhospitable coast-lands; they have
thereby retained their racial characteristics, and are now
the most typical of the Hottentot tribes. A nomadic
people, they continue to preserve many of their ancient
practices and customs.

It is apparent that, in their natural state, primitive
tribes cannot live in direct contact with European civilisation; as in other parts of the world, so in Africa we see
them receding farther and farther and perishing by degrees.
Wherever they have become assimilated with Europeans,
in whatever capacity, they have deteriorated. Our contact with them has not been for their good. They have
been hunted down, driven from their pastures, or enslaved.
But, where they have been free, they evince many bar-
baric virtues that are conspicuously absent in the half-
breeds. It is true they are inveterate cattle-lifters; but
this habit must be regarded in them as one form of hunting: like all nomadic and primitive peoples, they are essentially hunters. They are kind to one another, hospitable in
their way, and what is called "fond of music."

In other parts of Africa, but especially in the remote Pygmy tribes.
districts of the Equatorial forest zone, we recognise scattered
remnants of a primitive people in the various Pygmy tribes.
They are encountered, in a chain of small settlements extend-

Pygmy tribes.

ing right across the continent, from the Gulf of Guinea, where they were first observed by Mr. Du Chaillu, to the Albert Nyanza, and in the Middle Congo region. Of these tribes, the Akka average only four feet in height. Some of the dwarf tribes discovered by Mr. Stanley during his recent journey through the great Congo forest, if one may judge from the specimens he examined, are even more diminutive (39 to 50 inches) and equally well-proportioned. Mr. Stanley speaks of the Wambutti as the handsomest of the primitive peoples of Africa.

All the Pygmy tribes are nomads and hunters—the bow and arrow being their principal weapon—and they adopt more or less the dress and practices of their neighbours. But they are holding their own with difficulty, and must in time altogether disappear. Whether there exists any ethnical connection between them and the Bushmen is a debated point. They are undoubtedly of a primeval race, but, as Dr. Ratzel points out, of no lower mental development than the Negro, and very far from approximating to the ape type, as was so often asserted.

Negroes.

For purposes of general description, the other indigenous races of Africa may all be included under the generic term of Negroes. But before entering into particular references, it may be worth while to take a general survey, and endeavour to realise the Negro character and mode of life. It would be tedious to expatiate upon points in which one tribe differs from another; we must rest satisfied with broad generalisations.

Characteristics of Negroes.

The popular idea of the Negro is the travesty one sees of him on tobacco-labels or on the stage: an ebony complexion, coarse thick lips, and a flat nose: but this is a type found nowhere in Africa, except perhaps in the Niger Delta, where debased natives are frequently encountered. It is quite natural to infer that the Negro types undergo modifications in accordance with locality, and that both in regard to colour and features there are as many varieties as in manners and customs.

As regards mental characteristics, without presuming to dogmatise, a few well-known traits may be referred to in this place; but up to the present time we can scarcely claim to have discovered the genius of the Negro race. In its debased forms, as a stunted parasite in America or as Europeanised on the West Coast of Africa, we do not recognise the true race-development of the Negro. Under this limitation, therefore, we can only reproduce popular ideas on the subject.

It appears to us, then, that life has been so easy to the Negro in his African home that his character has undergone scarcely any evolution beyond that of man in the savage state. Wherever he has come in contact with a higher native civilisation—in the Súdan, for instance—he has developed along natural lines; but, grafted upon the alien civilisation of Europe, he has either retrograded or exhibited a mimetic, and therefore a spurious, nature. Left to himself, the Negro has, in all outward respects, been remarkably unprogressive. That the race, and far more the individual, is capable of development—of what we call progress—has been demonstrated over and over again. It is true we usually associate the progress of the Negro with his capacity to adopt the civilisation we impose on him. He is so clever at imitation, he so rapidly accommodates himself to altered circumstances, and, above all, he is so amenable to authority, that he easily adopts a hybrid civilisation. But, as Dr. Blyden points out,* this is not a true race-development: the Negro must go his own way, in his own home, if the race is to discover and nourish its inherent genius.

<small>Development of the Negro race.</small>

* *Christianity, Islam, and the Negro Race*, by E. W. Blyden.

Negro character.

The character of the Negro in his primitive state is that of the overgrown child. His superficial and impressionable nature is the cause of many virtues and failings in him. He is vain, self-indulgent, impulsive, demonstrative, and theatrical; but he has "a good heart." Livingstone, whose experience of the Negro character was unrivalled, appears to have come to the conclusion that, after all, the Negro is no better and no worse than the rest of the sons of men. And, indeed, we Europeans appear to unsophisticated savages a most immoral and wicked people: their judgment of us is, in fact, crippled by much the same limitation that prejudices our judgment of them. There is the same curious admixture of good and evil qualities in them as in us: it is merely a distinction of kind and a question of degree. The Negro is, in short, an untrained child of Nature; and want of self-control or of "character" generally—the products of civilisation—naturally accentuates his failings. Only those who have lived with him learn his many excellent qualities of heart and mind. M. Elisée Reclus, the eminent geographer, gives the Negroes of Africa a good character: he says they are docile and faithful, and have many "feminine" characteristics; they are timid, curious, jealous and coquettish, braggarts, lovers of secrets, fond of petty quarrels and speedy reconciliations; moreover, they are satisfied to obey and to be sacrificed for those who oppress and ill-use them.

Negro morals.

There is a popular notion that those tribes which go in a state of nature and are untouched by foreign influence are the most moral. Generalisations of this sort are tempting, but they are dangerous to accept. Lying and stealing, for instance, come naturally to an oppressed, primitive people; and, it is true, these failings are acquired in an extraordinary degree on the outskirts of civilisation. In South Africa this phenomenon has been most strikingly exemplified: our contact with the native races has resulted in their deterioration; for they have learnt our vices, and not our virtues. Only the Kafir tribes have been able to withstand our blighting influence. Cases there have been where natives have fertilised the seed of Christian teaching, but these examples are relatively few in number. It is also remarkable that crime and cruelty are most conspicuous among tribes that enjoy a relatively high social culture. But still, it is doubtful whether the generalisation referred to in the above: that the unclothed tribes are the most moral: be a fair conclusion. Dr. Ratzel, in commenting on the subject, considers that polygamy, with its attendant evils, would appear to exert the determining influence in this respect. An unclothed tribe is essentially a primitive one, and, being poor, cannot acquire wives by purchase. Although polygamy as an institution is universal in Africa, it is only the more advanced tribes which possess the capital (such as cattle) to indulge in any excess. Polygamy gives rise to the Slave Trade and a host of other evils; and we can readily realise its disastrous influences on a savage people. Envy of others' possessions is a leading characteristic of man, and human life is cheap in Africa.

The stamina and vitality of the Negro race must be very great, since it has withstood for centuries such devastating scourges as the Slave Trade, incessant tribal wars, barbarous practices (*e.g.*, human sacrifices, ordeals, witchcraft), and unchecked disease. But Negroes take life easily; their animal spirits are irrepressible; even when they are driven as cattle in a slave-caravan, the incidents of the march provoke their loud mirth, though their hearts, like their bodies, may be suffering. As an agriculturist, the Negro is unsurpassed: he is more efficient in this respect than the weaker Coolie or the more intelligent Chinaman. His *Negro labour.*

dexterity is remarkable in the practice of any new handicraft.
His precocity in book-learning is equally great; but his
ability is said to stop short of a high standard. He culti-
vates the land with the simplest implements, the hoe being
the chief, sometimes the only one. The Negro is capable of
great endurance. He is capable of work, too—of any amount
of work as a *free man*; but as a slave he will render no
more than his taskmaster exacts. And it is important
to bear in mind, that though the Chinaman or the Coolie
are good substitutes for the Negro labourer, they are only
makeshifts: the indigenous native is, after all, the best
agriculturist and workman.

Domestic life of Negroes. The domestic life of Negroes is what we might expect of
a primitive people. The bonds of family relationship are
very strong. The love of the mother for her child is as
potent a passion in the Negress as among her European
sisters; and her influence in the family (the tongue being
her most effective weapon) is much greater than that of its
nominal head, the father. The man performs the work which
is most fitted to his strength, whilst the woman is employed
on tasks requiring skill and endurance. Marriage is mostly
by purchase, especially among those tribes which raise cattle,
and is celebrated with great ceremony. Whilst polygamy
is general where the means of purchase exist, divorce is
rare, largely on account of the commercial character of marriage. Like most natural peoples, the natives of Africa are
very "musical:" that is to say, they have a highly developed
sense of rhythm and noise, and indulge it *ad nauseam*.

Forms of government. Their forms of government are half-patriarchal, half-
feudal. A benevolent despotism appears to be the best
for them: yet the great Zulu and Matabele leaders and
the Waganda potentates have not been the absolute despots
they appear to us, for their power was derived from their
chiefs. Their territories, though not having the advantage

of being mapped as "spheres of influence," are recognised by their neighbours to extend as far as their arms can reach to strike effectively; they are therefore subject to expansion and contraction. Foreign pressure has, undoubtedly, welded together tribes under recognised leaders; but the general absence of cohesion has rendered them easy victims to the European lust of territory.

The simple pomp of Negro courts is characteristic of the poverty of the land. But the Negro is naturally fond of ceremony; he dearly loves to talk and to argue, and is an astute diplomatist, as many Europeans have found to their cost. It is said that the reason why he likes trading is the opportunity it affords him to "haggle," and not the profits he derives. *Negro court life.*

Although tribes like the redoubtable Zulu evince a remarkably warlike spirit, the Negroes are too self-indulgent to be bellicose as a race. If their mode of warfare appears to us cruel, it is because human life is not of much value in Africa. They make excellent soldiers under a capable leader, and can show both courage and devotion in a cause. Their weapons of war are chiefly the spear and the club, constructed in various forms, and to a certain extent the axe and the knife—weapons that are essentially practical and workman-like. Bows and poisoned arrows are commonly used. When about to take the war-path, the warriors carefully anoint themselves with some preparation of fat, so that they shine like bronze statues; sometimes they use paint (red and white chiefly) in ingenious and awe-inspiring devices; and they bedeck themselves with all the finery they possess. *On the war-path.*

We can picture to ourselves very much the style of life led by the greater number of the natives of Africa when we recall the circumstances of their geographical position: a vast Tropical land, shut off from the outside world, in *Negro mode of life.*

which Nature for the most part provides the means of sustenance. The natives, living under such circumstances, easily satisfy their animal appetites. Most of them are agriculturists, some are herdsmen, some both. The raising of cattle is successfully pursued on the eastern side of the continent, where milk is the chief article of food and the blood of oxen is drunk. The derivatives of milk are used as articles of food only by the Arabs, Abyssinians, and Berbers. Sheep and goats are raised, but horses are unknown to the Bantu. The staple diet is a meat and vegetable one, for the most part, and salt is a commodity largely in demand.

Negro dwellings. The native dwellings are of the simplest possible construction, from materials ready to hand: mud walls, reeds and grasses, and what not. They are erected round a central point, and protected on the circumference by hedges of thorns or other impediments. Their chief essential is that they be safe against attack. The villages are, consequently, built in such a manner as to ensure this protection; hence, difficulty of access is sometimes further increased by ditches and palisades. The herdsmen often build for themselves stone walls, and cover them with skins, to keep out the drifting sand and the cold. Windows are entirely dispensed with, and the doors are very small. The best huts are made in the Upper Nile region; elsewhere they are of the most unsubstantial and uncomfortable character. The destruction of a native village entails, therefore, little loss on its owners. Pile-dwellings are erected by river and lake communities; and temporary forts are found in large trees; but nowhere do we meet with extensive wood-built villages. A Negro village is sometimes of considerable size, so as to closely surround the hut of the chief; but in the greater kingdoms this is not practicable, and the principal settlements are, in consequence, comparatively small and scattered over a wide area.

The dress of the natives is of many kinds, the demand **Negro dress.** being at present regulated by the supply of skins, cloths, or woollen materials. A bunch of grass, a twig, or a palm-leaf are always to be had, however, should other materials fail; and some of the inland tribes have no other covering to their bodies. The Negroes of South and Central Africa and of the Upper Nile region wear a sort of apron suspended from the waist in front and behind. Herdsmen wear skins; while the Wanyoro and Waganda, who manufacture excellent bark-cloth, drape themselves in its ample folds, and are the most "dressy" natives of Africa. Where woollen stuffs are easily procurable, as on the West Coast, they are largely used for clothing. Hats are worn only on special and solemn occasions; but grease in the hair proves a good protection against the sun. The free use of fat or grease on the body is, in fact, a very general custom, and they are sometimes mixed with colour or aromatic preparations.

Elaborate dressing of the hair is a fashion widely dis- **Negro fashions.** tributed, and the most fantastic designs are popular. Individual fancy rather than prescribed fashion appears to be the rule; but the Zulu and other peoples have a national mode of hair-dressing. The shaving of the head is in certain districts a sign of mourning, though some natives either crop the hair close or partly shave the head for decorative and other reasons. This practice of dressing the hair is, however, least conspicuous among the higher Negro tribes, such as the Waganda.

Tattooing is not an art that can be said to be widely **Negro practices.** practised: but the natives of the Middle Congo are very expert at it, and partial tattooing or the raising of cicatrices on the body are customs frequently followed: sometimes these serve as tribal marks. Piercing the ears, nostrils, or lips, and inserting ornaments, is a custom common among the Zambezi and Nyassa tribes and in the

Upper Nile territories; and filing or extracting certain front teeth is a frequent practice.

Religious ideas of Negroes. The religious customs of the indigenous Negro tribes point to a universal belief in spirits—if not in a divinity—and in a future life of some sort. They believe, says Ratzel, that the soul (? breath) dies with men, but that the spirit (? shade) goes into the earth and returns from thence. Burial-places are therefore sacred. Gross superstitions of course exist.

Negro superstition. The world to them is full of spirits; there is a spirit in everything, whether animate or inanimate objects. Thus, animals are supposed to possess the souls of men, and the worship of snakes is not uncommon. The wholesale practice of human sacrifices—wives, relatives, or slaves of the deceased, or even subordinate chiefs—is one of the main causes of depopulation in Africa; whilst " smelling out " witches and obnoxious individuals is another.

Fetishism. Fetish-worship is more apparent among the tribes in the Northern and Central than in the Southern and Eastern regions; on the West Coast it is quite a cult, for in those parts wooden idols or graven images are common, and they enjoy a certain order of precedence. Anything can be declared a fetish. This is decidedly a backward step, even for tribes in the lowest stage of culture. The fetish priest or magician is a dangerous enemy to Christianity. Apparently the Negroes cannot dispense with his services; for not only is he their doctor, but he is useful to them also in many affairs of life.

Trade and commerce. The Africans are born traders; and on this account commerce has been found to be the most effective civilising agency in the hands of Europeans—an agency potent for good or evil. Every village has its market, whilst a town may have several. If one wants to buy the simplest article, it involves the time-destroying process of " going to market." But external commerce, which was introduced by the Arabs and Portuguese, is as yet small, owing chiefly to the want of easy communications. The caravan-routes are, therefore, of immense importance for the introduction of European influence.

The caravan-traffic, which is concentrated on the East Coast, is there properly organised, whilst that on the West Coast has declined with the suppression of the Slave Trade. Farther to the north and east, however, caravans, owing to the enterprise of predatory natives, advance more like trains of war, in close order, and require to form strong encampments at night. The rate of march, for long journeys, is not, as a rule, less than 2¼ miles an hour, while some explorers have been able to advance at the rate of four miles an hour.

<small>Caravan traffic.</small>

Let us now make a closer inspection of some of the more representative native peoples in Africa. Our limits will only admit of a very hasty survey.* Commencing in South Africa, we shall gradually work our way northwards to the Súdan.

<small>Representative native peoples.</small>

The vigorous and energetic Kafir peoples living in the south-eastern corner of the continent—Kafraria, Natal, and Zulu-land—are composed of the Zulu, Swazi, Pondo, and three or four less known tribes. They are in many respects in advance of the other peoples of South-Central Africa, to whom ethnographically and linguistically they are allied. They occupy some of the finest lands of South Africa, live in a sub-Tropical and well-watered country, and possess herds. As herdsmen, they live a free, independent life, and are nourished by a wholesome meat and milk diet. Their contact with Europeans, though leading to many disastrous encounters, has resulted in many customs and ideas of Christendom being introduced among them, to their individual advantage; but in the domestic arts they are still behind many of the tribes of Central Africa.

<small>Kafir peoples.</small>

---

* In the foregoing and in the particulars that follow I am largely indebted to Dr. Ratzel's *Völkerkunde* for my *data*.

The Zulu.   Of all Kafir peoples the Zulu are the most powerful. From Chaka to Cetewayo, they have had many capable leaders, who, enjoying a limited despotism, have led them to victory upon victory. The military organisation of the Zulu has, above every other influence, been the main cause of their material progress. Like all herdsmen, their government and family relationship are strictly patriarchal, but with them in an extraordinary degree. The king is the father of his people. None are allowed to marry without his consent, and that is rarely given until after twenty years of military service, though sometimes a whole regiment may be married as a reward for conspicuous bravery in the field. The men are early trained to the use of arms and in the evolutions of warfare. The warriors are fed by the king, whose numerous "wives" cater for them. By fostering care such as this the Zulu army has become the most redoubtable of any savage people. Their arms are the spear and shield, the asssegai and the club.

Under these martial conditions, family life is sacrificed to the exigencies of the State, and women occupy a very subordinate position. Polygamy, though general, is restricted by the want of means to purchase wives: but the "fair captives" in time of war are plentiful enough.

The rearing of cattle is the principal occupation of the people. Though, as we have indicated, the Zulu are behind other races in the domestic arts, they are very skilful in the working of metals. Their dress is of the most primitive kind, consisting in most cases simply of an apron. In their mental endowments they are distinguishable for the strength and decision of their character and for their innate pride as a race of warriors; but they are none the less the victims of superstition and witchcraft.

Though what has been said of the Zulu is largely applicable to the other Kafir peoples, the former are the most notable and powerful, largely on amount of their political unity. The Zulu have, in fact, "eaten up" or dispersed many of the smaller tribes; and they have, moreover, been able to hold their own in the wars against white colonists.

The numerous Bechuana tribes occupy the central regions, between the Zulu on the east and the Ovaherero on the west, the Orange River in the south, and, say, the Zambezi River in the north. Their northern boundary is, however, uncertain; on the east the Draken Berge form a natural frontier, as on the west do the steppes of the Kalahari. Within this extensive tract of country the pacific tribes of the Bechuana pursue a pastoral life, the rearing of herds being their chief occupation. They are, of all the Kafir peoples, the least differentiated from the Negro tribes of Central Africa. Their history has in the main been determined for them by their geographical position. Surrounded as they are and have been by strong tribes, and occupying a country incapable of sustaining a dense population in any one particular place, they have become scattered: consequently, there is little cohesion among them. The chief tribes are the Basuto, Makololo, and Bamangwato. They are not a warlike people, though they have proved their prowess in war; on the contrary, they pursue the arts of peace, and are quite willing to work for Europeans, towards whom they are well disposed. Impressionable and of weak character, they are readily influenced for good or for evil.

We thus see that in the Bechuana we have a ready medium for the expansion of British influence through a healthy and rich country suitable to colonial life, and leading from a strong political base in the south to the banks of the Zambezi. Therein lies our opportunity and our responsibility. Fortunate it will be for us if we do not neglect the one nor abuse the other.

The Ovaherero.

The Ovaherero tribes lead a half-nomadic life in the barren country occupied by them between the Kalahari and the Atlantic. They are the only people of South Africa to whom agriculture is unknown; their sole occupation is the rearing of cattle, which regulates all the affairs of their life. They appear to have retrograded in civilisation, and, though bright and light-hearted, they are inaccessible and unprogressive.

The Ovambo.

The highly fruitful land on the south bank of the Kunéné is occupied by the Ovambo tribes. They are among the most peaceful and diligent of agricultural peoples in Africa, and they live in crowded communities. Besides cereals, they cultivate tobacco, which forms the currency of the country. What little we know of the Ovambo is very much to their credit, for they appear to possess an exceptional sense of honour. The other tribes on the Kunéné are allied to the Ovambo, but apparently are independent of them. From their proximity to the Portuguese, and therefore to the traffic in slaves and spirits, their manners and customs have undergone considerable modification for the worse.

Ethnological varieties.

The Zambezi Valley is, both in a physical and ethnological sense, the transition region between South and Central Africa. The tribes of the two regions, though apparently of the same stock, are remarkably differentiated in mental and social characteristics. The strongest tribes there, as elsewhere, occupy the richest countries. The Zulu peoples in the east would appear to bridge over the ethnological varieties that are met with in that region. The Central African tribes have not been welded together by the military organisations that exist in East Africa; there is, in consequence, not the same unity among them, and they are vastly inferior in moral qualities, being more cowardly and less trustworthy. They are, in fact, an undeveloped and an agricultural people, cattle being difficult to raise in consequence of the presence of the tsétsé fly. In some of the Zambezi tribes we recognise the remnants of a conquering people. Migratory movements appear to have taken place, not only from east to west, but also from south to north. The tribes, however, approximate more to those of Central than to those of South Africa.

The Makololo are one of the chief tribes of the Zambezi Valley. Owing to the occurrence of the tsétsé fly cattle-rearing is not pursued to any great extent; the people are mostly agriculturists. Dwelling on both banks of the Zambezi, and accustomed to a river-life, they have become expert boatmen. Unfortunately, the Makololo have deteriorated even within the time they have been known to us. The Bakoba, a river-people dwelling on the shores and islands of the Zambezi, appear to belong to the indigenous race of this region, though their origin, like that of the other tribes in their neighbourhood, was undoubtedly from the south.

<small>The Zambezi tribes.</small>

Proceeding from south to north, the first great kingdom encountered in the Upper Zambezi is that of the Barotsé and Mambunda (Marutsé-Mabunda), composed of as many as eighteen large tribes. In them also the absence of any military organisation is distinguishable: in its place we observe, rather, a despotism characterised by great cruelty.

Farther east, on the Zambezi, the Batoka bridge over the ethnological varieties between South Africa and the Lakes region; and they are an agricultural people. In the highly fertile and Tropical regions of the great Lakes, under the south-east monsoons, we enter one of the most interesting and promising parts of Africa.

To the south and west of Lake Nyassa and around Lake Shirwa, the Manganya or Wa-Nyassa, who are differentiated by a slight departure from the Negro type in their lesser

<small>Nyassa tribes.</small>

prognathism, exhibit striking traits of diligence and energy. Some of their better qualities have undoubtedly been suppressed by the invasions they have sustained, but on the whole they are a pacific and capable people. Their elaborate mode of head-dress and love of ornaments are noteworthy. One encounters in them the first occurrence of the hideous *pelélé*,—a ring inserted in, and at right angles to, the upper lip; and they also practise tattooing and file or extract certain teeth. Formerly they used to rear cattle in large numbers; at the present day they are one of the most advanced of Central African tribes, both in industrial arts and in agriculture. The Slave Trade has, however, practically destroyed their home industries, and has most probably brought about the absolute want of cohesion that characterises their political organisation. Their manners and customs are much the same as those in vogue among the Zambezi tribes.

East Coast tribes. Between Lake Nyassa and the East Coast, the tribes, though related to one another, have been widely dispersed and have suffered terribly, not only at the hands of Kafir conquerors from the south, but also through the Traffic in Slaves, which is rampant there. The allied tribes between Lakes Nyassa and Bangweolo, the Babisa, might almost be regarded as Hottentots; ethnologically they are united with the inhabitants of the kingdoms of Muata Yanvo, Kazembe, and Kasongo. Although they occupy strongly defended positions as agriculturists, only some of their chiefs possessing small herds, they have been oppressed and dispersed by the ruthless slave-hunters and -traders.

Ethnological dualism. Throughout Eastern Equatorial Africa it is seldom that we do not encounter, scattered among the agricultural communities, nomadic tribes who terrorise and dominate their neighbours. But this ethnological dualism is not without precedent in other parts of the world: we ourselves have the Gypsies. In Eastern Africa these marauding tribes have warlike habits; they not only live by robbery, but act also as agents for the Slave Trade. At the same time there are more pacific tribes, which are quite content to settle down next to agricultural peoples and rear cattle.*

Of all the half-nomadic and conquering tribes the Mata- bele are now the most prominent. Their original home was undoubtedly in the south. They are first-rate warriors and brigands, and probably derived their military instincts from the Zulu, to whom they are related. The Zulu peoples, in fact, would appear to extend on the eastern side of the continent throughout the entire distance from Natal to the Equator. Mosilikatse, the father of Lobengula, the present chief of the Matabele, was their first great leader and liberator; their actual separation from the Zulu proper appears to have occurred at a comparatively recent date. Again and again, in their feuds with the Batoka and Makalaka, they have shown themselves to be a wild and warlike people; and they have been conspicuous for their brutality and insatiable appetite for the destruction of human life. The Mashuna, living in their neighbourhood, have suffered, and continue to suffer, terribly from their depredations and oppression. The country between them has been devastated—but is supposed to be one of the richest gold-fields in Africa.

<small>The Matabele.</small>

The warlike shepherds of Galla-, Somál-, and Masai-lands are of Hamitic origin, but of very mixed race. The Galla are half-Negro, half-Arab. The Wollo-Galla, a fanatical Mohammedan people, are as conspicuous for their habits of theft and their untrustworthiness as the Pagan Galla in the south are notable for their fidelity and frankness. As agriculturists and herdsmen, and in the industrial arts,

<small>Tribes of Galla-, Somál-, and Masai-lands.</small>

---

* Cattle-raising, however, may be said scarcely to exist north of the Zambezi.

the Galla bordering on Abyssinia and the Somäl of the coast towns are the most advanced; but the purely nomadic tribes dispense with domestic utensils they cannot obtain by barter.* The warlike tribes are divided into two great classes—warriors and non-combatants. Only the latter are allowed to marry, to smoke, and to indulge in intoxicating drinks. The Masai, however, have also married warriors, who on occasions go upon the war-path. Incessant raids, chiefly to "lift" cattle, appear to be their chief occupation.

The Galla are partly under the influence of Islam, and have been profoundly affected by their contact with Abyssinia, with the history of which country they have been associated for 300 years. The Somäl and Danakil, and a large number of the Galla, have become converts to Islam, but their Pagan customs are conspicuously transparent under its thin veneer. The Galla appear, in fact, to have been deteriorated by Mohammedanism.

"Between the Devil and the deep sea."

The position of the peoples of the East Coast, situated as they are between the Coast Arabs and the brigand tribes, is a most embarrassing one. Yet in no other part of Africa are there more pronounced evidences of a capacity for development. The Traffic in Slaves and the raids of the Galla, Somäl, and Masai, have been the greatest enemies of progress. The weaker tribes have been dispersed, robbed, or annihilated, and any cohesion among them has been promptly destroyed. The Arab domination, in fact, does not appear to have been for the good of the natives, but quite the reverse.

Ethiopian tribes.

Two distinct peoples occupy the source-region of the Nile—Ethiopia in its widest sense: the sedentary agriculturists and the wandering herdsmen, the latter being of lighter colour, of nobler attributes, and in most cases

* The Masai, the most pronounced nomads, are specially conservative.

the dominant race. The Waganda are in every respect
the most prominent of these peoples, and they form the
basis of the population in Uganda. Then there are the
Wahuma, a shepherd people, who keep strictly apart from,
and consequently do not assimilate with, their neighbours;
yet the royal family of Uganda are Wahuma.

The Waganda and Wanyoro are outwardly distinguish- *Waganda and Wanyoro.*
able from most other African peoples by their dress, for
they clothe themselves from head to foot. The Waganda
pay great attention to this custom, and are said even
to punish with death anybody found in the streets insufficiently clothed. Yet, curiously enough, in their own
homes the women are accustomed to throw off their robes;
and the warriors who go to battle not only first divest
themselves of superfluous clothing, but also paint their
faces red or white. They have often been described by
travellers as exhibiting great taste in their graceful toga-
like draperies; and it is further notable that they avoid
any disfigurement of the body, such as tattooing. Their
dwellings are vastly superior to those commonly found in
Africa, and their industries are equally remarkable for
excellent workmanship. The women for the most part
engage in agriculture, while the men build houses and
serve as warriors. The Waganda are also great hunters,
and those who live on the Nyanza are expert fishermen.
Polygamy, owing to the great preponderance of women, is
general, and marriage is by purchase. King M'tesa is said
to have had as many as 7000 so-called wives.

Both the Waganda and Wanyoro are warlike, and they
are admirably equipped. They carry spears and shield
into battle, and occasionally bows and arrows; many also
possess muskets

Their political strength is due to the military organisation under which they are trained, for every efficient man is

Waganda. a warrior. Besides an excellent army, the Waganda possess a large fleet of canoes, well built, and usually manned by forty men in each.

Dr. Robert W. Felkin, in his admirable accounts of these people, has made us acquainted with their military strength and political organisation, their subtle diplomacy and comparatively high degree of social culture.

Feudalism underlies their form of government. Court ceremony is a potent factor in their lives, a certain savage pomp being maintained. Their love of music and social amusements brings the people constantly together. The governing body consists of the king, the prime minister, the great chiefs, and some court officials, such as the chief cook and brewer; and it is notorious for its cruel and barbarous enactments.

The Waganda have shown themselves open to foreign influence. Too curious to indulge in jealousy, they have readily availed themselves of foreign commerce. By their trade with the Zanzibar Arabs they have become more or less familiar with the Swahéli language. They have also permitted Christian missionaries to reside at court. The clever way in which M'tesa played off one Mission against the other, and both against the Arabs, was a striking example of native wit and diplomacy.

Tribes between Abyssinia and the Congo. There are a number of pure Negro tribes dwelling in the country between Abyssinia and the Congo watershed. Dr. Junker observed that the skin-colour of these tribes becomes darker and darker from north to south and east to west. On the other hand, the peoples on either side of this chain of settlements, the Abyssinians and Niam-Niam (Zandé), are light-coloured. These Negroes follow very closely the manners and customs of the shepherd tribes of East and South Africa, and they themselves engage in pastoral pursuits. They do not appear to have been long in possession of their present homes, but to have migrated or to have been driven there from the north.

The most northerly of these tribes at present known to us are the Shillúk, who are undoubtedly pure Negroes. Their warlike character has obtained for them an evil reputation; but it must be remembered that they have simply defended their homes against the Egyptian spoiler and the slave-trader. A branch of the Shillúk, the Jur, resemble them in every respect, while the numerous tribes of the Dinka, though disunited, are allied by blood. The Nuer, another warlike people, resemble the Shillúk and Dinka. The Bari are primitive and inaccessible, but are said to be intelligent. The Shuli and Madi, on the other hand, though standing in blood-relationship to the Bari, are a vigorous agricultural people, who very readily submitted to the Egyptian domination. {Upper Nile Negroes.}

The majority of these Upper Nile Negroes have adopted the most rudimentary forms of ornamentation. They tattoo themselves. The Dinka and Nuer, for instance, have tribal tattoo marks; but the Shillúk and Jur do not follow this barbarous practice. While all of them are satisfied with a modicum of clothing, the Shillúk, Jur, Nuer, and Bari very often have none. The Upper Nile territories were at one time among the most densely populated regions of Africa; but they have been devastated by the constant slave-raids: in consequence of which the shepherd people have, as a rule, for protective purposes, larger villages than the agricultural. Raiding for cattle has been the leading motive of all native military undertakings in Africa; and, in the Nile territories, the slave-traders have in this way robbed the shepherds in order to pay the agriculturists, besides securing for themselves the usual complement of victims. In the industrial arts, and particularly in the working of iron, the Upper Nile Negroes take high rank among the natives of Africa. Their family life, though differing in few respects from that of other Negroes, has been profoundly affected by the depredations of the slave-raiders.

Light-coloured peoples.

As regards the light-coloured peoples of the Upper Nile, the Niam-Niam (Zandé) should not be classified as Negroes, strictly speaking: their relationship belongs, rather, to the Galla and Somâl. More vigorous, both mentally and physically, than their Negro neighbours, they have also attained a higher degree of culture. Their occupations are chiefly agricultural; but, split up as they are into numerous tribes, there is no cohesion among them. The accounts of travellers concur in describing the Niam-Niam as the most inveterate cannibals.

Another cannibal people are the Monbuttu, who occupy an unique position among so-called Negroes. They also are light-coloured—among the very lightest in Africa—and their physiognomy approximates very closely to the Semitic type.

Central African tribes.

Of the tribes of Central Africa we know less and less as we penetrate into the Interior, the Middle Congo region excepted; but there is reason to believe that, ethnologically, they differ but slightly from other Negroes. Their languages are dialects of the Bantu. It is there that we encounter some of the most densely populated districts in Africa, such as in Manyema and on the banks of the Sankuru. The admixture of light and dark coloured peoples, which is so common on the East Coast, is observable also in the central regions of the continent. Reference has already been made to a race of people of diminutive stature, apparently of indigenous origin, who are found here and there in Central Africa dwelling in small isolated settlements.

Cannibalism would appear to be very widely distributed

as a custom among the Central tribes. Tattooing also is a practice frequently met with, though it is not usual among Negroes; in the Middle Congo region the natives ornament themselves in this way from head to foot. In spite of cruel and barbarous practices, and the cheapness of human life, the populations of Central Africa would appear to increase very considerably. The Slave Trade works havoc among them; but the Slave Trade is carried on chiefly from the outskirts. In the inland regions slaves are not so valuable as a commercial commodity, because there is not sufficient work for them in the fields. In presence of this disturbing element to social progress, internal commerce and the industrial arts have, it must be admitted, reached a relatively high degree of development.

Practices and customs.

In the Central regions south of the Súdan there is little or no cohesion among the tribes, for the slave-traders and raiders have destroyed it. Agriculture, in spite of the favourable conditions of soil and climate, is not carried on with any great care, and cattle-raising is not pursued to any extent.

The kingdom of the Muata * Yanvo, which at one time was said to be equal in area to Germany and to contain a population of two million souls, has recently broken up; but it was undoubtedly of very ancient origin. The actual Lunda peoples (Kalunda or Balunda) are the most widely distributed and influential, and form the basis of the population; while all are of the Bantu stock. They are well-built, somewhat light in colour, and have fairly regular features. The women practise tattooing, paint the body, and cut the hair short; but the men, as a rule, while abstaining from these customs, pay very great attention to the dressing of their hair. They engage almost exclusively in agriculture.

The Balunda.

As regards their political organisation, whatever their

* Muata = " Master."

cohesion at one time may have been, the numerous tributary chiefs at the present day affect greater and greater independence the farther they are removed from the central authority. A curious division of the administrative power is worth noting. The joint ruler with the Muata Yanvo is his "unmarried wife," a queen who has her own court and whose "husband"[*] is regarded as a woman. The two rulers are supported by an aristocracy; and there is also a sort of general assembly, which has given rise to a "public opinion." The capital town of each new Muata Yanvo is changed on his ascent to the throne. In Kazembe, a tributary state, very similar social conditions are observable.

<small>West African tribes.</small> The indigenous peoples of West Africa have naturally undergone radical modifications through their long and uninterrupted intercourse with the European colonists. Woollen stuffs, so readily obtainable, have been adopted as ordinary articles of dress; and the introduction of muskets and gin has played an important part in the life of the peoples. Their languages are divergent from the Bantu dialects. In the settlement of freed slaves at Sierra Leone, for instance, there are representatives of 200 Negro tribes, speaking as many as 151 different languages. Then, in the colonies, the European languages are spoken to a large extent, while Arabic and Fulbé are also current. Yet, in spite of these antagonistic elements, the natives are wonderfully alike in outward respects. While polygamy and the Slave Trade are largely responsible for the existence on the Coast of these heterogeneous phenomena, the repeated invasions from the Interior have been equally, if not in a greater degree, the fundamental cause of them. It is, moreover, natural to infer that these phenomena are more conspicuous in the less settled districts between the Portu-

---

[*] At the time of Bachner's visit, this unsexed individual is reported to have introduced himself as "only a woman, but the wife of a great person."

guese colonies in the south and the Niger Delta in the
north. While the Negroes of Angóla have a large proportion of Portuguese blood in their veins, they are very
closely allied to the natives of the Congo; and at Bihé,
for so long a slave-trading centre, the population is very
mixed.

The industries of West Africa have in like manner been greatly affected by the European domination. Foreign manufactures have practically stamped out the native industries; and only in shipbuilding has our contact been to the profit of the Africans. The native industries are therefore at a low stage. The capacity of the Negro for commerce is brought out on the West Coast in a marked degree. The Dualla are very advanced, and are a good type of the native trader; but they try to raise monopolies, like other people. In astuteness they are probably surpassed by the active Bangala. Where trade is vigorous, the native has an opportunity—the very best opportunity—for advancement. But this exerts the reactionary influence of making the individual independent of the central authority: thus, the native political organisations of the West Coast are less stable than those of the East Coast. Moreover, the teaching of Christian missionaries has naturally had the effect of divesting the native ruler of the sanctity which frequently attaches to his person; and, though he may be still the high-priest, he is not so unapproachable as was formerly the case. On the other hand, the same Christian teaching has inculcated a higher mental culture, which, quite apart from the weakness of native character, might have had a greater degree of permanence but for the immoral practices of irresponsible traders and the introduction of the gin-trade to supersede the Traffic in Slaves.

Trade and commerce on the West Coast.

Considering the extent to which the Slave Trade at one time raged on the West Coast, it is not to be sup-

Slavery and the Slave Trade.

posed that, since its abolition (which entirely ruined the organised caravan-traffic), slavery has been very greatly affected as a domestic institution. There are Negroes who still regard themselves as slaves. It is worth while noting in this respect, that whereas the more highly developed peoples (such as the Fulah and Moors) treat their slaves worse, those only slightly removed above the slaves in station treat them most leniently. There are slaves in every household on the West Coast: whilst the purchase of wives is a custom more prevalent there than anywhere else in Africa. Women are the most valuable marketable commodity, and, though polygamy* is indulged in to an extraordinary extent, they have their rights: in fact, Dr. Ratzel speaks of the West Coast as the land of Woman's Rights. While the household slaves appear to be well treated, those who work in the fields are regarded more as animals.

Negro kingdoms.

Organised armies are found in Dahomé, where women are the best soldiers, and in Ashanti, the only two self-founded Negro kingdoms in Africa. The famous Amazon-warriors do not marry; they are regarded as men, and occupy barracks in the king's palace, where they are waited upon by eunuchs.

Occupations of the natives on the West Coast.

Agriculture is generally pursued, except where the populations, from their position on the Coast, are better engaged in fishing or trading operations or in gathering oil-seeds. The Krú (Krú-boys) are a fraternity of native sailors who have been thoroughly trained by Europeans; every vessel working down the Coast employs them, so as to save the ship's crew from exertion under such perilous climatic conditions.

The Jolof and Mandingo.

On the North-West Coast, south of the Mohammedan States, there are peoples, undoubtedly of the Negro race,

---

* It is stated that the King of Ashanti may possess 3333 wives, but no more.

whom it is not easy to classify. The Jolof and Mandingo
portray Negro types, but types greatly modified by admixture
with a nobler race. Purely Negro characteristics, in fact, become less and less observable as one penetrates inland. In many respects the Pagan Negroes of the Niger-Benué district excel their Mohammedan neighbours, as in the construction of their huts and in agricultural pursuits; while their industrial arts have also reached a higher stage of progress. This is a phenomenon worth noting, since Islam is credited with the power of always elevating the Pagan peoples.

Pagan Negroes of Niger-Benué District.

Islam in the West-Central Sudan.

The Fulah, by their talents and perseverance, have risen from the lowest stage of native culture to the highest; but those who have remained herdsmen are still behind the other peoples in this respect. As conquerors, the Mandingo come next to the Fulah, but their power at the present day has decayed, and they themselves are dispersed, although originally they exercised the most potent power in North-West Africa. Prior to the Fulah domination, they were, in fact, the chief people of this region. The Hausa are, perhaps, not so capable as either the Fulah or Mandingo; but their past has been equally great, and their influence must at one time have been very extensive, if one may judge from the spread of their language. As far north as the Azben plateau it is still the prevailing tongue, although the Tuareg have ruled there from time immemorial; and it is the dominant language over wide regions to the south, in all the so-called Hausa States. As the language of commerce, also, it is spoken on the west side of the Niger and beyond. In their diligence, orderliness, and trustworthiness, the Hausa retain the stamp of an ancient civilisation. We ourselves employ them as police, with good results; and in the Niger Territories they are excellent herdsmen. Rohlfs, indeed, regards the Hausa as the highest in

The Fulah.

The Hausa.

intellectual development of any people between the Niger and the Benué.

<small>Islam in the Western Sudan.</small> Want of cohesion and weakness of political relations are characteristic of the Negroes of North-West Africa, in consequence of which they have fallen an easy prey to their light-coloured conquerors. The first ambition of a Moor or Fulah would appear to be to possess a drove of slaves, who in some cases have become the germ of a state. It has been truly said that every wandering Fulah in the Western Sudan is a seed of future dominion over the darker coloured peoples. Like the Arabs of the East Coast and the Jews of all countries, they insinuate themselves into positions of influence. In consequence of this disintegrating process, only the inaccessible tribes of the Interior are protected from dispersion. The ruling classes of this region are, of course, the Mohammedans. Rohlfs, however, estimates that between the Niger and Benué they form only one-third of the population. Acknowledged Mohammedans are, as a rule, only those living in the towns and the wandering Fulah and Mandingo who come from the north. To the Fulah, propagandism is the means and the end: conversion to Islam and the enrichment of the propagandists are, of course, synonymous.

That the progress of Islam has effected important changes in native culture requires no demonstration. Islam has rooted up many ill weeds in Pagan territories and planted better seed; more especially it has been the enemy of the archfiends, Superstition and Fetishism. In all that concerns the outward aspects of culture, Islam has undoubtedly improved the Negro. The Jolof, a weak people, evince the relative influences of Christianity and Islam where, as in Gorée and St. Louis, they have come in contact with Europeans and Arabs. Though learning European crafts, they have retained their own manners and customs; but they have very readily come under the ascendancy of the Arabs and have assimilated with them.

Enough has been said to draw certain conclusions in regard to the mental, moral, and material culture of the natives of Africa. We have seen that in his savage state the Negro leads a life of ease and self-indulgence. A child of Nature, he is contented to receive the sustenance so freely given to him, without experiencing any desire to emancipate himself from Nature's leading-strings. Some dim consciousness of a higher power and an immaterial world has indeed entered his soul, but his untutored mind invests these intuitions with a fantastic and mythical interpretation. His mind being freely open to receive impressions, and the harsh conditions of his social life having schooled him into unquestioning obedience to the powers that be, he has on occasions been raised to a higher stage of culture, from whatever source it has come, native or foreign, provided it has been adapted to his peculiar genius. Thus, the great Lunda, Zulu, and Waganda kingdoms of Central and South-Central Africa were built up and fused into a certain degree of compactness and cohesion by the genius of native leaders. With the death of their leaders, and in the absence of any competent successors, these kingdoms have gradually suffered disintegration: none the less, barbarous as they may appear in our eyes, they have shown an advance of native culture, a step forward towards progress, or potential civilisation. In a lesser degree we have seen the weaker tribes conquered and absorbed, driven back or dispersed, by stronger tribes: and the stronger tribes have either been herdsmen, living a healthier, more vigorous and freer life in the less enervating uplands, or of a more energetic race.

Native culture.

The examples that have been cited are the best test-cases, for the disturbing factor of European or alien influences has not played so potent a part in these Central

Disturbing influences.

Disturbing influences. native kingdoms as in the coast-lands and in North and South Africa. This disturbing factor, which has acted like an electric current, is one with which we shall deal in the next chapter. In the main it has been a spiritual force: positive Islam and negative Christianity. The great Mandingo kingdom and the other Negro kingdoms in West Africa, Dahomé and Ashanti, have been too much under its influence to admit of their progress being fairly criticised apart. As for the Republic of Liberia, it has been wholly founded by foreign agencies and populated by freed slaves; so that it, too, is not to be cited as an example of untrammelled native culture; as an experiment, it is, of course, most instructive.

The Slave Trade and its ramifications, the introduction of vile spirits and of guns and gunpowder, and the advance of conquering Europe on the one hand, of proselytising Islam on the other, are also so inseparably associated with native life and culture, that, until we have fully considered these matters, we cannot hope to attain a correct appreciation of the forces working for good and for evil in Africa. In the meantime, it is proper in this place to emphasise the fact that, from what we have so far seen of native culture generally, the wide-spread institution of polygamy, and the inherent disposition of the Negro to lead a life of ease and self-indulgence, are predisposing causes in favour of all outside influences not antagonistic to their growth. In a word, if—at the risk of an unfair comparison—we accept self-sacrifice as the central principle of Christianity and self-indulgence as that of Islam, we see at a glance how it is that Islam gains ground where Christianity must retire humbled and mortified.

In the regions populated by the Pagan Bantu, between the Sûdan and Cape Colony, we may fairly conclude that the natives, in their primitive and untrammelled state, have

made little or no progress, but evince, rather, an arrested *Native civilisation.*
development of culture. When, however, from their impressionable nature, they have come individually or collectively under the domination of relatively stronger tribes, they have readily assimilated with them; but this process of absorption has, of course, raised them no higher than the stage to which their conquerors had attained.

From the comparative absence of political cohesion *The European domination.*
among the Bantu, it is evident that little or no resistance can be offered against the forces which Europe can control. By the European domination, therefore, the obstacles to be overcome in this respect are slight. As the pioneers of civilisation in Africa, and especially in the Pagan regions, it is our duty to implant the civilisation to which we ourselves have attained; but it must be adapted to its new home. We must either raise the African up to our own level, or sink to his; too often we see the latter result. Native rights should be respected, of course; but while "natural rights" are recognised, we should not risk being carried away by sentiment when drastic measures are called for. As Professor Huxley points out,* tigers have a "natural right" to prey on men; but men have an equal right to defend their lives. It is, therefore, logical to infer that, if we regard it as a duty to carry our civilisation to those parts of the world where *European responsibility.*
circumstances have driven us, it may be necessary for its execution that the few should suffer for the many. Not that we are at all squeamish in this matter, quite the reverse; but our responsibility in adopting force when persuasion fails acts in two ways: we ourselves must practise what we preach. For example, if we suppress the Slave Trade because it is not good for our African *protégés*, we must also suppress the traffic in spirituous liquors and

* *Nineteenth Century*, February 1890.

effectually control the importation of arms and ammunition. Our duty in these respects is clear: it were rank hypocrisy to adopt the one course of action and neglect the other. By continuing such a short-sighted policy as this, we ourselves will in the end be the sufferers, for native interests and European interests are identical in so far as public morality is concerned. No half measures are possible; according as we accept or neglect our responsibilities we shall inevitably bring about either the assimilation or the extermination of the natives under our control.

CHAPTER V.

ISLAM AND CHRISTIANITY.

HISTORICAL SKETCH OF THE PROGRESS OF ISLAM AND THE EXTENSION OF ARAB INFLUENCE—THE BORDER-LAND OF ISLAM IN THE SOUTH—SIGNS OF THE TIMES—HISTORICAL SKETCH OF THE PROGRESS OF CHRISTIAN MISSIONS—RESULTS OF MISSIONARY ENTERPRISE—METHODS OF MOHAMMEDAN PROPAGANDISM AND ARAB RULE, AS COMPARED WITH THOSE ADOPTED BY CHRISTIAN MISSIONS AND EUROPEAN RULE: IN THEIR EFFECT UPON THE PAGAN POPULATIONS—CONCLUSIONS.

MAP.

RELIGIONS, AND MISSIONARY STATIONS   *Plate* XI.

ISLAM AND CHRISTIANITY.

OF the forces which war against barbarism, and which are most potent in the promotion of civilisation in Africa, none are more conspicuous than the propagandism of Islam and the enterprise of Christian missions. In both instances the means and the end have proved to be very much the same. The propagandists of Islam, who, for their own material advantage, have imposed their rule on the Pagan populations, have been inspired by a faith in their mission equal to that of the Christian missionaries, in whose train European commerce and conquest have followed on an ever-increasing scale. Rival forces.

Islam, or Arab influence, advances with the sword in one hand and the Koran in the other,—as it appears to us. Christianity, or European influence, advances with the sword or paper-treaties in one hand and the Bible or a case of gin in the other,—as it appears to the native mind. It is no use quarrelling with the comparison: it is a just and faithful one. We should see ourselves as others see us—in our acts; and not as we too often see ourselves—in our proclamations. From the time when Prince Henry the Navigator sent forth his valiant captains to conquer new worlds up to the present precipitate scramble for African lands, all the European nations—if we were to believe them—have been inspired chiefly by love of their fellow-man in their endeavours to promote civilisation. Civilisation! The cant phrase * falls glibly enough from the Their weapons.

---

* "Progress and Development are the fundamental ideas contained in the word civilisation."—*Histoire de la Civilisation* (Guizot).

lips of Europeans, who have sought to hide their own selfish designs under the cloak of philanthropy. What degree of civilisation have we introduced into Africa, and in how far have we improved the condition of our African brethren?

It will be our purpose to inquire into this matter: to trace the progress of Islam and Arab influence, of Christianity and European influence, and to endeavour to discover the methods by which both have supplanted paganism and barbarism. After dwelling upon their methods and results, we shall be in a better position to arrive at a just appreciation of the relative merits of Islam and Christianity in the attempt to raise the indigenous populations of Africa to the level of nineteenth-century civilisation.

Cross and Crescent.

Without exactly foretelling a crescentade or a crusade in Africa, it is obvious that these antagonistic elements are bound to clash wherever rivalries of territorial expansion may exist. Africa, indeed, bids fair to become the chief, if not the last, battlefield of Cross and Crescent.

Disposition of their forces.

The whole of the northern portion of the continent has been held or dominated for ten centuries by the compact forces of Islam. In South Africa Christianity has a strong, if a somewhat more restricted, base, and, with powerful reinforcements in the east and the west, it has boldly advanced upon the Pagan Interior. Skirmishes at the outposts of Islam have occurred; but our main forces cannot for several generations take up a sufficiently strong position to venture upon a general attack.

Early Christianity.

Unhappily, of these opposing forces, Islam shows a more or less united front, whilst Christianity has often undermined its strength by dissensions in its own camp.* The early Christian Church is an example of this disunion. The

---

* The disunion between the Christian missions in Uganda—one of the most glorious and fruitful fields of Christianity in Africa—is a lamentable example in modern times.

sedentary Jews, it is true, were at no time propagandists, but lived, as they live now, in exclusive communities. To Cyrenaica, however, at the time of the Phœnician culture, they migrated in large numbers, and also for a long distance up the Nile Valley. But the early Christians, split up into innumerable sects, were always wrangling and fighting for dogmas, and were in consequence unable to exercise any influence over those they regarded as Pagans, to whose level they themselves eventually sank. When, therefore, the tide of Islam, carrying its simple doctrine, swept over the shores of North Africa, all were engulfed in its relentless progress. It even flowed across the desert of the Sahara. But in the twelve hundred years of its supremacy in North Africa it has obliterated all the earlier culture, of which only a few monuments now remain. *The tide of Islam.*

This advance of Islam from the north and east went on, as has been indicated, for a thousand years after the lapse of the early Christian Church. The attention of Europe was not again directed to Africa until the fifteenth century, when the pioneer explorers re-discovered the outline of the lost continent. Roman Catholic missionaries then set out, and, for a period, achieved brilliant results in the accomplishment of their high calling; but before the close of last century their influence had waned. It has been reserved for the nineteenth century to witness other Christian missions enter the abandoned field, not only with renewed enthusiasm, but with the most far-reaching consequences. The march of our modern commercial crusaders will scarcely be impeded until their forces are collected outside the frowning ramparts of Islam. *Later Christian efforts.*

The spread of Islam, and with it the extension of Arab influence in Africa, covers a period of 1250 years, and may be divided into three distinct, though only approximately dated, phases. Its progress at the present day in *Spread of Islam.*

the Súdan and in Galla-land proves that its forces are not yet enervated, though in other parts of the continent they may appear to be so. For instance, to use the picturesque and forcible phrase of Mr. Joseph Thomson, Morocco now-a-days is no more than a "back-water" of Islam: stagnant, impure, unwholesome.

Islam: First phase of conquest. The first phase of its extension occurred in the seventh century, and covered a period of only about seventy years. In the year 640, a lieutenant of the Khalif Omar, Amru Ibn al Aassi by name, invaded Egypt with an army of 4000 men, and in the following year seized Alexandria. He and his successors earnestly promoted the cause of Islam, which rapidly extended westwards till it reached the Atlantic. In short, it took less than seventy years for the Arabs to become the masters of North Africa. The Berber tribes offered some resistance, on one occasion at least with notable success, but in the end they were forced to accept Islam and to adopt the Arab language. Arab rule at that time was undoubtedly a beneficial one: not only did it grant religious tolerance, but all that was best in the earlier civilisation it supplanted was carefully fostered. The large towns were, in consequence, inhabited by industrious and progressive populations. Outside the towns, however, and among the masses, Berber customs were preserved, and in a degree more and more marked from east to west: for, from Egypt to the Atlantic, the Arabs decreased in numbers. North Africa in those flourishing times evinced a higher degree of culture than was found in Europe, except Byzantium; and the position of women was very much better than it is now.* Only the nomad peoples and those living outside the influence of Arab settlements were untouched by this wave of progress; and

* The position of women among the Berbers of Morocco at the present day is higher than among the Arabs. They are quite satisfied with one wife.

only they were spared the decline that, in the sixteenth
century, followed in the track of the Turk.

Mohammedan influence, in the first phase of its extension, stopped short of the desert zone. Here was a natural barrier from sea to sea; but even that was eventually overcome. The second phase, from the eleventh to the seventeenth century, was inaugurated by the large Arab migrations from Egypt westwards. Numerous nomad tribes, with all their belongings, migrated to North-West Africa. Arab writers compute their numbers to have been as high as one million; others have estimated them at only 250,000. It is probable that other tribes soon followed along the road thus opened up. This migration lasted from the middle of the eleventh to the thirteenth century, and resulted in Islam planting its banners in Songhai and Kanem, and on the East Coast. According to Dr. Lenz,* the States of the Middle Niger have ever since remained the chief bulwark of Islam and the centre of an advanced civilisation. The history of Timbuktu, which was founded in 1077 by the Tuareg, shows, however, that the progress of Islam was not unattended by checks of one sort and another. Its domination over Kanem came somewhat later. As for the Fulah, they may or may not have come under its influence at this period: it is not possible to determine.

<small>Islam: Second phase of conquest.</small>

The Arabs crossed the Red Sea in the seventh century; but it is not until the ninth century that we hear of any extensive migrations, and not until the eleventh century, or the commencement of the twelfth, that they reached the confines of Abyssinia. Somál traditions lead one to infer that the Arabs also established themselves in their country and in other parts of East Africa, and warred against the Pagans in the south. The Portuguese, at least, when they first reached this coast early in the sixteenth century, spoke

---

* *Timbuktu*, vol. ii. p. 162.

of the powerful and inimical Mussulman rulers of the great
"Adal" kingdom between Tajura and Cape Guardafui.

In the sixteenth and seventeenth centuries Islam extended its sway over other of the remaining countries of the Súdan. In Kordofan there are traces of its influence having been established as early as the fourteenth century, if not before. The evidence as regards Darfur and Wadai is uncertain; though, as regards the latter, Barth considers that Islam had no footing there until 1640. The Bagirmi received Islam at the close of the sixteenth century, the Katsena in the seventeenth century, and the inhabitants of Kano a little later. But Barth states that the Hausa populations remained Pagans until forced by the Fulah to make a public confession of their own faith. The influence of Islam during the second phase of its extension thus appears to have reached to the ninth parallel of north latitude, roughly speaking, and to have penetrated along the East Coast as far south as the Equator.

<small>Islam: Third phase of conquest.</small>

The third and last phase of the progress of Islam and of the Arab domination has had its chief development within the present century, and is due to the enterprise of the proselytising Fulah. Their religious zeal at the commencement of the century became too great to rest satisfied with founding agricultural colonies in the Central Súdan; they carried their conquests far to the south and east, and to the shores of the Atlantic. After conquest followed reconstruction. Through the warlike operations of the Fulah and the extension of commerce by the Hausa the Mohammedans have now reached even the Gulf of Guinea.

Not only is this religious propagandism apparent on the southern frontier of Islam, but also in the very heart of the Súdan and in North Africa. In the main it has been carried on in those parts by the Senusi, a puritan Mohammedan sect, whose relations, though scattered, are far-reaching, intimate, and powerful. Their strict discipline and the abundant resources at their disposal constitute the Senusi a formidable opponent to European enterprise. They are well informed as to events transpiring in the Mohammedan world, and do not scruple to adopt any means for the promotion of their interests. Every year the present chief of the sect, at the oasis of Jarabub, near the oasis of Siwah, sends out hundreds of missionaries.

M. Marc Fournel states * that "in Wadai the Sheikh el-Mahdi could mobilise in a few weeks an army ten times stronger and more enthusiastic than that which crushed (sic) the English and Egyptians in the Súdan, and it is stated that his *zawia* contains enough modern fire-arms to render his forces sufficiently redoubtable against those of any European power." Wadai is, in fact, the present centre of Mohammedan propagandism, and the Senusi are in power there.† The dominion of the native Sultan extends far beyond the limits of Wadai proper. Dr. Nachtigal, one of the few European travellers in that country who have returned alive, and upon whose descriptions we largely rely for the scanty information in our possession, states that the Sultan of Wadai rules over a country probably 150,000 square miles in area, and having a population of 2,600,000 souls. The people are inimical to the Mahdists, and only recently we heard of a great battle fought between them, probably for dominion.

Interesting as it would be to fix the southern limit of Islam in Africa, it is evident that authorities must differ in estimating the actual power and number of the Moham-

Southern limit of Islam.

---

* *L'Afrique Explorée et Civilisée*, February 1888.
† The Maba comprise the aristocracy of the country, and belong to the Senusi sect. They speak an "isolated" language (F. Muller), or a language closely akin to that of Fur (Lepsius).

medans among the semi-Pagan tribes in the border-land of Arab influence. But we may safely assume that Mr. Ravenstein, in the map illustrating this chapter, has given the approximate boundary of Islam in the south.

Cohesion of Mohammedan forces.

It is well worth noting that, whereas we are disposed to imagine the cohesion of the forces of Islam is equally great all along the line—that is to say, in the southern border-lands — the most trustworthy European travellers in those lands have directed our attention to many weak points, where Islam either has not affected the Pagan populations at all, or only in so slight a degree that it may be said merely to have inoculated them. Let us take a few examples. The Mandingo and the inhabitants of Futa Jallon have adopted Islam either *pro forma* or not at all (Dr. Lenz). The Wolof and Bambara are mostly Pagans (Le Brun-Renaud). On the Coast of Guinea there are Mohammedans on the island of Sherboro; there are over 5000 in Sierra Leone; they outnumber the Pagans in Liberia; and in the town of Lagos they number some 10,000. In Bagirmi there are a number of Pagan tribes (Dr. Nachtigal). And the farther east we go, the more uncertain becomes the domination of Islam. Thus, in the source-region of the Nile, where the political supremacy of the Arab rather than the extension of Islam has been attempted, we find numerous Pagan tribes: of such are the Dinka, Bari, Bongo, Madi, Shuli, and Niam-Niam.* The Shilluk and others are only partly Mohammedan; but the Bagara and Kababish, to the west of the White Nile and south of Kordofan, and the inhabitants of Galabat and Takela, are entirely Mohammedan.

Outposts of Islam.

As regards the remaining regions of Africa south of this border-land of Islam, it may be stated in general

---

* Dr. Ratzel, our former authority, states, on the other hand, that the Upper Nile region is under Mohammedan domination.

terms that Islam has no footing and institutes no systematic propaganda. Of the Eastern Horn it has already been said that the Somâl are in the main Mohammedan, and that, though some of the Galla have accepted Islam, there remain several Pagan tribes. The inhabitants of the so-called Swahéli Coast are Mohammedans; and we find Arabs or Mohammedans in almost every large town, especially in Eastern Equatorial Africa; but, living in families or communities, they do not sensibly affect the populations.

In the last few years, it is true, we have seen something very closely resembling concerted action on the part of Arabs—or so-called Arabs, many of whom were simply the "sweepings" of the East Coast—to repel foreign influences; but it is obvious that this action was inspired by a desire on their part to protect and maintain the time-honoured institution of the Slave Trade, and was in no sense a religious movement. In the Upper Congo, in the region of the great Lakes, and on the East Coast, conflicts of this character and significance have recently taken place; but they should be regarded simply as the death-throes of the Slave Trade and of Arab dominion. That they were partially successful is evidence of the impotence of the European Powers in Africa to deal promptly and effectually at any distance from the coast with elements subversive of law and order; but, given the power to act, it must be merely a question of time, and, it may be added, of sincerity, on the part of Europe to successfully suppress all such symptoms of anarchy. *Recent hostilities.*

It is an entirely different matter when we come to consider the elements hostile to European influence, and too strong for its control—at least, at the present time— in those regions of Africa where Islam has taken a firm *Strongholds of Islam.*

Strongholds of Islam.

stand. It is true that in Lower Egypt, where Islam has penetrated most deeply, Great Britain has exercised, and is exercising, a wise and beneficent control, and that in Algeria France has established * the Roman Catholic religion; but those countries, as has so often been insisted on in this book, scarcely belong politically to Continental Africa. The strongholds of Islam, as far as their power for dominating Africa is concerned, are situated, not on the shores of the Mediterranean, but in the vast, inaccessible Súdan. Among the Tuareg of the Sahara the *marabut* are the missionaries, judges, and teachers; and in the Súdan the Fulah have schools everywhere, even in the smallest communities. The Koran, the Arabic language, and several treatises in the vernacular are studied; and one hears even of libraries, such as that discovered by Dr. Nachtigal in Bornu: so that, on the whole, one is surprised at the intellectual culture that is found in many parts of the Súdan. We have already alluded to the high degree of development of native industries and the organised governments in the Central and Western Súdan. That these political phenomena are strong elements antagonistic to the introduction of alien influences cannot be doubted. At the same time they furnish a substratum of hope that, with the introduction of legitimate—really legitimate—commerce, by which European intercourse with the Súdan will be promoted, the more advanced peoples will come more and more under our influence. Not all of them are fanatics, and few would be willing to forego any material advantage arising out of such intercourse. The treaties which Mr. Joseph Thomson recently concluded with the Sultans of Sokoto and Gandu are inspiring examples. Our hopeful-

Súdan.

---

* In Algeria the *mufti* and *imam* have little influence; the *marabut* have more; and the *kuan* (monks) direct the Pan-Islam movement: their strong organisation gives them the power (Rinn).

ness in this respect is not discounted by reference to local conditions until we enter the more primitive regions to the east. In Kordofan, according to Wilson and Felkin, the people are superstitious and have scarcely any religious ideas. But the fanatics of Galabat, the Mahdists, the Senusi, —these are very different factors to reckon with. Now that Emin Pacha has been forced to evacuate his province, which was so effectively situated for operations in the Upper Nile territories, we have lost our last footing there; and it must be confessed that the outlook is very black indeed. It is useless to repine; but it will take years of labour and lavish expenditure to recover the position we have thus lost by our own folly and negligence. *[margin: Upper Nile.]*

Uganda, whose influence in this region is so potent, has in recent years been the battlefield of Paganism, Islam, and Christianity; it presents an unique and typical example of the interaction of these forces in Africa. Arab traders had been at court for many years before King M'tesa, through Mr. Stanley, invited Christian missionaries to take up their abode in his country; but Islam had in the meantime made little progress, for the Arabs were traders, not propagandists. That they exercised a certain influence is true, and that they endeavoured to bring about the expulsion of European missionaries is equally true; but it was on account of their commercial interests, and not for the Mohammedan faith, that they adopted and pursued this hostile line of action. M'tesa himself refused to submit to the distinctive Mohammedan rite, and burnt one hundred of his young men who had done so; but neither was he at heart a Christian, nor were his people for some time perceptibly influenced by this intercourse with foreigners. *[margin: Uganda: a modern battlefield.]*

On the death of M'tesa, however, and the ascent to the throne of the cruel boy-king M'wanga, we witnessed, not only a political crisis, but one of the most remarkable

<small>Waganda martyrs.</small>

and significant events in Africa—hundreds of Waganda, Christian converts, dying for their faith at the stake. That this measure of success should have been obtained by Christian missionaries is a most encouraging and notable sign of the times. Not that the Christian missions, Roman Catholic and Protestant, were themselves entirely in accord: unhappily this does not appear to have been always the case; but that, after the revolutions and the defeat of the Arab puppet-king, M'wanga himself—the slaughterer of converts—should have appealed to the Christians for support and assistance against the usurpers of his throne, and have promised any number of reforms, worthless as such promises may be regarded. We see, in fact, in this horrible tragedy of butchery and barbarism, glorified as it was by the native martyrdoms, the elements of progress which, were European influence more than a name, would inevitably produce substantial results.

Before turning to the work and progress of Christian missions in Africa, a passing reference may be made to the Jews and Copts. And here I may express my indebtedness to Dr. Oppel, whose admirable paper, *Die religiösen Verhältnisse in Afrika*,* has been of so much assistance to me in the construction of this chapter, that I may be said to have based it entirely on his *data*.

<small>Jews.</small>

In spite of their oppressed state the Jews are said to be increasing in numbers; but in North Africa, as we have said, they exercise no influence. In Morocco, where they are widely distributed, and especially in the coast towns, they pursue an industrious life as artisans; elsewhere they engage in trade. Their position in Algeria and Tunis, in consequence of the French administration, has been improved; in other parts they appear to lead an isolated but contented life.

---

* *Zeitschrift der Gesellschaft für Erdkunde zu Berlin* (1887).

The Copts are found more especially in the northern **Copts.**
towns of Lower Egypt, in Siut and other centres of population. In Khartûm there is, or was, a Coptic Church. A
relict of the Christian Church, the Coptic is now in a very
corrupted state; and the same may be said of its daughter
church in Abyssinia. Christianity established itself in
Abyssinia in the fourth century, and at first made great
progress; but its debased forms in that country at the
present day exhibit scarcely a trace of the old faith:
Pagan, Jewish and Mohammedan influences are everywhere
apparent. The innumerable churches and monasteries,
priests, monks, and nuns in Abyssinia tend to maintain
outward forms. The Jesuits and others have never made
any lasting impression upon them.

We thus encounter in the province of Islam scattered
oases of Christian sects which have suffered from the unfavourable conditions of their environment. All attempts
to implant or revive Christianity in North Africa have
so far failed. It is otherwise when we enter the Pagan
lands where Christian missionaries have led the way to
European discovery and settlement.

Missionary enterprise and geographical discovery in **Phases of Christian missionary enterprise.**
Equatorial and South Africa are inseparably associated,
and may be divided into two distinct phases. The first
phase is exclusively restricted to the enterprise of the
Roman Catholic Church in the sixteenth century; the
second and more important phase, from last century to the
present time, embraces the foundation and growth of other
Christian missions in Africa. Practically the whole of
Roman Catholic and Protestant Europe, assisted by North
America, has taken part in this movement, the progress and
results of which we may now consider.

All the early Portuguese navigators took with them their **First phase.**
complement of priests and missionaries. After Diego Caõ's

Christian missionary enterprise: first phase.

voyage (1484), the so-called King of Congo received innumerable Franciscans and Dominicans; and the so-called King of Benin also asked for missionaries to his people. The experimental missions in Upper Guinea, though they made many converts, lost them all when the Portuguese settlements were abandoned; and their apparent temporary success was due to political expediency on the part of the native chiefs rather than from religious conviction. In the kingdom of Congo, on the other hand, Christianity established itself more firmly. According to Werner, the diocese of Mbazi (San Salvador), embracing the kingdoms of Congo, Angóla, and Benguela, was established by Pope Clemens VIII. in 1596. The early successes of the Roman Catholic Church would appear to have been notable, judging from accounts published at the time; but it is certain they fell off considerably with the decline of the Portuguese dominion and the dissolution of the Jesuit order in 1773. In 1840 there were said to be 700,000 Negro Christians; but when Livingstone, in 1854, visited Angóla, he found the monasteries deserted, though, to his astonishment, there were numerous Negroes who could read and write. At the present day all traces of Christianity are merged in the grossest paganism.

Christianity, in the first epoch, would appear to have had a footing also on the East Coast, between the mouth of the Zambezi and the Equator: but *data* as to its extent and success are wanting. In the Sudan and in Senegal, in the islands of Mauritius and Réunion, missions were planted; but only in Réunion was any success reaped.

Second phase.

No new Roman Catholic missions were established between the years 1767 and 1829. Protestant missions had, however, taken the field during that period. The first Dutch missionary landed at the Cape as early as 1665, and many others followed; but it was not before

1737 that Protestant missions earnestly entered upon their work, not only at the Cape, but in Upper Guinea. The first native church in South Africa was built in 1800, from which year dates the practical foundation of the Christian missions that now hold undisputed sway over the whole of Cape Colony and beyond.

The following are the spheres in which Christian missions have been and are most active:—(1.) In West Africa, the coastal lands, and for some distance inland between the Senegal and Kunéné rivers; (2.) in South Africa, all the territories to the south of an imaginary line drawn from the Kunéné to the Limpopo; (3.) in East Africa, the coastal lands from the Limpopo to Abyssinia and the region of the Great Lakes; and (4.) in North Africa. To them should be added, to be more explicit, (5) the missions that have recently sprung up on the track of discovery in the Congo basin. Each of these spheres may be briefly discussed. *Spheres of Christian missionary enterprise.*

With the exception of the Ivory Coast,* all the populated regions of West Africa are studded with mission-stations. English Societies, except in the ancient spheres of the Catholics, largely predominate, though in Upper Guinea many of them are American; and German Societies are active on the Gold and Slave Coasts and in the Camarons. It would be tedious to particularise any further, nor need we venture on a computation of the converts claimed by each mission. In their own way they claim in different parts, according to the political conditions under which they work, a success more or less problematical, but at any rate earnestly striven after. If their efforts had not been discounted by the immoral and subversive effects arising out of European political rivalries and commercial greed, it is obvious that the success of Christian *West Coast missions.*

* From Cape Palmas to Cape Three Points.

missions in West Africa would have been much more marked than it actually is; but it is not the missionaries who should be held morally responsible for this abortive action.

<small>South African mission-fields.</small>

South Africa may be now regarded as a Christian land: about half of the entire number of mission-stations in Africa are located there. It has been found a most fruitful soil for nourishing missions, the success of which has, however, been due mainly to the more settled and effective conditions of administrative control.

<small>East Coast missions.</small>

Although parts of the East Coast were among the first of the Portuguese possessions in Africa, their missionary enterprise there has not met with a tithe of the success that characterised it in Angola. Any achievements of Christianity in East Africa have been due to other and later missions. Indeed, in the province of Mozambique, we see not only no traces of missionary success, but debased "vestiges" of its failure. The missionary enterprise of other nations has endeavoured to enter the Interior from the coast-lands between the mouth of the River Zambezi and the port of Mombaza, but more especially from the coast opposite Zanzibar. Its success, however, has not been nearly so great as on the West Coast and in South Africa: in fact, it may be said to have so far failed. Reasons for this comparative failure are ascribable to the facts that: (1.) the East Coast has been for so long under Mohammedan influence; (2.) the missions have penetrated into the Interior like exploring parties, without first establishing a base on the Coast; (3.) European influence has not until quite recently taken any hold on the mainland; (4.) the natives are more warlike, energetic, and untractable than in West and South Africa; and (5.) wholesale annexations of territory have caused mistrust of all Europeans.

In the vicinity of the great Lakes, and especially in

Nyassa-land, the English and Scottish missionaries have taken up a firm position; but there again their power for good has been discounted, if not for a time thwarted, by complications of a political character. In the basin of the Congo missionary enterprise is only in its earliest, and therefore exploratory, stage of growth. In North Africa the missions are chiefly Roman Catholic, as one might suppose from the political conditions that exist there. Other missionary stations.

The Roman Catholic stations in Africa are said to number 250; those of Protestant missions, 600. As to the number of converts claimed by each mission, it were more prudent to avoid statistics. Dr. Oppel asserts that during the present century some 10,000 native adherents to Christianity have annually been secured. But the *Church Missionary Gleaner* for February, 1890, remarks: "In 1885 two American Societies published statistics of Protestant Foreign Missions, based upon and enlarged from tables compiled by Dr. R. Grundemann. These gave for Africa, 600 missionaries, 7000 native teachers, 576,000 native Christian adherents, 160,000 communicants, 190,000 scholars. But Madagascar is included, and also (apparently) a good many colonists in South Africa. Probably the number of missionaries should be reduced to 500, and all the other figures *halved*." Let us therefore rest satisfied with the general remark that Christian missions in Africa, embracing workers from nearly all European countries and from North America, have planted stations and erected churches in all the regions of Equatorial and South Africa to which access can at present be obtained, and they have made numerous native converts. Number of mission stations, missionaries, and native converts.

It will now be our task to ascertain, as far as we can, what have been the results of missionary enterprise.

The missions in Madagascar and South Africa have made good progress, in West Africa moderate progress, in

K

Results of missionary enterprise. East Africa little progress, and in North Africa no progress at all. This appears to be the general result, according to Dr. Oppel, who partly accounts for the inequality by the fact that Christianity has found the greatest difficulty in making any impression on peoples who have been long under Islam, or in those countries where the attitude of the native rulers has been hostile. The latter conclusion is just enough, but the former is perhaps subject to qualification: since, as Dr. Blyden assures us,* not all Mohammedans are fanatics. In the main, however, Dr. Oppel's verdict may be regarded as a true finding. It is chiefly in the Pagan countries where Christianity has met, and must continue to meet, with most success. The oppressed and dispersed peoples of Africa are naturally more accessible than those living under a strong and despotic administration. But the chief guarantee of the success of Christian missions, over and above the character and position of the native peoples, is, after all, the presence of a strong government behind. Security of life and property, just laws, and good example are the factors which, more than any others, account for the success of missionary enterprise. These conditions appear to be improving all round Africa, with only a few notable and lamentable exceptions. In South and West Africa, though they vary in value, they are none the less apparent: and in East Africa they are slightly better than they were. But in North Africa, so long as Mohammedan rule is tolerated, Christianity cannot expect to receive much encouragement. Paganism withdraws every year more and more into the Interior. The Arabs, though

---

* "We entertain the deliberate conviction—gathered not from reading at home, but from travels among the people—that whatever it may be in other lands, in Africa the work of Islam is preliminary and preparatory. . . . The African Mohammedans, as far as we have observed, are tolerant and accessible, anxious for light and improvement from any quarter."—*Christianity, Islam, and the Negro Race*, p. 28.

numerically stronger and more easily acclimatised, cannot
command the means that Europeans so easily secure. Is it
not, then, merely a question of time for Christian Europe
to impose its domination and its creed upon the greater
part of Africa?

We tread very uncertain ground, on which numerous
disputants have fought, when we come to consider the
methods by which Islam has promoted its cause, and to
compare them with those adopted by Christianity,—in their
effect upon the Pagan populations. But we cannot shirk
the responsibility of discussing this momentous question.
With Islam we, of course, associate Arab rule; with Christianity, the domination of Europe. *[sidenote: Methods adopted by Islam and by Christianity.]*

In the first place, let us hear what some of the leading
African travellers have to say in the matter.

In general the verdict has been given against Islam; so
much is certain. But to this there have been at least two
notable exceptions. In an article in the *Contemporary
Review*, Mr. Joseph Thomson, a close and conscientious
observer, states, when comparing the degraded populations
of the Coast of Guinea and the banks of the Lower
Niger with those of the Central Súdan, that what he
saw there gave him a very different impression from what
he had expected to see. He found in the Súdan large
and well-built towns, well-clothed people, behaving with
self-possessed dignity, and signs on all sides of an industrious community, considerably advanced on the path of
civilisation, and carrying on different trades. The various
metals were worked, stuffs were spun and dyed, and the
markets were thronged. Savage tribes had been transformed into semi-civilised nations. Fetishism, with its degrading superstitions, had disappeared before Islam, which
had inspired the Negroes with a new and vigorous life.
These were the impressions made on Mr. Joseph Thomson *[sidenote: Verdicts in favour of Islam.]*

during the course of his journey up the Niger to Sokoto and Gandu. Later on we shall examine his "spectacles."

Dr. Flegel, another competent traveller, in discussing (*Lose Blätter*, p. 17) the very same region, points to the freemasonry of Islam, by which all Mohammedans are considered as equal, and which secures to them the consideration they expect of others, thus leading to pacific annexations of territory, &c. But, though true in theory, this is very far from being the case in practice. Thus, a Mohammedan cannot legally be made a slave; but once a slave, always a slave: so that there is really no sanctuary in Islam for the Pagan-born. And again, the course of history shows that, as a general rule, the Pagan tribes have been conquered in the first instance by the sword, and not by the Koran.

Verdicts against Islam.

Dr. Oscar Lenz, on the other hand, states * that Islam is an enemy to all progress, as compared with European standards, and that it exists by reason of its own inertia, when left undisturbed (*wenn er völlig intakt bleibt*). The Koran is the Alpha and Omega of the pious Moslem. The result is—religious intolerance, expressed in the most brutal manner to dependants; and, accompanying this fanaticism, an unbridled covetousness, often greater than religious intolerance itself. Moreover, lying to and deception of the "Unfaithful" are, according to Dr. Lenz, the direct legacy of Islam to its adherents. His opinion, in short, appears to be that Islam is the greatest enemy to European culture in Africa.

Dr. Hugo Zöller expresses his views in almost similar terms, though, like others, he admits that, in outward respects, Mohammedanism grafts great improvements on the Pagan. He says † there is no greater promoter of

---

* *Timbuktu*, vol. ii. p. 375.
† *Die Deutschen Besitzungen*, &c., iii. p. 93.

barbarism in Africa than Islam. Yet Dr. Blyden states*
that "between Sierra Leone and Egypt the Mohammedans
are the only great intellectual, moral, and commercial power.
The tribes intervening have for more than three hundred
years been under the influence of Islam. It has taken
possession of, and has shaped the social, political, and
religious life of the most intelligent tribes. Its adherents
control the politics and commerce of nearly all Africa north
of the Equator."

Between these diverse authorities who is to decide? **Diverse authorities.**
Missionaries and their supporters at home are naturally
severe critics of Islam: they inveigh against its sensuality
and immoralities.

If we turn to arm-chair geographers and critics, our
judgment is still further confused. M. Elisée Reclus, for
instance, says† that since the fall of Carthage and the decadence of Egyptian civilisation, the most notable event for
Africa has been the spread of Mohammedanism. Its simple
doctrine, the zeal of its apostles, its cohesion and numbers,
are the forces which have conquered where Christianity
must fail. The Christian missionary cannot assimilate
with the people: he is an alien; he will not give his
daughter in marriage with a native Christian. Moreover,
the Arabs speak in the language of the people—the principal vehicle of civilisation.

Finally, Canon Taylor apologises: ‡ "Another accusation
is that Islam is sterile and unprogressive. But the same
may be said of other Oriental religions. It is a question
of race and climate rather than of creed."

The only conclusion to which this conflicting evidence **The evidence examined.**
seems to lead is, that either all are right or all are wrong, or

---

* *Christianity, Islam, and the Negro Race*, p. 260.
† *Nouvelle Géographie Universelle*, x., p. 30.
‡ *Leaves from an Egyptian Note-Book*, p. 111.

The evidence examined.

—which is far more reasonable—that there are two sides to the question, and that the truth will be found in a judicious compromise. Let us, then, endeavour to sift the evidence.

In the first place, we must eliminate the personal element, which may fairly be supposed to bias the writers. It is obvious that the travellers in Africa are our most trustworthy authorities, for only they have seen the practical working of the systems they either extol or condemn. How, then, do we account for Mr. Joseph Thomson's views?

It must be remembered that Mr. Thomson's journey to Sokoto and Gandu was a flying visit, speed having been essential to its success; and that he passed rapidly from the mouth of the Niger, where the most degraded populations in Africa are found, and from a coast that has been debased by the demoralising traffic in gin, to the most advanced centres of Islam. Can we wonder that he was struck by the contrast in the outward culture and civilisation of the respective regions, or that, in comparing them to the East Coast, where Islam has no propaganda and whose adherents are brutalised Arab slavers, he should have seen this contrast still further emphasised? For it is in the Western Súdan and on the Gulf of Guinea that Islam and Christianity, Arab and European influence, have their typical development in Africa. No; the wonder would have been, had Mr. Thomson not noted the superiority in the outward culture and civilisation of the Mohammedan peoples over those of the debased Negroes. Had he, however, visited some of the independent Negro peoples between the Niger and Benué, whose culture, Pagans though they are, Dr. Ratzel (*Völkerkunde*, i. p. 635) regards as in many respects higher than that of their Mohammedan neighbours, he might have modified his opinions.

Moreover, in assuming that this culture and civilisation of the Mohammedans are *outward* or external only, we have the opinion of Dr. Oscar Lenz to support us. Dr. Lenz, an accomplished traveller, whose experience of the peoples of the Mohammedan Súdan is unrivalled, says,[*] "Islam in its outward aspects is somewhat imposing when we see it in all its purity and greatness, but it becomes a caricature when it stoops to concessions." And its most marked concession in the Súdan is, according to him, the subordination of doctrine to unbridled covetousness. We have already seen the futility of Dr. Flegel's reasoning as regards Mohammedans being safe against enslavement; and it is further to be noted that the domestic immoralities ascribed to Mohammedans—which are too well known to be particularised—are in themselves a cause of the Slave Trade.

The evidence examined.

When men like Dr. Blyden pronounce in favour of Islam, we are compelled to recognise the fact that they and their critics do not argue from the same premises. The authoritative judgment of Dr. Blyden on such a question[†] is undoubted: for he is a full-blooded Negro, a statesman, a scholar, and himself a Christian. When he speaks of Islam being the most intelligent force in the Súdan, he compares it, no doubt, with paganism and fetishism, on the one hand, and with the methods of Christianity on the other, —not Christianity as we know it, but Christianism, if the term may be allowed, on the West Coast of Africa. He sees Christian Europe preaching its noble doctrine, but practising the very reverse of it, by conniving at slavery whilst pretending to suppress it, and by introducing the accursed traffic in gin and gunpowder. He sees

---
[*] *Timbuktu*, vol. ii. p. 375.
[†] During a voyage last year from Tenerife to Liverpool I had many opportunities of eliciting Dr. Blyden's views. We were passengers together.

The evidence examined. Islam preaching temperance—the moral safety of the natives—and for the most part practising it. Furthermore, he sees Europeans sinking to the level of the natives, and Mohammedans raising the latter up to their own level —whatever that may be.

To turn to the other authorities we have quoted, M. Elisée Reclus justly ascribes the remarkable progress of Islam to its simple doctrine, the zeal of its apostles, its cohesion and numbers, and its power of assimilation. But one at least of his arguments is open to attack. The cohesion of Islam, though apparently great, and certainly greater than the cohesion of Christian Europe, has its weak points, which were indicated in the early part of this chapter. That its simple doctrine and its power of assimilation are forces in its favour cannot be doubted; and that, as an ancient indigenous power, numerically strong, it has made more rapid strides than Christianity, accompanied as the latter has been by the alien influence of Europe, is no less obvious. But time and opportunity, should these be turned to proper account, will profoundly affect these conditions; for hitherto we have only experimented in Africa, whilst now we are called upon to colonise it.

Finally, Canon Taylor's argument, that the sterility and unprogressiveness of Islam are a question of race and climate rather than of creed, is one not to be proved or disproved; the phenomena of race and climate are so inseparably connected with creed that to dissociate them is unfair. It is not to be gainsaid that an Oriental religion is adapted to an Oriental people, to whom Christianity must be, as Mr. Thomson expresses it, "a delicate exotic;" but that does not dispose of our responsibility in dealing with the African natives under our protection, nor of our duty to raise them up to our own standard of civilisation, if it be possible. It only raises the question as to the best methods of acclimatising Christianity under the arid and torrid conditions of Africa. *The evidence examined.*

To speak of acclimatisation implies concession,—a compromise of the methods at present in vogue. We do not, of course, expect the missionaries to assimilate with the natives, and thereby sacrifice so many centuries of civilisation, but we do expect them to make greater allowances for native prejudice and native depravity, and, whilst themselves living an industrious, educative, and exemplary life, to endeavour to instil into their charges the principles and practices rather than the (to them) incomprehensible dogmas of Christianity. We have no right to expect of the natives of Africa the miracle of sudden conversion by the power of faith nor the intelligence to grasp the abstract truths of Christianity; at the same time we must pursue the most direct and intelligent course to their hearts and minds.

As a conquering power, Islam would appear to have a certain advantage over Christianity: it is a religion of forms rather than of principles underlying human actions, and it can at once raise up the conquered to its own level. A conqueror must either assimilate the conquered or be assimilated with them. But it is obvious, from reference to past experience, that our methods of conquest so far have not been the best possible.

The more we learn of Africa—for the dark clouds that have hidden it for centuries have been only gradually dispersed—the more vividly is the impression borne in upon us that, if we cannot at once root up the noxious weeds that poison the atmosphere of that great suffering continent, we can at least plant healthier growths, which may mitigate the deadly exhalations of barbarism. But our moral plantations must be suited to the climate, or they cannot be expected to thrive. Our experiments so far have been on a *Summing up.*

Summing up. comparatively small scale, so that we can scarcely expect their influence in this respect to be great; but the conviction is forced upon us that, even in the modest attempts we have made, not sufficient attention has been paid to the laws of acclimatisation, to the conditions of life in Africa. We have been enthusiastic weeders, it is true, but we have not yet planted the healthiest growths: for surely gin and gunpowder, and the disregard of native rights and native prejudices, are not the best means to influence savages. Living example is to them far more potent than dry precept: and, as we shall see later on, we have failed entirely to carry into our African policy the highest example of Christian Europe.

Unlike savages in other parts of the world who have perished at the breath of Europe, the African Negro evinces a vitality superior to the vicissitudes of his life and a capacity for taking on a higher civilisation than that which he at present enjoys. But to expect that at the touch of Christianity the devil of savagedom should come out of him, and that—to again quote Mr. Thomson—he should sit at the feet of the missionary, clothed and in his right mind, is to expect no less than a miracle. The process of development must be a much slower one, and not only a slower but a more natural one than the wholly alien processes that at the present day are being forced upon him by his well-meaning but misguided friends. The Negro must be guided gradually along the lines which Nature herself has pointed out. His impressionable mind, his child-like character, and his adaptiveness are all instruments in the hand of his reformer. He must be provided with something better and more wholesome to replace what all agree in regarding as the poisons of his existence. Polygamy and slavery, two of his worst enemies, have prevailed in Africa from time immemorial, and cannot be destroyed at a blow. On the other hand, the introduction of spirits and weapons of destruction, the most widely spread agencies of European influence, can be immediately stopped without detriment to the African.

On the West Coast this abominable traffic * is notorious for its deteriorating effects on our "customers:" it paralyses all the efforts of missionary and philanthropic enterprise; and it is associated in the native mind with Christianity in the same way as the Slave Trade is associated by us with Islam. We support, or at least do not suppress, the one, and we decry and endeavour to stamp out the other; yet both are equally scandalous and blood-guilty: our hypocrisy in the matter is transparent even to the native mind. In short, it is no exaggeration to say that progress in Africa is impossible until the traffic in both these abominations is destroyed.

In Southern Africa the natives have for the most part either given way entirely before the advance of a vigorous alien race, like the Dutch and the English, or they have become enslaved and deteriorated by absorption: the step from the one degree of culture to the other has been too great. Only the strong Zulu tribes have maintained their integrity, and that not wholly. In the Súdan, on the other hand, contact with a civilisation in a sense suited to the conditions of climate and the genius of the people has resulted in a more natural fusion between Pagan and Mohammedan. The conditions in this case have worked for progress. In the Upper Nile territories we have seen the Egyptian domination fall to pieces by reason of its utter rottenness; and in East Africa the Arab ascendancy has also decayed. Both of them, nourished by the Slave Trade, have done little or nothing to advance native culture. With these few examples before us, it is evident

Summing up.

---

* Statistics will be given in a subsequent chapter.

that no systematic attempt has been made to extirpate what is worst and to encourage what is best in the native civilisations of Africa. The Slave Trade, injustice, and cruelty have characterised Egyptian and Arab rule; while Europeans themselves have shown very little advance upon these methods, and have, moreover, debased the natives with spirituous liquors and introduced other agencies for the easier destruction of their homes.

The suppression or adequate restriction of the traffic in gin, guns, and gunpowder would, therefore, appear to be one of the first steps to be taken by us, if our desire to reform the Negro is a sincere one, and not a mask for unbridled license.

Anti-Slavery Conference, 1889-90.

The Anti-Slavery Conference of 1889–90, after several months' deliberation at Brussels, drew up an admirable programme for the suppression of the Traffic in Slaves. The General Act, if ratified, will also go far to regulate the traffic in firearms, but not far enough towards the suppression of that in spirits. It is gratifying to note that the Powers represented at the Conference made a genuine effort to grapple with these two crying evils; but they were not strong enough to put aside the "trade interests" involved by their total suppression. A middle course was therefore adopted. The traffic in firearms will, it is hoped, be regulated in such a manner as to check the former indiscriminate distribution; and it must be confessed, considering the difficulties and dangers of this complicated question, the measures approved by the Conference promise to be as effective as can reasonably be expected at the present time. But it is greatly to be deplored that more stringent measures were not adopted for the immediate or ultimate suppression of the traffic in cheap spirits. It is true that those regions of Africa not already infected are to be protected from the flood of poisonous spirits now being poured into the continent

by unprincipled merchants; but the traffic is too vast to be
dealt with in this half-hearted manner: it should be totally
destroyed. Raising the duty to 1½d. per quart will do
little or no good. The trade interests of a few Europeans
should not have been allowed to overrule the spiritual
interests of a continent at the mercy of its invaders.
Such a cowardly concession as this augurs impotence in
carrying out other enactments by the Conference, and
engenders the fear that what has been gained in principle
will be lost in practice. In a word, the traffic in firearms
has been more or less effectively dealt with, because it
placed weapons in the hands of the natives of Africa
that might at any moment be turned against ourselves;
but the traffic in spirits, which can only destroy our
victims, though condemned in principle, has been condoned
by the measures adopted for its nominal restriction.

CHAPTER VI.

THE TRAFFIC IN SLAVES.

THE SOURCES, CONDITIONS, AND EXTENT OF THE SLAVE TRADE—DISCUSSION OF REMEDIAL MEASURES.

MAP.

COMMERCIAL PRODUCTS   *Plate* VIII.

THE TRAFFIC IN SLAVES.

THE continent of Africa bears evidence of an arrested *Civilisation of Africa.* development which no one can satisfactorily explain. The civilisation of North Africa, at one time so high, has decayed; whilst contact for 400 years with the culture of Europe at other points on the Coasts has been productive of nothing more striking than the deterioration of the natives.

Critics who have endeavoured to account for this pheno- *Main causes of its arrested development.* menon are fairly unanimous in expressing the opinion that the Slave Trade is the principal cause by which the progress of Africa has been retarded. Those who have been among the foremost in effecting her ruin, by maintaining the Slave Trade, have also been the foremost in working for her regeneration, namely, those whose pride it is, and always has been, to call themselves freemen—the English. Other European nations, some generously, some grudgingly, have in like manner recorded their verdict against man-hunting. First a murmur of conscience, at witnessing the patient suffering of a helpless continent; then a more heartfelt expression of sympathy; and, finally, a cry of horror and of shame: these symptoms have characterised the growth of public opinion in regard to the inhuman traffic by which countless millions of men, women, and children have been ruthlessly torn from their homes and treated with a relentless cruelty that no pen can fitly describe.

I have before said that the trade in spirituous

Degradation of Africa.

liquors has had an equal, if not a greater, share in the degradation of modern Africa; but, as the drink-traffic is a European monopoly, its suppression has been persistently shirked. Dosing with vile spirits is, of course, not exactly the sort of treatment to be applied: and that is a point we have yet more thoroughly to appreciate, when public opinion becomes too strong for the reckless traders, whose ill-gotten wealth out of the prostitution of European enterprise in Africa is a scandal of our times and a living lie to our pretensions of philanthropy. With this passing anathema—and because enough has been said on the subject—we may confine ourselves in this chapter to the Slave Trade.

The revolting traffic in human life must be removed from Africa at any cost. But it has so grown into her system that it cannot be eradicated in a generation or two: any precipitate action or ill-considered treatment may, in fact, result only in sacrificing the life of the patient. Homœopathic doses of philanthropy will do no harm, nor will they do much good. The entire social system of Africa must be strengthened, physically as well as morally, in order that she may be able to absorb or throw off the insidious poisons which have for so long embittered her existence. I hope to be able to show, after discussing this question of the Slave Trade, what remedial measures may be safely attempted in the meantime; but only Time and careful nursing can ever win back Africa to a higher life among the nations.

What, then, is the exact position?

Slavery and the Traffic in Slaves.

In one form or another, slavery, and in a greater or lesser degree the Traffic in Slaves, exist throughout the whole of Africa. This is not in the least astonishing. Every country and every race on earth have at some stage of their existence groaned under the curse of slavery. Only

when men have recognised in themselves the dignity and
strength of manhood and of freedom have they been able to
break their fetters and stand up for their rights. And how
long does it take, in the life of a race, in the history of a
country, for this product of moral and social development
to take root and blossom? Why, it is only the other
day, though we may call it four centuries, that there
were public slave-marts at Seville and Lisbon, and even
at Bristol.* Though slavery in the present year of grace
does not exist in Europe, except in the Turkish dominions,
it is still indigenous in many advanced Asiatic states:
Arabia, Afghanistan, Beluchistan, Borneo, China, Persia,
Siam, Syria, and Turkey. The New World has finally
abolished it, once and for all; but by its aid were built
up the colonies, republics, and empires that more or less
flourish there. Africa alone is the last continent, as a
continent, where it exists. And the export Slave Trade in
Africa was for a certain period a monopoly † for which the
maritime powers of Europe wrangled and fought, until, by
solemn decree (the "*assiento*," 1713–39), it was awarded
to Great Britain. To what base uses we turned our
maritime supremacy, in depopulating extensive regions of
West Africa, and in trapping men, women, and children in
our slave-preserves to assist in the rough work of opening
up the American colonies, are facts too notorious to dwell
on. It is estimated that millions and millions were thus
deported to America; and it would be scarcely possible to
say how many millions at the present day are the direct
descendants of those kidnapped Negroes.

The Abolition of Slavery in 1833, and the noble Act of
Emancipation, by which the slaves were set free at a cost to

---

* It is said that at Bristol English criminals—*e.g.* convicted thieves—were
at one time sold as slaves to Jamaica planters.

† Contract for supplying the Spanish colonies with 4800 Negroes annually.

Europe and the Slave Trade.

the British people of twenty million pounds sterling, though they stand to our credit, only palliate the crime against humanity of which we have been guilty. Our debt to Africa can only be repaid by continued unselfish devotion to its service. Other European Powers, who have been equally blood-guilty, have not had even the grace to do so much; at most, they have given grudging consent to any initiative undertaken by Great Britain for the suppression of the Slave Trade, and in a few instances have co-operated in a half-hearted kind of way. At the present day the people whose proud national motto is "Liberty, Equality, Fraternity," is the one great nation whose refusal to admit the "right of search"—an absolutely essential measure for checking the export Traffic—is zealously upheld, though the implication is denied. Do the French really realise that they are trafficking in indulgences? One cannot believe it; yet such is the case. The possession of the French flag,* easily obtained, gives rascally Arabs the practical right to carry their human cattle from the shores of Africa into foreign ports. This sort of merchandise is playfully called "Black ivory." A slave, it seems, has no soul and no rights: he is only a "thing."

Under these circumstances, it is not surprising that slavery, as an institution, and the Slave Trade, in accordance with the natural operation of demand and supply, should still exist in Africa. The wonder would be if it did not. Where "Might is right" the weaker must always be at the mercy of the stronger, in the absence of an effective public opinion.

To associate the Slave Trade with the propagandism of

---

* At the recent (1889-90) Anti-Slavery Conference in Brussels, France, whilst still maintaining her position in refusing the "right of search," has nevertheless agreed to increased restrictions and vigilance in regard to vessels of under 500 tons obtaining the protection of her flag. Only time and experience can show what results these new measures may produce.

Islam is, as we have already explained, quite as unjust as *Islam and the Slave* to couple the gin-traffic with the progress of Christianity. *Trade.* We have also demonstrated that the profession of the Mohammedan faith does not in itself protect the Pagan-born against enslavement. Nor does Islam encourage slavery; on the contrary, it attempts to regulate this universal and established custom and advocates manumission.

What, then, is the leading incentive to the Slave Trade? *Fundamental* Can any one, not ignorant of the true facts nor biassed *cause of the Slave* against their acceptance, refuse to admit that its funda- *Trade.* mental cause is—to put it brutally—the desire of gain? If there is a demand, there will be a supply, no matter what the commodity may be. In Africa there is a demand for slaves; the supply, therefore, is inevitable, and it is drawn from sources that are nearest to hand. Destroy the demand, and the need of supply is obviated. It is of no use forming a "ring" and trying to stamp out the supply; for, as surely as water finds its own level, any obstacle placed in the way of the natural flow of the supply will not dam its course but only divert it. And the mischief is, that by deflecting the course of natural events, the risk is run of hurting the cause itself.

We may, therefore, consider our subject under the two vital aspects of demand and supply.

There is a demand for slaves—eunuchs, women, and *Operation* boys—in all Mohammedan countries. It is immediately *of the law of demand* supplied. The natives who are hunted down in the *and supply.* Sûdan are taken to Tripoli, Egypt, Turkey, Arabia, and Persia. Some are retained for home consumption, so to speak.

There is a demand for slaves on the plantations in the East African islands and on the East Coast. It is openly supplied.

There is a demand, though a diminished one, for slaves on the West Coast of Africa. It is easily met.

There *was* a demand—though, happily, it has been withdrawn—for slaves in the American colonies and lands. In the absence of this demand, at the present day, no more slaves are exported from the West Coast. The export-trade has, therefore, died a natural death. The exceptions to the contrary are comparatively trivial.

Could anything be plainer?

<small>Adjuncts of the Slave Trade.</small> Now we may further consider the supply. And in regard to this matter we must start with one very important statement, the truth of which has been fully established: it is, *that the Slave Trade in itself does not pay*. It is not very romantic, but it is a fact. The Slave Trade not paying in itself it must, in consequence, be made to pay somehow, because there is a demand. Hence it is that the traffic in slaves and the traffic in ivory have always worked hand in hand. We have only to look at a map to convince ourselves of this coincidence. *All slave-routes are trade-routes.* As ivory is by far the most valuable product of Africa, it is traded in conjunction with the next most valuable product—slaves. If gums were the most valuable commodity of commerce, they would take the place of ivory. And besides, the only method at present in vogue for transporting goods from the less accessible places of supply to the places of demand is on the shoulders of men. Few commodities in Africa would admit of fair wages being given to these human beasts of burden: consequently, carriers must be obtained somehow.*

Is it not obvious, from a consideration of these facts, that

---

* It is stated that hired porters are not more costly to the Traders than the slaves they impress into their service. This point demands further inquiry.

if we wish to extirpate the African Slave Trade, we must use the weapons of commerce and not those of war? The wholly inadequate though well-meaning measure of blockading the Coasts has been demonstrated over and over again to be futile. If we determined to arrest a gang of burglars, should we despatch to the scene of their depredations a *posse* of police escorted by a fire-engine and a brass band? Only very few slavers fall into meshes the exact position of which they know beforehand, though, of course, those few are better than no prizes at all; and, far from discouraging this patrol of the Coasts, I would advocate that the number of vessels should be increased. But it is against half-measures of this kind we should be most guarded, since they are liable to render us too easily satisfied. Nor should we adopt the plan initiated by the Congo Independent State of setting a thief to catch a thief,—by appointing Tippu Tib, prince of slavers, Governor of the Stanley Falls Station.*

Measures against the Slave Trade.

Bearing in mind these preliminary observations, we may refer in the fewest essential words to the actual condition and extent of the Slave Trade in Africa.†

Condition and extent of the Slave Trade.

The slave-preserves are situated wholly in Tropical Africa, between latitudes 15° N. and 15° S. For purposes of description, the subject may be divided into the following three natural divisions: (1.) the Red Sea Traffic; (2.) the

Slave-preserves in Tropical Africa.

---

* Mr. Stanley, under orders from Brussels, founded in 1883 the Stanley Falls Station to check the Arab Slave Trade. The station was attacked by the Arabs and was evacuated in 1886. The following year Tippu Tib was appointed Governor.

† My *data* and statistics are derived mainly from the Report to the Brussels Conference (1889) of Mr. W. H. Wylde, for twenty years Superintendent of the Slave Trade Department in the British Foreign Office; from a paper in the *Revue de Géographie* (August 1889) by M. A. Spont; Mr. Easton Teall's *Memoranda*; and Mr. James Stevenson's Slave Trade map (Ravenstein).

Desert Traffic; (3.) the West Coast Traffic; and (4.) the
East Coast Traffic.

The Red Sea Traffic. The Red Sea Traffic has grown out of the demand for
slaves in Turkey, Arabia, and Persia. At one time it was
satisfied by the supply drawn from Southern Europe; but
at the commencement of the present century this source
was cut off. Africa, from whence only a few slaves
were formerly drawn, then became the source-region of this
degrading commerce. The agents are chiefly Arabs from
Arabia and the Persian Gulf; but it would appear that a
certain amount of this export-trade is carried on in driblets
as private ventures. The native craft used for that purpose
carry small consignments only, of from five to thirty or
forty head, and rarely numbering a hundred; and they know
very well how to elude the vigilance of British cruisers.
The slave-preserves of the Red Sea Traffic are the Central Súdan and the Upper Nile region, Abyssinia and the
country to the south. The chief trade-centres are Abeshr
(Wadai), Fasher (Darfur), Khartúm, Galabat, and Dongola.
From thence the slaves are taken to ports and creeks on
the Red Sea and Gulf of Aden. In Arabia, Jeddah is
the principal port where they are received, and Mecca
and Hodeida are the chief depôts whence they are distributed.*

The Great Desert Traffic. In the West-Central and Western Súdan, the slaves are
drawn from the regions to the south of Lake Tsad and
between the Niger and Benué. The chief centres are
Timbuktu, Kano (Sokoto), and Kuka (Bornu). From
Timbuktu, Bornu, and Wadai, some fifteen to twenty large
caravans cross by the terrible desert-route to Morocco and

---

* M. Spont estimates that from 15,000 to 18,000 slaves go by the Red
Sea route to Arabia and beyond, whereas formerly they found their
way down the Nile to Egypt, a route which is now blocked by British
troops.

Tripoli * every year, though Morocco receives only a comparatively small number of the slaves. M. Spont estimates that from 10,000 to 12,000 slaves are annually taken alive across the desert.

Travellers have given heart-rending descriptions of the Great Desert Traffic. Bornu derives its wealth from it, and from thence in the last twenty years the export-traffic has increased by leaps and bounds. Rohlfs on one occasion saw a caravan of 4000 slaves set out from Kuka; a fortnight elapsed before the last batch took the road. One can scarcely exaggerate the terrible sufferings of the slaves, marching across the Desert for 800 miles to Murzuk, under a burning sun, and exposed to attack from the nomad Tuareg and to the relentless cruelty of their drivers. It is estimated that one in five perish on the way. Rohlfs states that the track is marked on either side by the blanched bones of slaves, and might easily be followed by a traveller who did not himself know the way. And these ghastly mile-stones mark the slave-routes in other parts of Africa.

The West Coast export-trade having ceased, for reasons already stated, the slaves drawn from those Equatorial regions are carried mostly to the North and East. Those brought to the coast are, according to Mr. Wylde, employed in large numbers by the native chiefs and traders for domestic and agricultural purposes. *The West Coast Traffic.*

The Traffic on the East Coast has increased in an alarming manner. We knew nothing of it until the revelations of explorers in the middle of this century. But we are assured that the whole of the East Coast Traffic, which was not very brisk in the last century, has since then grown into its present enormous proportions. For a long time *The East Coast Traffic.*

---

* The Slave Trade has more than once been "abolished" in Tripoli ! But we should not rail at "the Turk," for other European Powers know how to abolish in principle what they retain in practice, as regards abuses in Africa.

The East Coast Traffic.

the Eastern Traffic was slight; the Arabs were content to wait for the arrival of caravans on the Coast; but at the present day it is more extensive than any other in Africa. It has been variously estimated that from 20,000 to 40,000 slaves annually reach the Coast, where a certain number are retained as domestic and agricultural servants; the remainder are exported in dhows to the islands of Pemba (5000 to 6000 annually), Zanzibar, Madagascar, Comoro, Réunion, and to the Persian Gulf. The death-rate of slaves marched to the East Coast is estimated at one in ten.

"The French Possessions," says Mr. Wylde, "must be mentioned as places where slaves are absorbed, because it is notorious that Africans are introduced as free labourers into the islands mentioned, having been purchased and redeemed with a view to their introduction." It has already been stated that a certain amount of this export-traffic is carried on under the French flag.

The two chief centres of the Eastern Traffic are: (1.) Unyanyembe (Tabora), where slaves are drawn from as far west as Nyangwé and from as far north as Uganda; and (2.) the Nyassa region. The latter is at present the most prolific. All the ports and many of the creeks on the East Coast are more or less used for the export-traffic, but the caravans from the Interior prefer Kilwa, Dar-es-Salaam, Bagamoyo, and Pangani.

Total annual number of victims.

In regard to the total annual number of victims to the Slave Trade in Africa, authorities differ so widely that it seems impossible to arrive at any but the roughest estimate. We have so far quoted only the number of slaves who safely reach their destination; but it must be remembered that these represent only a tithe of the victims to the Slave Trade. Apart from the innumerable deaths on the march, we have to account for the untold thousands who are butchered in the raids when these slaves are captured.

M. Spont's estimate of the total annual number of victims is 200,000 to 250,000; that of Livingstone, Cameron, and others is 500,000; whilst that of Cardinal Lavigerie is as high as 2,000,000. Probably half a million were nearest the mark; and surely they are enough, when one considers the amount of misery crammed into the life of a single captive.

Before considering repressive measures, it may be well to mention some of the predisposing causes of slavery and the conditions under which the Slave Trade is carried on in Africa. When people talk of one-half of the population being slaves to the other half, they must not be taken literally, although it is perfectly true that slavery, as an institution, has deep-seated roots in Africa. If domestic slavery were alone the demand which it is the province of the slave-trader to supply, nothing like the depredations which now characterise the Traffic would be necessary. As in other countries and other times, so in Africa, captives of war are enslaved; but mere bondage is better than butchery, and even marks a certain advance in the social life of savages. In the Central and Western Sudan religious intolerance or zeal may be one incentive to the enslavement of the Pagan populations; but, as we have already seen, it is entirely subordinate to the utilitarian purposes to which the slaves are turned. In the Upper Nile region, the Slave Trade is, more strictly speaking, a commercial venture to meet the large demand made for slaves in Asia. In the Eastern Traffic, ivory, which so largely controls the remuneration of slave-raiding, is its Alpha and Omega, for it would never pay to bring slaves empty-handed to the Coast. Ivory, in fact, throughout the greater part of Africa, is one of the predisposing causes of, if not the chief incentive to, the Slave Trade.

Later on, when we come to consider the commercial

Predisposing causes of slavery.

products of Africa, we shall see not only that the trade-routes by which ivory is carried to the coasts and the slave-routes are identical, but that the same coincidence is observable in regard to the elephant-hunting grounds and the slave-trading preserves.

<small>Methods of man-hunting.</small>

The methods by which the Arabs* of the East Coast carry out their *razzias* are simplicity itself. They settle down near to peaceable communities, and acquire land and property, ivory, &c. Openly they plant their useful vegetable seeds, but in secret they sow the seed of discord: so that tribe is set against tribe, and individual against individual, while the Arabs themselves daily increase in public estimation, power, and wealth. When the time of their vile harvest arrives, that is to say, when they have collected a sufficient amount of ivory, the blow is struck. Upon some pretext, or upon no pretext, a quarrel is picked, and, either alone or with assistance, an attack is made by them on their inoffensive and too confiding neighbours. Those who offer resistance are shot down; the rest are dragged into slavery,—men, women, and children. With their superior arms, the Arabs have an easy victory. We thus see that, besides pursuing their nefarious trade, the Arabs sow discord and dissension wherever they go. Extensive regions to the west of the Great Lakes have been depopulated in this manner. In the Súdán, on the contrary, and especially in the Upper Nile territories, the methods pursued by the slavers were at one time, whatever they may be now, even bolder in conception and execution: *zeribas* were formed with the avowed object of slave-hunting, which was carried out in a business-like and wholesale way.

We have already mentioned that the slave-traders also

---

* We call them Arabs by courtesy, but most of them are the "scum" of the Coast or half-caste Portuguese.

employ nomad and warlike tribes to raid for them, while
individual natives, under this demoralising influence, occasionally do a little slave-catching on their own account.
Professor Drummond amusingly says: one cannot send
three men on an errand without running the risk of two
of them conspiring together and making a slave of the
third. And quite recently we heard of a caravan in East
Africa which, falling short of supplies, paid its way by sell-
ing one another into bondage.

Resources.

Dr. Livingstone refers to the following sources of slavery
in East Africa: (1.) criminals who are sold for their crimes;
(2.) witchcraft; (3.) reprisals and kidnapping.

It may be asked, how is it that the slave-traders, who
are numerically so insignificant, have the power to work
such havoc? The answer to this very natural question is,
that they and their followers are well armed with weapons
of precision and have plenty of ammunition: so that the
natives, being provided only with primitive arms, have
little or no chance against them. Hence the importation
of arms and munitions of war into Africa is one of the
principal things to control, if Europeans honestly intend to
suppress the Traffic in Slaves. Attempts have been made
and are being made in this direction; but they can never
be altogether successful. It has been found absolutely
impossible to prevent guns and gunpowder from being
imported, or smuggled into, such an immense continent
as Africa. And besides, by placing obstacles in the way,
one runs the risk of altogether shutting off the supply
of arms and ammunition, upon which Europeans in the
Interior themselves depend for their protection. We
must, therefore, rest satisfied with the recent enactments
of the Brussels Conference for counteracting this evil.

The supply of arms and ammuni- tion.

The consideration of these questions fittingly introduces
the measures which have been undertaken in the past and

those now proposed for the suppression of the Slave Trade.

<small>Measures against the Traffic in Slaves.</small>

Since the first years of this century to the present day the objection to slavery has gradually grown into a feeling of abhorrence which no nation dare defy. The European Powers, beginning with Denmark and followed by Britain, one by one have declared against the Slave Trade, and have emancipated the slaves in their respective colonies. Conference after Conference, at which the question was discussed, has passed Resolutions and enactments against the Traffic.* The Anti-Slavery Society of London has persistently kept the subject alive, and, besides educating public opinion, has done much in the fifty years of its existence to bring about favourable results. Sierra Leone and Liberia were created chiefly as a nucleus against slavery and the Slave Trade. The navigation of the Niger, and the opening up of commerce in those regions, were undertaken with much the same prospects in view, and the Congo Independent State was founded with similar objects. Nor should we forget the operations of Sir Samuel Baker, of General Gordon, and of their successors, in the Upper Nile territories. Their aim was to raise there barriers against the Slave Trade, by planting the rule of Egypt, by opening up routes, and by encouraging legitimate commerce. Treaties and agreements between Great Britain and native chiefs, such as those concluded with the sultans of Zanzibar, and political action in the coastal lands, besides the partial blockade of the Coasts, are among the other measures that have been undertaken with the main object of suppressing the Slave Trade. Yet, as we have seen, the Traffic still exists; and

---

* The Conferences and Congresses at which questions relating to slavery and the Slave Trade have been discussed were the following :—Vienna, 1815; Aix-la-Chapelle, 1818; Verona, 1822; Brussels, 1876; Berlin, 1878; Berlin, 1885; and Brussels, 1889-90.

not only does it exist, but in some regions it is actually increasing.

That, following upon the repeated "abolition" of slavery, and the fines and penalties to which slave-traders have been subjected in various parts of Africa, there should have grown up a sort of legalised Slave Trade or compulsory labour in its stead, is no more than might have been expected. Those who are best able to judge state that the export Slave Trade can never be effectually suppressed until, by unanimous agreement, if not by international law, it be proclaimed piracy, or equal to piracy, to engage in it. Moreover, all are agreed that the legal status of slavery must be abolished: for they argue that, as long as this legal status is recognised, so long will escaped slaves be under the power of their captors and masters; and that, unless slave-traders are summarily dealt with as pirates, they will not be deterred, by the infliction of a fine, from pursuing their abominable calling. The Sultan of Zanzibar, in August last, issued a proclamation which, if realised, will doubtless lead to the ultimate abolition of the legal status of slavery in East Africa. Similar measures have, it is true, been approved of or adopted by former sultans of Zanzibar; but there is room for hope that, with a British Protectorate over the island, this final enactment will be carried into effect. <small>The legal status of slavery.</small>

What to do with manumitted or freed slaves is another serious question. The danger of releasing a large section of the community from the obligations, however unjust, which slavery imposes upon them, is very great; but it is a danger that has been faced in other countries and other times, and one that it should not be impossible to overcome, provided the Powers are sincere in their philanthropic objects. Some method of gradually relaxing the bonds of slavery might surely be found. A kind of servitude or serfdom, <small>Manumission.</small>

for instance, by which slaves can work out their freedom within a certain number of years, has before now been tried with success. Old men and children might safely be released at once. By gradual stages the new order of things might be made to replace the old. But, as we have too frequently experienced, it is no use making regulations of this kind unless we see them faithfully observed; and it is worse than useless framing laws that offer a loophole through which guilty parties can escape their penalties.

We may, in conclusion, specially apply the principles laid down by these observations in regard to the various regions of Africa harried by slave-raiders.

Suppression of the Traffic in various regions.

At the outset we are met with one very serious obstruction: the greater part of the Súdan is closed to Europe. The Central regions have always been, and for many years are likely to remain, a sphere in which European influence must be insignificant. The Eastern regions have been the theatre of serious, and to a certain extent successful, operations against the slave-traders. At one time, shortly after the appointment of Emin Pacha to the Egyptian Equatorial Provinces, the Slave Trade was crushed or crippled in most of the Territories of the Upper Nile; and the Red Sea Traffic was considerably hampered by the vigilance of our cruisers. But now that Emin has fallen, we have lost our last hold on the region which his position, had it been rendered more stable, might have dominated. He himself stated that, with outside support, he could easily have retaken Khartúm. Many years must elapse before our position on the Upper Nile can be regained. Under favourable circumstances, however, with the Red Sea or the East Coast as a base, it would appear quite possible to gradually introduce legitimate commerce and to check the Slave Trade by its pacific means, supported by police supervision. But our greatest hope lies, for the present, in those parts of the Sudan which are accessible from the Niger and Benué, and which are being rapidly opened up by commerce.

Suppression of the Slave Trade in various regions.

In the Equatorial regions and the Lakes country to the south we have a more hopeful, if somewhat more complicated, task to perform. The export-trade is not beyond our control, provided the Traffic in Slaves be declared equal to piracy, and that at least a limited "right of search" be accorded by international agreement. Unfortunately, matters have been complicated on the Coast by the rash and ill-considered action of the German East Africa Company, which led to a general rising of the Arabs and the destruction of European influence. The drastic military measures of Major Wissmann, the German Commissioner, have resulted so far in the restoration of German rule at certain coast towns, at the cost of much bloodshed. But measures of this sort, though at times they may become necessary, are the very worst for the development of the country, upon the success of which, after all, will depend the power of Germany to deal with the Slave Trade.

In regard to the regions to the south it may be safely assumed that, though very little effective assistance can be expected from Portugal on the Mozambique Coast, as soon as British rule is consolidated in Nyassa-land the Traffic there will be promptly checked.

It is not improbable that the question as to the suppression of the Slave Trade in Southern Equatorial Africa will first be solved by the Congo Independent State.* On the

* The Slave Trade is rife within the basin of the Congo. Excellent enactments against the Traffic have been made by the State, though these remain for the most part a dead letter, owing to the impossibility of enforcing them beyond the restricted limits of the few stations on the river. With the increased powers derived from the Brussels Conference (1889-90) it is to be hoped that something will be done to deserve the confidence of Europe in this respect.

Upper Congo, between Stanley Falls and Nyangwé, the
Arabs hold a strong position. At their head stands Tippu
Tib, the uncrowned Sultan of Central Africa. On the lower
reaches of the Congo, the Independent State is slowly consolidating its administrative system—so slowly, and at such
immense cost to its sovereign, King Leopold, that, by a
recent deed of gift, his Majesty, in consideration of financial
support, has relinquished his acquired rights in favour of
Belgium, into whose hands the government of the State
will thus ultimately fall. With Arabs in the East and
Europeans in the West—slave-traders and anti-slave-traders—is it not obvious that sooner or later there must
come a final struggle for supremacy? It will not be a contest between Cross and Crescent but between the ivory-traders and legitimate commerce; and upon its issue will
largely depend the future of the Slave Traffic. I am not
one of those who believe that, by the extinction of the
elephant, and therefore of ivory, the Slave Trade must
die a natural death: on the contrary, I am convinced
that some other export-commodity would at once take the
place of ivory.

Pacific measures. And now, beyond the merely legal course of undermining the Slave Trade, what are the best pacific measures
to be adopted in the Interior? We may put altogether
out of account, as likely to do far more harm than good,
the scheme of Cardinal Lavigerie, in so far as armed
expeditions against the slave-traders are concerned. Even
if it were possible for European expeditions to carry out
effective operations in the Interior, the conditions of climate
would militate against their permanent success. I am convinced that the process of undermining and destroying the
Slave Trade must be a much slower and a much less romantic
one. It must be controlled by sound commercial principles.
With a firm base on the coast, it should seek to advance

THE TRAFFIC IN SLAVES. 179

into the Interior step by step, taking advantage of the *Pacific measures* healthiest sites for the establishment of settlements, which could and must be made self-supporting. We should send out to Africa vigorous young men—not worn-out, disillusioned adventurers—who are able and willing to turn their hands to anything. They would take possession of the best lands—such as in Usambara and Kilima-njaro— and develop them and the commerce of the surrounding districts. A chain of settlements, within touch of one another and the coast, could thus be formed right across the continent, such as it was the object of the Berlin Conference (1884-85) to achieve. They would give protection and assistance not only to European travellers and explorers but also to the natives in their neighbourhood, who could then rest in some degree of security against the slave-raiders, and have at least a chance of cultivating their own lands.

In connection with, and as a protection to, this commercial and agricultural scheme, it would of course be necessary to organise a system of police,—native levies under European command, whose duty it would be to protect the stations, uphold order, and keep careful watch over the Slave Traffic. The Eastern slave-routes at the present time intersect the chain of Lakes almost at right angles. With gunboats on the Lakes, it would therefore be a comparatively easy task for such a vigilant supervision being exercised that very few of the native craft carrying slaves could escape unobserved. *Police measures.*

These and other obvious measures are perfectly feasible and practicable within a limited degree, provided the European Powers who claim authority over the regions under consideration recognise their responsibilities and cordially co-operate in discharging them. The most serious obstacle to their fulfilment is, of course, that of climate.

It has yet to be proved that European settlements are possible in the less favourable districts of Tropical Africa. On the other hand, the stations need not be large, and the number of Europeans required for their administration need not be great. Doubtless, if a call for such men were made, it would be generously answered.

Conquest by assimilation.

In laying these proposals before the reader, and in advocating their adoption, I do not presume to have discovered any original policy. Some of them have been the result of independent inquiry, but all of them are apparently supported by the best authorities, even if we have occasionally to read between the lines of their published statements. It is not too much to say that, until these or similar measures are introduced for the suppression of the Slave Trade—namely, by assimilation and not by conquest—no permanent success is likely to be achieved.

CHAPTER VII.

PROGRESS OF EXPLORATION.

HISTORICAL SKETCH OF THE PROGRESS OF DISCOVERY AND OF EXPLORATORY WORK IN AFRICA—LIMITS TO OUR PRESENT KNOWLEDGE—THE TASK OF THE FUTURE, ITS PROBABLE DIRECTION, AND THE SPIRIT IN WHICH IT SHOULD BE UNDERTAKEN.

MAP.

Progress of Exploration . . . . *Plate* XII.

PROGRESS OF EXPLORATION.

ALTHOUGH it is true, to a qualified extent, that the modern exploration of Africa partakes of the nature of re-discovery, we do not require to go very far back to determine the genesis of our present accurate knowledge. The scientific exploration of the continent falls almost exclusively within the last hundred years. *Exploration of Africa.*

It is a subject of controversy, and one into which we do not require to enter at any length, as to how much or how little of Africa was known to the ancients. That many of the broad features of its geography were familiar to Herodotus (B.C. 450), Eratosthenes (B.C. 200), Ptolemy (A.D. 150), Edrisi (A.D. 1154), and others, we have cartographical evidence at these dates to prove. The most conspicuous and best known instance is that afforded by Ptolemy's description of the source-region of the Nile. His lake-reservoirs and "Mountains of the Moon"—regarded up to D'Anville's time (1761) as absolute facts, and subsequently as dubious or mythical—have been finally revived and re-christened by modern explorers.* *Ancient geography.*

The Mediterranean and Red Sea lands, Egypt, and the Lower Nile regions were, of course, fairly well known many centuries ago; but the desert zone presented then, as in a lesser degree it presents now, almost insuperable difficulties to the exploitation of Inner Africa,—difficulties which the Arab incursionists, by the introduction of the camel or "ship of the desert," were able only partly to overcome.

* Mr. Stanley claims for his recent discovery, Ruwenzori, that it is identical with the "Mountains of the Moon."

Of exactly how much or how little of the East and West Coasts was familiar to the ancients it is not possible to say. But the probability is that the West Coast was known to the Senegal or Sierra Leone (*cf. Periplus* of Hanno), and the East Coast down to 7° S. latitude (*cf. Periplus of the Erythræan Sea* and Ptolemy's *Geography*). Even beyond those limits the coast was not quite unknown, though it is doubtful whether Phœnician mariners ever circumnavigated the continent.

Portuguese pioneers. It was not until after the epoch-making voyages of the Portuguese pioneers—the emissaries of Prince Henry the Navigator—that we may be said to have acquired any precise information in regard to the coasts of Africa south of the desert zone. These bold mariners were the first to outline its shores, to open up the continent to the enterprise of Europe, and to break down the barriers between East and West.* They discovered a new world in the route to India, and established themselves at the most favourable localities, though on the East Coast of Africa they had to displace or fraternise with powerful Arab chiefs, whose predecessors had built imposing cities for themselves, and for centuries had been nursing a thriving trade. In their wake followed the maritime nations of Europe, who planted their colonies in the coastal lands.

The systematic, scientific exploration of Africa † dates from

---

* Cape Bojador was doubled in 1434, Cape Blanco in 1441, Cape Verde in 1445; Fernando Po was reached in 1471; the Congo was discovered by Diego Cão in 1484; the Cape was passed (unseen) by Diaz in 1487; in 1497 and 1498 Vasco da Gama discovered the ports of the South-East Coast; Sofala and Kilwa were taken in 1505-6.

† My data in this respect are derived mainly from Dr. Supan's admirable review of *Ein Jahrhundert der Afrika-Forschung*, in *Petermanns Mitteilungen* (vol. xxxiv. No. 6), to which I am greatly indebted; and some passages are taken direct from my own report on *The Achievements of Seedsmen during the Nineteenth Century in the Fields of Geographical Exploration and Research* to the Paris Geographical International Congress (1889).

the foundation in London, in the year 1788, of the African *Systematic scientific exploration.* Association. It is, however, to be noted that between the years 1768–73, James Bruce led the first great scientific expedition into Africa; on which occasion he travelled from Massawa to the sources of the Blue Nile, and from thence through Sennar and the Nubian Desert back to Egypt. Other though less important journeys had also been made; but it was due to the African Association that, in place of isolated individual effort, a system of connected scientific exploration was introduced.

At that time (1788) our acquaintance with Africa was *Our acquaintance with Africa up to 1788.* restricted to the coastal zone. Even at the best known parts, where missionaries and traders were settled, our knowledge of the Interior extended for about only two or three hundred miles. In Egypt and Senegambia alone had any serious attempts been made in the scientific exploration of the country. The Gold and Slave Coasts were, and had been for centuries — precisely on account of the gold and the slaves — the chief points of colonial attraction; but of the vast Interior little or nothing was accurately known, and that little was based mainly on the reports of Jesuit and other missionaries. It was the policy of the Portuguese and other pioneer colonists to keep all information concerning new countries as far as possible to themselves, and to regard their discoveries as exclusive fields for commercial ventures. The only notable exceptions to this uncertain knowledge of African lands were Egypt and the Nile Valley.

In those brilliant days for the discoverer and the buccaneer, the West Coast was more or less the sphere of commercial, and the East Coast that of missionary, enterprise.

The fabled riches of Timbuktu in the west, and the far-famed though mythical kingdom of Prester John (Abyssinia) in the east, were originally the respective goals. The foundation in 1618 of an English company of merchants,

Our acquaintance with Africa up to 1788.

whose object was to reach Timbuktu, and the despatch in 1490 of the Portuguese mission to Abyssinia, may be said to have kindled the torch of knowledge which subsequent emissaries of Europe have borne into the darkest recesses of Africa.

Up to the second half of the eighteenth century, then, we were mainly dependent on the Jesuit and other missionaries for our information in regard to Inner Africa; while the Portuguese had been the first to obtain any precise knowledge of Tropical South Africa. But, as we have said, the interests of the traders were in no sense geographical, and in most cases were confined to the slave-preserves and gold-fields of the coastal lands. At the Cape a very different set of conditions existed: for there, onwards from the year 1652, the Dutch in large numbers had entered the interior lands,—not as exploiters and robbers, but as genuine colonists. The expeditions undertaken by the Dutch Government into the unknown regions were, it is true, kept strictly secret: and it is therefore difficult to ascertain how far their knowledge of the Interior really extended.

In a word, we may summarise and define our precise knowledge of Africa in the year 1788 as having been restricted to a narrow border of the coastal zone. A more extensive acquaintance with Inner Africa was enjoyed only in Morocco, Algeria, Tunis, Senegambia, the Gold and Slave Coasts, Lower Guinea, the Cape, the Lower Zambezi Valley, and the region between the Red Sea and the Nile Valley.

Fields of exploratory enterprise.

From the peculiar configuration of the continent, the effect of which upon political settlement has been demonstrated, we are prepared to observe certain well-defined fields or spheres of exploratory enterprise. Access from the coasts into the Interior has in the main been by way of the great river-valleys, which present the fewest natural obstacles to the advance of caravans. The distinctive spheres of discovery and exploration in Africa may be defined as follows:—(1.) Morocco, Algeria, and Tunis, as far south as the Atlas Mountains, Tidikelt and Ghat; (2.) Tripoli, as far south as Ghat and Murzuk; (3.) Lower Egypt, the Mediterranean shores as far west as the Barka peninsula, and the entire Nile Valley district to the shores of the Red Sea, as far south as the Wellé River and the Victoria Nyanza, and as far west as the Libyan Desert and the Tsad water-parting; (4.) the Galla and Somál Coast-lands; (5.) the East Coast, between the Equator in the north and the Zambezi in the south, and as far west as the Upper Congo, along, say, the 25th meridian of E. longitude; (6.) South Africa up to the banks of the Zambezi; (7.) the West Coast, from the Camarons in the north to the River Kunéné in the south, including the valleys of the Congo and its tributaries and the upper course of the Zambezi; (8.) the Upper Guinea Coast, the valleys of the Lower and Middle Niger and of the Benué; (9.) the Central Súdan; and (10.) the Western Sahara Coastal zone and the country between Senegambia and Timbuktu, mainly in the valley of the Upper Niger.

<small>Distinctive spheres of discovery and exploration.</small>

As regards the character and extent of the work accomplished, it may be said that the regions which have been thoroughly explored, to a large extent through official agencies, are few and restricted. They are mainly the following:—(1.) Algeria and Tunis; (2.) the Lower and Middle Nile valleys, the Egyptian Súdan, Abyssinia, and the source-regions of the Nile; (3.) patches of country between the East Coast and the Lakes region; (4.) South Africa up to the Limpopo; and (5.) patches of country on the West Coast, chiefly in the French Congo Territories, in Senegambia, and on the immediate shores of the Gulf of Guinea. In

<small>Character and extent of explorations.</small>

the remaining, and especially in the interior parts of Africa, threads of topographical knowledge intersect like so many channels of communication, and mainly follow the great river-valleys. To the south of the Equator explorers' routes cross and recross one another in every direction.

Unknown or unexplored lands.

Patches of unexplored or unknown country occur here and there, but are chiefly confined to the following regions: —(1.) The Sahara, where there are immense areas of unexplored country, especially in the east and contiguous to the Súdan border-land; (2.) inland from Liberia;[*] (3.) within the basin of the Congo, in the lands intervening between the main arm of the river and its numerous tributaries; (4.) the interior lands behind the Camarons and the French Congo Territories, contiguous to the Congo watershed; (5.) numerous patches of country between the routes of explorers, in the central regions of Southern Equatorial Africa, but mainly between the watersheds of the Congo and Zambezi; and (6.) some of the Somál lands of the Eastern Horn.

It is, therefore, evident that plenty of work remains for the African explorer to accomplish. And of all these regions the most interesting is likely to be found to the north of the Congo, in the lands which form the watersheds between the Congo, Nile, Shari, and Niger, in the very heart of Africa.

Periods of exploratory work.

Dr. Supan thus divides the periods of exploratory work in Africa:—

1. Epoch 1788–1850. Periods of individual exploration in the north and south.
    (*a.*) 1788–1830. Niger problem.
    (*b.*) 1830–1850. Slow progress in Nile Territories and in South Africa.

---

[*] Mandingo-land, however, has more recently (1889) been revealed by Captain Binger, a French traveller.

2. Epoch 1850–1888.* Periods during which the explorations in Northern and Southern Equatorial Africa were connected with one another.
    (*a.*) 1850–1862. Nile and Zambezi problems. Explorations in the Sahara Desert and in the Sûdan.
    (*b.*) 1862–1877. Congo problem. Connection between explorations in Eastern and Western Equatorial Africa.
    (*c.*) 1877–1888. Filling in of details, and the extension of colonisation in Tropical Africa.

The above affords an excellent index to our subject.

We may now proceed to systematically review, as far as possible in chronological order, the progress of exploration in Africa. It will be necessary for us to refer only to those travellers whose pioneer work may be regarded as instrumental in breaking new ground. As far as possible we shall ignore supplementary work. *Progress of exploration, 1788–1888.*

The main object of the African Association was to promote the exploration of Inner Africa. The problem of the Niger, the solution of which had been attempted for over a century, was, for utilitarian as well as for scientific purposes, the first to engage their attention. Simultaneous attempts to reach Timbuktu, the fabulous wealth and power of which exercised an unfailing attraction, were made by Ledyard from the Nile, by Lucas from Tripoli, and by Houghton from the Gambia. Alexander Gordon Laing, who had travelled on the Sierra Leone Coast and in Tripoli, was, however, probably the first European to *The Niger problem.*

---

* The date 1888 is not a fixed quantity, but simply indicates the centenary of the foundation of the African Association, in honour of which Dr. Supan's paper was written. The present arrangement is, however, retained, subsequent explorations being detailed apart.

The Niger problem. reach Timbuktu (1826).* Very great uncertainty existed as to the actual course of the Upper Niger, though most geographers made it flow to the east; and the wildest speculations were entertained as to its lower course, some connecting it with the Nile, and some with an inland sea. Although the final identification of the Quorra with the lower course of the Niger was not actually established until, in 1830, the brothers Lander traced the river to its mouth, the problem of the Niger was long before solved in its main features. The first journey (1795-97) of the distinguished Scottish explorer, Mungo Park, through the vast unknown lands of the Niger basin, proved the existence of a watershed between that river and the rivers of the West Coast, and also that the Niger, in its upper course, flowed to the east. As the agent of the African Association, Mungo Park undertook his second journey (1805), from which he never returned. Although he himself did not actually solve the so-called problem of the Niger, his name and his fame are most intimately associated with the exploration of the river, and have earned for him the title of its "discoverer."

No less remarkable was the journey (1798) of Hornemann, from Cairo to Murzuk, for a great part through unknown lands. His object was to reach the Niger: but he was diverted to Tripoli, whence he made a fresh start south (1800), and was never again heard of. Numerous though abortive journeys, with the same object, ensued. The most important were those of Tuckey and Peddie (1816), the former proceeding up the Congo, the latter following Park's route down the Upper Niger, in the

---

* A sailor named Adams was supposed to have reached Timbuktu in 1810; and the French assert that Caillié entered the town before the advent of Laing. The following are other claims to this distinction:—the Portuguese, Benedetti Dei (fifteenth century); the Frenchman, Paul Imbert (seventeenth century); and the English sailor, Riley (1815).

hope of their eventually meeting somewhere in the Interior.

The actual and final solution of the Niger problem was due to Clapperton and his servant, Richard Lander. In company with Denham and Oudney, Clapperton made that still famous journey (1822-24) from Tripoli across the Sahara to the Mohammedan States of the Central Súdan. At Bornu, Denham and Clapperton separated, the former going south, the latter—in company with Oudney (who died on the way)—proceeding west. Clapperton and Denham returned together to England in 1825. They were the first Europeans after Hornemann to cross the Great Desert, to see and describe the great inland lake (Tsad) of which the Arab geographers had spoken, and to bear witness to the extent and power of the Mohammedan States of the Central Súdan. Although they were able only partly to solve the hydrographical problems of the regions through which they passed, their careful astronomical observations gave to the map of North Africa an accuracy it did not before possess. Clapperton's second journey (1825-27) was made under the auspices of the British Government, for the purpose of opening up commercial relations with the Sultan of Sokoto; and he hoped at the same time to discover the unknown course of the Niger. Accompanied by three companions, who died on the way, and Richard Lander, Clapperton started for the Interior from the Bight of Benin, and reached Sokoto. His death (at Changary, 1827), from the vexations and hardships of the journey, defeated his cherished purpose; but it is to be noted that he was the first European to reach the Niger and the Súdan from the south. It was reserved for Richard Lander, as we have said, and his brother John, to prove subsequently that the Quorra or Niger emptied its waters through several mouths into the Bight of Benin. This long-vexed problem

Final solution.

was thus solved in its leading features, and entirely through the agency of British explorers.

Main incentive to exploration of the Niger. Although the chief incentive to the exploration of the Niger was the desire to open up the inland territories to our commerce, the ostensible purpose was the suppression of the Slave Trade. The British Government and a company of Liverpool merchants, at whose head stood Macgregor Laird, despatched several expeditions to open up the navigation of the Niger. Baikie commanded the *Pleiad* (1854), which ascended the Chadda (Benué) for 150 miles beyond a point previously reached; and he afterwards conducted (1857–62) expeditions on the Niger proper.

French enterprise. The French, with the object of securing commercial supremacy, were making similar, and in a sense more successful journeys, from Senegambia to the Niger. They made sustained efforts to reach Timbuktu; and, up to the present day, they have persisted in the task of opening up a route thither. This phase of their activity was ushered in by the discovery (1818) of the sources of the Senegal and the Gambia by Mollien. De Beaufort failed to reach Timbuktu in 1824. Two years later, the Paris Geographical Society offered a prize to the explorer who should penetrate to this coveted goal. This led to the remarkable overland journey of Caillié (1827–28) from the Upper Niger, *via* Timbuktu, across the Atlas Mountains to Tangiers.

The conquest of Algeria by the French in 1830 was a decisive event in the history of North Africa. The native resistance necessitated expedition after expedition being undertaken, thereby leading to excellent geographical results. Moreover, the attention of Europe was for a time directed to Africa.

Sahara: overland journeys. In 1845–46 Richardson made his journey to Murzuk, Ghat, and Ghadames. Three years later, he proposed to the

British Government to undertake from Tripoli a journey *Sahara and Súdan.*
across the desert to the Súdan, with the object of promoting
commercial relations, and thereby contributing to the suppression of the Slave Trade. The geographical results of
this journey were, however, due rather to his German companions, Barth and Overweg. Barth, between 1850 and
1855, traversed and carefully examined some entirely new
country: he twice crossed the Desert, reached Adamawa
and discovered the Upper Benué, explored Kanem and the
country to the south of Lake Tsad, and visited Timbuktu.
Other worthy compatriots and followers in his path, from
Tripoli to the Central Súdan, were:—Vogel (1853–56),
who determined astronomically several important positions;
Rohlfs (1865–67), who crossed from the Gulf of the Syrtes
to the Gulf of Guinea, after having previously (from 1862)
travelled in Morocco, Algeria, and Tunis; and Nachtigal,
who was the last explorer to use the caravan-route from
Tripoli to Kuka, from whence he started on his remarkable journeys through unknown lands to Tibesti (1869),
Borku (1871), Wadai (1873), and thence through Darfur
and Kordofan to the Nile.

The discovery of the Benué raised high expectations *A pause in discovery.*
of a new route into Central Africa. Between 1879–85
some excellent work was accomplished by Flegel, who
obtained precise cartographical *data* for the Adamawa
plateau. But on the Guinea Coast, for so long the scene
of European enterprise, relatively slight progress was made
in the survey of interior lands. Explorations in Sierra
Leone and Senegambia were carried on intermittently, but
rarely passed beyond the watershed. Attempts to reach
the Niger from Senegambia resulted, between the years
1855–65, in revealing a considerable extent of new country.
The hope of connecting Senegambia, by railway or otherwise, with Algeria, has been the dream of the French from

1850 to the present day, and has led to several journeys being made across the intervening desert.

The Nile problem. After the solution of the Niger problem, the attention of explorers was directed to the Nile. In 1831 the African Association was absorbed by the Royal Geographical Society of London, by whom the new hydrographical problem was energetically attacked. Bonaparte's expedition into Egypt (1798-1801) had already focussed the attention of Europe on Africa, and French *savants* began earnestly to study that ancient land. Mehemet Ali initiated (1805-48) a vigorous and enterprising policy, in the wake of which numerous travellers and adventurers flocked into the Nile Valley. The exploration of the Eastern Súdan was not seriously undertaken until after the conquest of Kordofan in 1823.

The prospect of finding gold lured the Egyptians farther and farther into the Súdan. It would be tedious to enumerate the countless journeys undertaken by the early travellers in the Upper Nile territories. Step by step the countries were explored and made known. From 1772, when Bruce left Abyssinia, up to 1830, only British expeditions visited (1805 and 1810) that country. But after 1830 the exploration of the Abyssinian highlands steadily progressed, and arose largely from the jealousy between France and Britain for political and commercial supremacy on the Red Sea. Both these Powers, and more recently Italy, have now secured there the best strategical positions.

Blue Nile. Beke (1840-43) settled the question as to the sources of the Blue Nile. But the brothers D'Abbadie, who resided in Abyssinia between 1837 and 1848, contributed more than any other explorers to the accurate cartography of that country. The British expedition (1867-68), which led to the overthrow and death of King Theodore, was fruitful in geographical results. Subsequent explorers filled in topographical details. To the south of Abyssinia, for instance,

the Italians have accomplished excellent work within the
last twelve years. Route after route from the Red Sea to
the Nile basin has been opened up.

As regards the exploration of the White Nile, reference White Nile.
has been made to the earliest views concerning the source-
region. Ptolemy described the river as issuing from two
lakes (the one in 6° S. and 25½° E.; the other in 7° S.
and 33° E.) and (according to Agathodæmon) its tributaries
as flowing from the "Mountains of the Moon" in 12½° S.
and between 25° and 35° E. Up to D'Anville's time
(say, 1761), cartographers, while allowing these *data* to
stand, regarded the Blue Nile as the true source-stream,
and frequently associated the Lake region of the White
Nile with the Niger system. D'Anville, however, sharply
dissociated the two arms of the Nile, and brought the
"Mountains of the Moon" to the north of the Equator.
Even Caillaud, in 1821, when he stood at the confluence,
imagined that the White Nile came from the west. The
Egyptian Government, though it founded Khartúm (1823),
had no scientific interest in the question. The modern
exploration of the river commenced in 1827 with the
travels of Linant de Bellefonds, an agent of the African
Association, who reached 13° 6′ N. lat., and attested
that the White Nile, from the nature of the deposits held
in solution, must issue out of a large lake, the latitude
of which, however, was regarded as in about 7° N. The
parallel of 13° N. was not passed in 1839, when Mehemet
Ali fitted out two expeditions: the first (1840) of these
reached 6½° N., and the second (1841) 4° 42′ N. The supposed locality * of the "Mountains of the Moon" was thus
passed; but opinions continued to be diverse in regard to
the precise course of the river. As the ivory-trade extended westwards along the White Nile, a portion of the

* Compare D'Anville's, Browne's (1799), and Caillaud's maps.

Bahr-el-Ghazal became known. Petherick's journey in the Upper Nile region (1858) carried our knowledge to 4° N. lat., and furnished the most trustworthy observations on those parts; but the discovery of the western tributaries served only to confuse the main question of the true course of the Nile proper.

Here we must turn aside, in order to preserve as far as possible the chronology of events, and refer to the progress of discovery in Equatorial Africa.

Discoveries in Equatorial Africa.
In the early part of this century it was supposed that Southern Equatorial Africa was entirely deficient in fine waterways. Karl Ritter, writing in 1817 (*Erdkunde*, i. 77), emphasised this particular point. Tuckey's abortive expedition (1816) up the Congo discouraged Europeans, who little dreamt of the magnificent network of rivers that lay beyond his furthest point. Yet, up to 1840, Tropical South Africa was the sphere of Portuguese political, commercial, and geographical enterprise. The most notable contributions were the maps of Bowdich, who himself had carried out explorations in the Gabún country (1817). Those of Congo, Benguela, and Angóla (1824) were based on the MSS. maps of Mendes (1785) and Furtado (1790). By investigating old Portuguese reports it was found that two *pombeiros*, or half-caste traders, had, as early as 1802 and 1814, actually crossed the continent, passing through the Muata Yanvo's kingdom, from Angóla to Tete, on the Zambezi. But the results of Portuguese explorations in Southern Equatorial Africa, whether great or small, were not sufficiently known; and it was reserved for British explorers to independently discover, or rediscover, the regions in question.

The existence inland from Mozambique of a large lake, called "Maravi," was believed in from 1518 onwards; and it was in turn associated with the hydrographical systems of the Nile, Congo, and Zambezi. Cooley, whose diligent researches in this direction were embodied in his maps (1845 and 1853), was probably the first to introduce the native appellation of Nyassa. This mysterious sheet of water was made alternately to expand and contract in order to accommodate its position to the views of geographers. The discovery (1849) of the snow-capped mountains of Kilimanjaro by Rebmann and of Kénia by Krapf, together with the information these explorers elicited as to the surrounding lands, gave the impulse to the decisive journey (1858) of Burton and Speke. Having together reached Tanganika, and Speke alone the southern shores of the Victoria Nyanza, it was ascertained that there were two lakes instead of one. Speke and Grant in 1862 definitely established the outflow of the Victoria Nyanza to be the true source of the Nile; and their successful labours were further completed by Baker's journey (1864) to the Muta Nzigé (now called the Albert Nyanza). *Discovery of the true source of the Nile.*

With the extension and temporary consolidation of Egyptian rule in the lands of the Upper Nile, the work of exploration received renewed impulse, especially (from 1874) under Gordon. Stanley bore witness (1875) to the vast size of the Victoria Nyanza, and, by circumnavigating it, to its unity. Baker had established the connection of the Muta Nzigé with the Nile system; and Mason and Gessi afterwards circumnavigated the lake. Emin and Lupton carried out capital work (from 1880) on the Bahr-el-Jebel and in the country to the south of Lado. *Further explorations in the Upper Nile region.*

Schweinfurth's journeys (1869–71) in the Bahr-el-Ghazal were of the greatest interest and importance. In 1870 he crossed the Nile-Congo water-parting and discovered the Wellé River, which at that time he regarded as the upper course of the Shari; and in the following year he broke entirely new ground in Dar Fertit. Junker's travels

in the Bahr-el-Ghazal and Niam-Niam countries were of
equal value. His first journey (1877–78) took him into
the source-region of the Wellé, and his subsequent travels
(1880–86) in the basin of that river were, to a large extent,
through little known or entirely unknown lands.

The Mahdist rising in 1884, however, closed the whole
of the Upper Nile region to the explorer.

Explorations in South Africa. We may now turn to South Africa. Cape Colony became a British possession for the first time in 1795.
Barrow, who was entrusted by the Government with the
task of surveying the colony, was the first to give (1797–
98) reliable information in this respect : and his map was a
fairly good one. Travellers and missionaries contributed to
the increase of our geographical knowledge, which coincided
with the progress of colonisation in the north and east.
During the opening years of this century, the land of the
Bojesmans (Bushmen) was first entered, the Orange River
was crossed, and a route into Bechuana-land was opened up.
Campbell, a Scottish missionary, determined (1812) the
course of the Orange River, and subsequently reached the
source-region of the Limpopo (Kurichane, $24\frac{1}{2}°$ S. lat.). After
the withdrawal of the Boers (about 1835) from the Cape
Colony proper, exploration and colonisation advanced rapidly.

The Orange River practically limited our knowledge of
the inland countries in the west until Alexander revealed
(1836–37) portions of Namaqua-land and Damara-land.
The 23rd parallel of south latitude, which marked the limit
of our knowledge of South Africa towards the close of 1840,
was in 1849 passed by Livingstone, who, in company with
Oswell and Murray, braved the dangers of the dreaded Kalahari Desert, and discovered the long-sought Lake N'gami.

Livingstone initiates a new epoch of discovery. From this date a new epoch of discovery commenced
for Tropical South Africa. Filled with enthusiasm at his
success, Livingstone re-visited Lake N'gami in the follow-

ing year (1850). In 1851 he discovered farther north
a mighty fluvial system (the Zambezi), of the extent of
which no anticipation had previously existed, and the chief
or main artery of which native report designated as the
Liambai. Two years later he ascended this river, crossed
the upper courses of the western tributaries of the Congo,
and reached (1854) the West Coast at Loanda. After a
brief rest, he set himself the task of solving the Liambai
problem. Turning eastwards, and following with few
deviations his former route as far as Sesheke, he discovered
the magnificent fall of water on the Zambezi which he
christened the Victoria Falls, and came out (1856) on the
East Coast at Kilimani (Quilimane). This notable journey
won for him the distinction of being the first European to
cross the continent of Africa.

But the Liambai problem was still unsolved. Living- *The Liambai problem.*
stone had no doubt that the Liambai was the upper course
of the Zambezi, which the early cartographers had made to
take its rise in the Monomotapa Mountains (Matabele-land).
His hypothesis was subsequently (about 1860) proved to
be correct, after the unknown regions of the Zambezi had
been explored.

These valuable additions to our knowledge of the Zambezi *Livingstone in the Lakes region.*
basin were enriched by Livingstone's discoveries and ex-
plorations farther east, in the Lakes region. At the head
of an expedition entrusted to him by the British Government, and accompanied by his brother, Charles, and Kirk,
Livingstone again started for the Zambezi in 1858. The
expedition lasted five years, and was fruitful in results.
Lake Shirwa was discovered, and Lake Nyassa, though not
actually discovered, was made known and accurately mapped
for the first time.

Livingstone's journeys during 1866–73 were devoted *Problem of the Luapula.*
to solving the problem of the Luapula, a river which at

one time was thought to be the ultimate source of the Nile. Ascending the Rovuma River, of which he had previous knowledge, he reached Nyassa, and, in 1867, the south end of Tanganika, the true orientation of which was due to him. He was the first European, since Monteiro (1831–32), to enter Kazembe's kingdom. On this journey he discovered Lake Moëro, and (in 1868) Lake Bangweolo * and the head-waters of the Congo (Luapula). In 1870 he crossed Manyuema, reaching Nyangwé (Congo) in the following year. This was the period when universal anxiety was felt for news of his existence.

Stanley and Livingstone.

After Stanley, on his famous journey of discovery (1871–72), had met Livingstone at Ujiji, the two explorers together visited the north end of Tanganika, and found that the lake had no outlet into the Nile basin. Ptolemy's hypothesis (as understood at that time, at least) was thus disposed of. In the midst of preparations in Europe to follow up the discoveries of Livingstone in the Luapula-Lualaba hydrographic system, the great missionary-pioneer and explorer died (1st May 1873) at the south end of Lake Bangweolo.

Explorations in Eastern Equatorial Africa.

Excepting the results of Von der Decken's journeys (1860–65), comparatively slow progress was made, after the return of Speke, in the country between the East Coast and the Lakes. Stanley, in his search for Livingstone, started from Bagamoyo and for some distance followed a new path to Tanganika. Cameron (1873–75), also starting from the East Coast, was the next to break new ground. He explored Tanganika and discovered its outlet (the Lukuga) into the Congo basin, reached Nyangwé, and, striking south-west, completed his remarkable overland journey by coming out on the West Coast at Benguela. To a large extent his

---

* It is claimed by the Portuguese that their earlier travellers had visited these lakes. Livingstone at least, was the first, not only to discover them to Europe, but also to map them accurately.

route led through unknown country. Among other results, he was enabled to establish the fact that the Lualaba, from its altitude above sea-level and from the volume of its discharge, could not belong to the Nile system.

Simultaneously with this brilliant period of discovery in Eastern Equatorial Africa, attempts were being made from the West Coast to reach the Congo basin. Up to 1850 several concomitant conditions had contributed to restrain or repel geographical exploration on the West Coast: of such were the political and social reaction ensuing from the decadence of Portuguese power, the depredations of the slave-traders, and the immense difficulty of organising caravans. It should be added, that the configuration of the coast-lands, by which the rivers, in forcing their way down from the inland plateau, are rendered unnavigable in their lower courses by rapids, was yet another cause of hindering the advance of European travellers and pioneers. The modern history of exploration on the West Coast dates from the foundation of the French colony on the Gabún (1843) and the travels in that country of Paul Du Chaillu, which attracted a great deal of attention.

Explorations on the West Coast.

Several journeys were undertaken from Benguela into the Interior. Magyar carried out explorations (1850-51-55) on the upper courses of the Kubango and Zambezi, and penetrated for a considerable distance north into the basin of the Kasai. Silva Porto established (1853) a connection between the old Bihé route and the Upper Zambezi. Bastian, starting from Ambriz, visited (1857) San Salvador, and thereby attracted the attention of his compatriots, leading to the foundation of the German African Association. The work of this Association deserves as honourable mention as that of its sister association in London; but it has now ceased to exist, its programme being performed by the Imperial German Government.

The Congo problem. The mighty Congo system was discovered, not from the West Coast, as might have been expected, but from the East. The lower course of the river was well known, and had often been visited up to 1870; but beyond that region everything was uncertain. It was the honourable task of Stanley, in a single journey (1874-77), to reveal this magnificent hydrographical system to the world. Starting from Bagamoyo, he marched to the Victoria Nyanza; circumnavigated the lake and visited Uganda; explored the Muta Nzigé (Albert Edward Nyanza) and the Congo-Nile water-parting; proceeded south to Tanganika, which he circumnavigated; and from thence, by the Lukuga outlet, reached Nyangwé, and entered the threshold of the unknown Congo basin. **Its solution.** He traced the river down to its mouth. The brilliant achievement of this journey, besides establishing several vital points in regard to the hydrography of the source-region of the Nile and the water-parting between that river and the Congo, most effectually solved the last great hydrographical problem in Africa—the origin, course, and magnitude of the Congo River.

Practical results. Livingstone's travels had previously awakened a lively and universal interest in Africa, but Stanley's feat resulted in riveting the attention of Europe to the "Dark Continent." In 1876 the International African Association was established, and His Majesty the King of the Belgians, its founder, became its chosen head. Equally important, in their practical bearing on the development of Africa, were the consolidation of the French Congo Territories, the founding of the Congo Independent State, and the ensuing delimitation of "spheres of influence" in Africa by the Signatory Powers at the Berlin Conference (1884-85).

Explorations in the Congo basin. In Tropical South Africa the basin of the Congo became the chief domain of exploration. The German African Association was busy in the south, with its base of operations on the West Coast. The impression that the main southern tributaries of the Congo flowed parallel to each other in a north and north-west direction was corrected by the discovery (1885) of the magnificent Kasaï-Sankuru system, through the explorations of Wissmann, von François, Grenfell, Wolf, Kund, and Tappenbeck. Stanley, who, at the instance of the King of the Belgians, returned to the Congo to set up the administration of the infant State, discovered (1882-83) Lakes Leopold and Mantumba. Grenfell navigated (1884-85) the M'bangi, and Van Gèle finally established (1887) the identity of that river with the Wellé. Numerous minor journeys were at the same time carried out in the basin of the Congo by Belgian officials and others.

In the French Congo Territories, De Brazza initiated (from 1876) a most important series of explorations. He himself established (1877) the unity of the Ogowé, and reached (1880) the Congo itself. Details were rapidly filled in by competent French surveyors.

Even the Portuguese, in this golden period of activity, were roused to deeds worthy of their past history in Africa. Serpa Pinto crossed the continent (1877-79) by a route which traversed some new country, between Benguela and the Upper Zambezi; and Capello and Ivens accomplished a still more important overland journey, which was mainly through unknown lands, between the Luapula and the Zambezi. The southerly-flowing tributaries in the little-known country to the west of the Zambezi system were rapidly investigated. *New routes opened up.*

In response to the representations of Livingstone regarding the introduction of missionary effort and commercial enterprise in the highlands round Nyassa, as being the best or only method to check the hateful Traffic in Slaves and to emancipate and elevate the native populations, the Established and Free Churches of Scotland created mission- *Occupation and survey of the Lakes region.*

stations, and the African Lakes Company was founded (1878) in Glasgow with the object of opening up, by way of the Zambezi and Shiré Rivers and the great Lakes, a new and almost continuous fluvial highway into the heart of Africa. Between 1877 and 1880 Stewart thoroughly surveyed the shores of Lake Nyassa; and details were subsequently filled in by the zealous officers of the African Lakes Company.

Further discoveries in Eastern Equatorial Africa.

In Eastern Equatorial Africa, the thread of exploration was taken up by Joseph Thomson, who succeeded to the leadership of the expedition which started under Keith Johnston, junior. Thomson explored (1878–80) the country between Dar-es-Salaam on the East Coast and the north end of Nyassa, and between the Nyassa and the south end of Tanganika, skirting the western shores of the latter lake up to its outlet, the Lukuga, which had at the time of his arrival resumed its drainage functions. Proceeding to the west, along the banks of the Lukuga, and subsequently to the south-west through Urua, but driven back when within a day's journey of the Congo, he reached the south end of Tanganika, and returned to the East Coast by way of Fipa and Unyanyembe. He was the first European to see Lake Hikwa, which, owing to its numerous appellations, he re-christened Lake Leopold, after His Majesty the King of the Belgians. The districts through which he passed on the above journey were thus explored and mapped for the first time, though at parts he crossed the routes of Livingstone.

New routes opened up.

In the country between Lake Nyassa and the Mozambique Coast, in which only the Rovuma basin was fairly well known, a number of new routes were opened up after 1880 by Johnston (1880–82), Maples (1881), O'Neill (1883–84), and Serpa Pinto and Cardozo (1885–86).

Farther west, in the Congo basin, the German East

African Expedition under Kaiser, Böhm, and Reichard carried out explorations (1880-84) between the Upper Lualaba and Luapula, across the route of Giraud, who was the first after Livingstone to visit (1883) Lake Bangweolo.

The repeated but ineffectual attempts to pass from the East Coast to the Lakes region through Masai-land did not deter Joseph Thomson, who, in the course of his successful journey (1883-84), explored the country lying between Mombaza and the north-east corner of the Victoria Nyanza. He was the first to map the northern aspect of Mount Kilima-njaro, the plateaus of Kikuyu, Kapté, and Guaso Ngishu, the mountain masses of the Aberdare Range and Kénia, and the lakes Naivasha, Nakuro, and Baringo. Dr. Fischer about the same time (1883) reached Kilima-njaro and Lake Naivasha; and later (1885-86) connected the Masai route with that in the south between Ugogo and Kageyi.

The exploration of Kilima-njaro thus received a new impulse. Since Von der Decken's time (1862) it has been repeatedly climbed: to the snow-line by New (1871); a little higher by H. H. Johnston (1884), and by Ehlers (1888); and twice by Meyer (1887 and 1889), who, on the second occasion, reached the summit of Kibo (19,680 feet). *Ascents of Mount Kilima-njaro.*

Between the River Tana, which the Denhardts navigated in 1878, and the Red Sea, several attempts to explore Somäl-land have been made since 1880. The most successful was that of James, who, starting from Berbera—and not from the East Coast—penetrated (1885) as far south as the River Webi. *Somäl land.*

We have yet to refer to the progress of exploration to the south of the Zambezi and Kunéné Rivers. The discovery of Lake N'gami, as already indicated, led to the exploration of Damara-land, which had been neglected. As early as 1850-51, Galton and Charles Anderssen had *Explorations south of the Zambezi.*

endeavoured, though unsuccessfully, to open up a route to Lake N'gami from Walvisch Bay, and to them we owe our first knowledge of the eastern portions of Damara-land and Ovampo-land. Anderssen in 1853 was finally successful in reaching the Lake. Since that time, South-West Africa has been frequently visited and to a large extent exploited. Damara-land and Great Namaqua-land have more recently been explored by German missionaries.

South Africa. The progress of exploration at the Cape and in the country to the north went, as before mentioned, hand in hand with colonisation and political expansion. We require, therefore, to give only a few dates in order to roughly indicate its march. The Orange River was not crossed until 1871, when the discovery of diamonds in Griqua-land attracted general attention. Farther east, British dominion had been extended over a portion of Kafraria (1853), Basuto-land (1868), &c. The upper course of the Limpopo was known as early as 1830, but its subsequent course was a problem that engaged considerable attention, and was not solved until the journey (1868) of Erskine, who traced the Olifant River to its confluence with the Limpopo, and followed the latter river to its mouth. Elton, two years later, substantiated these results by navigating the Limpopo. Zoutpansberg was the most northerly Boer settlement in 1851. From 1860 onwards, the Transvaal was topographically examined by three German travellers: Jeppe, Mauch, and Merensky. The discovery of gold-fields in Matabele-land and in the Transvaal, and of diamonds on the Vaal River, gave fresh impulses to the exploration of South-East Africa. Mauch's journeys (1865-69) in the Central plateau-country to $17\frac{1}{2}°$ S. lat., and (1872) from the Limpopo to Sena, on the Zambezi, were the first to open up new vistas to the explorer and exploiter. Details were rapidly filled in.

So far, our survey of the progress of exploration in Africa has not included the results of the past two or three years, it having been based on, and largely drawn from, Dr. Supan's paper on the centenary (1788-1888) following the foundation of the London African Association. But in a few words we can bring this record up to date.

The most characteristic feature of geographical progress in Africa during the last two or three years has been the steady work initiated by the various European Powers and Chartered Companies, not only in the survey of their territories, but also in prospecting for railways, concluding treaties with native chiefs, and defining boundaries. This initial work in the development of a country has been carried out with spirit in the French possessions on the Senegal and on the Congo, the German West African possessions, the Congo Independent State, and the British possessions in South and East Africa.

Progress of explorations between 1888 and 1890.

The Chartered Companies in particular have not allowed the grass to grow under their feet. Mr. Thomson's spirited journey (1885) to Sokoto and Gandu, with the sultans of which countries he concluded treaties on behalf of the Royal Niger Company, is an example of a forward policy that has been followed by others in the various regions of Africa. The French, on their part, have steadily pursued their aim of opening up trade-routes between the Senegal and the Niger, and have despatched several gunboats to Timbuktu. Colin's work in Bambuk, which had important geographical results, and that of Crampel and Fourneaux in the Gabún, are only isolated instances of French activity. Perhaps the most important journey was that of Binger (1887-89) within the great bend of the Niger. Binger, besides correcting our previous ideas as to the extent of the basin of the Upper Niger, by showing that the Comoë and Volta rivers, among others, drained a large tract of

West Africa.

country sloping to the Guinea Coast, demonstrated that the watershed is not nearly so high as has hitherto been supposed : it is simply a gently rising land or plateau, and the " Kong Mountains" as a range do not exist. His information in regard to the almost unknown parts of Mandingo-land is of the highest geographical interest. The Germans, on their part, with very much the same incentive—the desire to acquire political and commercial supremacy in the Niger basin—have been equally active. Among their travellers in West Africa, von François, Wolf, Zintgraff, Zöller, Kund, Tappenbeck, and Weissenborn have all done excellent work. In the Camarons especially, the *Hinterland* is being rapidly surveyed, and Zintgraff has recently been successful in opening up a route to the Benué. Yet, no further back than 1887, the country inland from the Camarons Coast, excepting the course of the Campo River, was a blank on the map.

Congo basin.

In the Congo Independent State we note the survey for a railway now in process of construction past the rapids on the lower course of the river, the valuable explorations of Bouvier on the Kwilu and in the country to the north of Manyanga, and of Cambier along the south bank of the Congo, between Matadi and Leopoldville. Lannoy de Bissey's excellent maps embody a vast amount of conscientious work carried out by the French officials in the Congo Territories. In other parts of the basin of the Congo, the officials of the State, *e.g.* Coquilhat, have done good work ; while independent travellers, like Grenfell and Baumann, have been equally active. Delcommune's navigation of the Lomami, up to the latitude of Nyangwé, revealed an important new highway into Central Africa.

Farther south, the independent work of the missionary Arnot, who has spent over seven years in Central Africa, chiefly in Katanga (Garenganzé) and the Barotsé Valley, has been instrumental in revealing a large extent of new 1888-90. country, and in solving some of the hydrographical problems of this interesting region. He has proved, for instance, that Livingstone's "Leeba" is the Zambezi itself, and not the stream which flows out of Lake Dilolo.

In Eastern Equatorial Africa, O'Neill obtained an im- Eastern Equatorial portant series of astronomical observations during a journey Africa. he undertook from Kilimani to the north end of Lake Nyassa, which showed that the lake had been placed too far to the west by about from 6′ to 8′ of longitude. The discovery by Rankin of an unused navigable channel (R. Chindé) in the delta of the Zambezi may prove to be valuable for commerce.

The Arab disturbances in Eastern Equatorial Africa and the rising on the Zanzibar Coast have interrupted exploration to a certain extent. But the agents of the British East Africa Company have been busy within their sphere of interest, and have enabled Mr. Ravenstein to construct a large new map of their territories. The most important of recent discoveries in that region have been those of Teleki and Höhnel (1887–88), to the north of Lake Baringo, where what was formerly known vaguely as Lake Samburru has been accurately mapped by them and christened Lake Rudolf. Borelli's work south-west from Tajura Bay, in Shoa and its tributary states, has been valuable; he succeeded also in penetrating for some distance into Galla-land.

Stanley's most recent journey (1887–89), undertaken for the relief of Emin Pacha, has been of the highest geographical importance. At the head of a large expedition, he proceeded up the Congo, and, by way of its tributary, the Aruwimi, reached the Albert Nyanza. The Aruwimi, or, as it is called in its upper course, the Ituri, was discovered to flow through a densely afforested region of indefinite extent. At the south end of the Albert Nyanza,

Eastern Equatorial Africa, 1888–90. Stanley traced the course of the Kikibbi (which Emin had previously examined at its confluence with the lake), and he discovered that it flowed from the Muta Nzigé (Albert Edward Nyanza)—that, in fact, the two lakes were thereby connected. The Kikibbi, otherwise called the Semliki, was found to receive innumerable tributary streams from a mighty snow-capped mountain-mass, the Ruwenzori, which possibly rivals even the mountains of Kilima-njaro and Kénia in altitude, although it was actually ascended by Lieutenant Stairs only to 10,677 feet. The Muta Nzigé —or, as it is now named, the Albert Edward Nyanza —was found to include the "Beatrice Gulf," previously discovered by Stanley, and to be of lesser area than was formerly supposed; it is thus the south-western source of the Nile. On the homeward journey to the East Coast, viâ Uniamwesi and M'pwapwa, the south-western shores of the Victoria Nyanza were ascertained to have a considerable southerly extension beyond the limit formerly assigned to them.

Conclusion. While the above have been the most notable contributions to the progress during the last hundred years of geographical discovery and exploration in Africa, we have been constrained by the limits of our space to greatly restrict our view, so that much excellent work and many profitable journeys have been entirely overlooked. We have but to compare the maps of each decade since 1788 to see how rapid this progress has been, and in order to estimate the activity of our explorers, travellers, and colonists. How great in this respect is our debt to missionary-pioneers we may recall with gratitude, for, in many instances, they have been the first to enter the unknown.

Though it may be held somewhat invidious to institute a comparison between the results which the various European nations have contributed to the discovery and the precise exploration of Africa in modern times, we may safely confine ourselves to a few general remarks.

The Portuguese were the first to open up Continental Africa to the policy of Europe; but, since the decline of their power, they have done comparatively little to promote exploration. The French have been eminently practical in the efforts they have made to open up new lands, by confining their activities to the districts where, with an effective base on the coasts, their colonies have been established. To them, also, we owe the earliest precise topographical information in regard to Lower Egypt, during the Occupation. Elsewhere in Africa, French travellers have contributed comparatively few results. The continent has only once been crossed by a Frenchman, Trivier, and this was accomplished in 1888-89. In the main, the work of French explorers, in the territories over which the national flag flies or is adventurously carried, has been scientific, valuable, and permanent. The Germans, now that they have colonial possessions of their own, are following the example of the French; but, before this comparatively recent departure, German travellers explored in all parts of Africa, and the work they accomplished is unrivalled for its thoroughness, its accuracy, and its importance. Though we may claim for British explorers the principal pioneer-work in Southern Equatorial Africa, it is to German travellers we chiefly owe our knowledge of the Sahara and Súdan. The activity of the Italians has been more restricted, and has in the main received its impulse through political aspirations. Between the Red Sea and Ethiopia they have appropriated a profitable field for their labours. The Belgians have done some good work in the Congo basin, under the ægis of their philanthropic king. Finally, British explorers, though more recently directing their attention to practical ends, have

Comparative view of European exploration in Africa.

been active in all parts of Africa. They have been inspired by the spirit of adventure and discovery no less than by the desire of commercial gain. It is to them we mainly owe the pioneer discoveries, from which nearly all the European nations have derived benefits equal to or greater than those that Britain has retained for her guerdon.

Unknown regions. It will be observed that the regions of Africa still to be regarded as "unknown" lie behind the spheres of European influence on the coasts. It is a curious fact that, so far, in the exploration of the continent, all the great hydrographical discoveries have been made, not by the more obvious process of tracing the great river-systems from their mouths to their sources, but in precisely the reverse way. The task of exploration in the future, however, will be to fill in details from the coasts inland. It is a task that will be all the more readily undertaken on account of the new impulse that has been given to colonisation, and because—the continent having been so rapidly partitioned off among the European Powers—it will become more and more necessary not only to adjust boundaries but also to define their precise limits. The interior lands will thus gradually be explored and exploited.

Mention has been made of the character of the work accomplished in the exploration and survey of African lands, and it is well to bear in mind how much more supplementary work will be required before we can regard our maps with any degree of satisfaction and confidence. Even for pioneer journeys there is plenty of scope left. Witness Stanley's last journey and that of Binger.

Character of expeditions. A word as to the character of expeditions. The ideal African traveller is he who adventures alone, or with a small personal escort, into the unknown, and returns with an accurate survey and supplementary information. Those who follow in his footsteps may be fairly confident of a friendly reception by the indigenous populations. In a number of notable instances it has been such men who have brought out of Africa the most valuable and permanent geographical results. The larger the expedition the greater the difficulty of obtaining—at least, by honest and pacific means—the necessary supplies, and the greater the danger of arousing the hostile passions of the natives. At the same time, there are some parts of Africa through which a traveller accompanied by only a small escort or a weakly-armed caravan could never penetrate. Happily, such regions are few, and they are becoming fewer every day.

These remarks are introduced with the object of recording the fact that, in the past, independent travellers have been able to accomplish—what big fighting expeditions could never have achieved—the best result of exploration in Africa, namely, the discovery of new fields for pacific occupation and development.

Small expeditions the best.

CHAPTER VIII.

COMMERCIAL RESOURCES.

PROGRESS OF EXPLOITATION — COMMERCE THE MOST IMPORTANT INITIAL FACTOR IN AFRICAN POLITICS—COMMERCIAL SUPREMACY RATHER THAN EMPIRE THE UNDERLYING MOTIVE OF EUROPEAN ENTERPRISE — THE REIGN OF COMMERCE — THE VALUE OF AFRICAN LANDS — GEOGRAPHICAL DISTRIBUTION OF PRODUCTS, AND THE MOVEMENTS OF COMMERCE — GEOGRAPHICAL DISTRIBUTION OF IVORY—COINCIDENCE OF SLAVE-ROUTES WITH TRADE-ROUTES, IVORY BEING THE PRINCIPAL ARTICLE OF EXPORT — THE LIQUOR TRAFFIC — THE LABOUR PROBLEM — COLONISATION—CHARTERED COMPANIES—" ROBBER-ECONOMY" —HONESTY THE BEST POLICY.

MAP.

COMMERCIAL PRODUCTS *Plate* VIII.

COMMERCIAL RESOURCES.

THE development of Africa as a field for European commercial enterprise has been very rapid in the past few years. It was not so long ago that Dr. Schweinfurth, in comparing the zones of social culture with the movements of commerce in Africa, divided the continent into three domains: (1.) the sphere of fire-arms, nearest to the coasts, in which intimate commercial relations were maintained with Europe; (2.) the transition region inland, into which native traders carried the cotton goods and manufactures of Europe; and (3.) the heart of Central Africa, into which European enterprise had not penetrated. Africa thus presented, in those days, the picture of a fortress, which was being stormed by the pioneers of commerce; but, since then, rampart after rampart has been broken down, redoubt after redoubt has been taken, and Commerce, entering by the great river valleys, has planted its flag in the very heart of the continent. The popular myth that the simple requirements of the indigenous peoples of Africa could be met with "moral pocket-handkerchiefs" is no longer tenable throughout the greater portion of the interior regions. Perhaps, in the cycle of social evolution, the natives may "hark back" in this respect, just as in our own day and in our own country the possession of a pocket-handkerchief marks an individual stage of social progress. But what with competition among the European Powers for political and commercial supremacy in Africa, and the growth of their colonies as markets for home manufactures, we have

Report of progress.

now to deal with very different conditions of demand and supply. The exploitation of Africa has, in the passage of time, besides revealing mineral riches in many parts of the continent, opened up prospects of commercial development which have been eagerly seized upon by chartered companies; and though relatively few regions have shown any immediate return for the capital introduced into them, capitalists have not been daunted, but, on the plea of philanthropy and patriotism, have advanced boldly upon new conquests, in the hope perhaps of their ultimately yielding some material advantages.

Value of African lands.

In the present chapter we shall deal with the marketable commodities of Africa. By defining the geographical distribution of the leading products in reference to the physical and political conditions of each distinctive region, we may be enabled to estimate, if only approximately, the value of African lands. We cannot pay too great attention to this subject, since it is commerce that takes us to Africa, and by commerce only that we can remain there, at least with any profit to ourselves. For, with the exception of a few strategical points, mainly on the Mediterranean and Red Seas—the route to the East—and at the Cape, the possession of African territory is of no special value at present in international politics, except, it may be, as a lever against the interests of one's neighbours. Unless the colonies in Africa can be self-supporting, it is difficult to see the value of them to the mother-country.* It is by commerce also, if our motive in colonising Africa be purely philanthropic, that we can best influence the indigenous populations, and it is by commerce that we can root up the evils that embitter their existence. Thus we see that, from whatever point of view we regard the development of Africa, commerce must

The factor of commerce.

---

* Portugal, however, appears to derive a kind of patriotic satisfaction in meeting the heavy annual deficit of her Mozambique province.

be reckoned with as an important political factor. It is, of course, rather too soon to speak with confidence of the commercial possibilities of the continent—we still know so little of it and its inhabitants—but the more vigorous nations of Europe are not likely to fail in subduing to their use any new field for enterprise, no matter what the initial cost may be. And so we may fairly conclude, now that some of them have finally entered in earnest upon commercial and political campaigns in Africa, that success will be to the valiant and to the successful. It has been a race—in the last few years a breathless race—not altogether for empire, nor for a crusade, but for commercial supremacy.

What prospects, then, does Africa offer as a field for European commercial enterprise?

In the southern shores of the Mediterranean we again recognise in this place a transition region between Africa and Europe, in which the climate and products approximate to those of the southern parts of Spain and Italy. Consequently, we find that colonisation by the people of those countries has been more successful than by the people of Northern Europe: only they, up to the present, have become in part acclimatised, and only in their case has the birth-rate exceeded the death-rate. *Mediterranean Littoral.*

Algeria and Tunis may be considered together, though, in respect of their economical progress, they stand in striking contrast. Algeria has been a French province for sixty years, Tunis a French protectorate for nine years; yet the latter, even apart from its more favourable natural conditions, would appear to have the more hopeful future. It is true that, during the French administration, Algeria has been converted from a desert into "a smiling province:" thousands of miles of road have been made, railways have been constructed, wells sunk, and all kinds of improvements introduced. Yet, even to-day, Algeria costs the mother- *Algeria and Tunis.*

Algeria and Tunis. country from seventy to eighty million francs annually, the expenditure nearly always exceeding the receipts. The European element—for the most part composed of Italians, Spaniards, and Maltese, besides the French themselves—though it has doubled its numbers, still bears a small proportion (about 10 per cent.) to the native populations, composed of Berbers (Kabyles) and Arabs; while the latter show no signs of assimilation. And the reason of this comparative want of success in Algeria would appear to be "red-tape." The native populations are in turn either persecuted or supported, or attempts are made at assimilating them with the European colonists. By being persecuted they are driven away; by being supported they obtain an undue supremacy; and attempts at assimilation have failed because of the exceedingly varied ethnic elements. Colonisation is at one time promoted, at another time obstructed; and for the most part it remains under Government auspices. Thus, Algeria is neither a settlement nor a plantation.* Tunis, on the other hand, is a commercial colony; there is no official immigration, and private enterprise has more scope, as is evidenced by the numerous local undertakings at present on foot. Though, as in all new colonies, the imports have exceeded the exports in Tunis, this is due to the Army of Occupation, which has to be provided for. By comparing Algeria and Tunis, therefore, we have a good example of officialism and private enterprise working side by side. Tunis, so far at least, appears to have fully realised the expectations that were formed of it in France.

In both Algeria and Tunis, and indeed in North Africa generally, viticulture would, according to Sir Lambert Playfair, appear to be the most hopeful industry for the future. Some, too, speak of wheat, for the growth of which many districts—such as the valley of the Mejerda—possess suit-

* *L'Algérie et la Tunisie* (P. Leroy-Beaulieu, 1887).

able soils and climate. Alfa or esparto grass grows wild, and
is, or was at one time, largely exported to Great Britain
for the manufacture of paper. Wool and early potatoes are
also valuable export-commodities. Cork in the forests and
iron ore in the mountains, besides other natural riches,
are among the remaining resources of the country. It therefore cannot be doubted that, in time, France will develop
her African possessions, which lie almost at her door, even
if she fails to extend her empire to the south and west.

Very different is the prospect in the fanatical Moham- *Morocco.*
medan State of Morocco, which, in spite of its supposed
mineral riches, its highly fertile soil, and favourable natural
conditions, lies stagnating "in the name of Allah." The
magnificent squalor of the towns, the dumb evidences of
a down-trodden people, whose only advantage under political rule is the opportunity to escape it—these and other
phenomena of a decaying and subversive power cry out
for reparation. Christians are despised, and can only live
with security and independence under the ægis of their
political representatives; foreign imports are crushed by
heavy dues; exports are crippled by a prohibitive tariff;
and the native industries are paralysed. If a native display
prosperity, far less wealth, he is at once made the victim
of courteous attentions on the part of the Sultan and his
officials. Under such political conditions it is not to be
expected that Morocco could possibly develop its great
natural resources; though Sir Henry Drummond-Hay, in
a recent report, speaks of a slight improvement in the
movements of commerce. France and Great Britain have
participated for the most part in the exterior commerce
of Morocco, but Germany is now taking a foremost place.
The chief exports are cereals and leather.

Between these countries and Egypt, the Turkish province *Tripoli.*
of Tripoli is so barren that, beyond esparto grass, fruits

and vegetables, its products are not at present of any considerable value. The port of Tripoli is, however, the terminus of the caravan-trade across the Sahara, and the oasis of Murzuk, in Fezzan, is another important trade-centre. Fez and Morocco city are other centres of the caravan-traffic of the Sahara, the principal "commodity" of which would appear to be slaves.

Sahara.   The camel-caravans that cross the Sahara, coming from the Súdan, trade also in ostrich feathers, spices, gums, rock-salt, &c., which are exchanged for the manufactures of Europe. In the Western Sahara, the salt mines and deposits are the chief wealth of the country; and the salt finds its way in the first instance to Timbuktu, one of the chief centres of its distribution. Ghadames and other oases in the Sahara are also objective points for caravans. But, owing to the unsettled political state and the predatory habits of the tribes in the Sahara, not to speak of the insecurity of life and the adverse conditions of climate, it is not possible for this caravan-traffic to be largely used in the future by European commerce; far less is it likely to compete with other and more practicable routes from the coast. Thus, even though the French may eventually establish some sort of communication between Algeria and Senegambia, it is difficult to see what advantages they hope to reap thereby, beyond the more or less illusory one of political aggrandisement. Elsewhere we have shown that the true access to the Central Súdan is by way of the River Niger.

The Nile Valley.   In the Nile Valley we have the most striking example of the value of water in Africa, and how, by a judicious system of irrigation, barren land can be made fertile. The Nile, periodically overflowing its banks, is the life-fluid of the desert country through which it passes; the regularity of its rise and fall can absolutely be relied upon, though on occasions, of course, an abnormally high or low Nile may be

experienced. At Khartúm the river begins to rise towards
the end of June, in consequence of the heavy monsoon rains
that fall on its upper catchment-basin; before the first day
of September it is at its fullest, but after the last day of
that month it decreases regularly, until the next summer
solstice. All along the banks of the Nile, from Khartúm to
the Delta, advantage is taken of these inundations by the
riverain people to reclaim from the desert a narrow parallel
zone of cultivable land. In no place does this zone of
artificial cultivation exceed four miles in breadth, whilst at
several spots the desert rules supreme.

In Lower Egypt the advantage which the Nile offers for irrigation purposes has been turned to exceptional account, and extensive works have been erected by the English and Scottish engineers in charge. By the restoration of the *barrage*,* which had been in disuse for twenty years, and the construction of numerous interlacing canals, the Deltaic lands have been converted into a rich agricultural region, supporting a dense population. According to Mr. Chisholm (*Handbook of Commercial Geography*, p. 348)—"Though the distance in a direct line from Wady Halfa to the shores of the Mediterranean is about 680 miles, equal to the distance from the Scilly Isles to the northern extremity of the Shetland Islands, the entire area fit for cultivation is less that 10,000 square miles, or about two-thirds larger than Yorkshire; and in this area is crowded a population of nearly 8,000,000, almost wholly dependent on agriculture." The labour for the up-keep of the embankments in this system of irrigation was at one time supplied by the natives themselves, who were subject to the *corvée*; but this system of forced labour is now abolished. The initial cost of construction must have exceeded one million pounds sterling.

Lower Egypt.

---

* The *barrage* is a dam thrown across the two heads of the Nile branches at the apex of the Delta.

Lower Egypt.

but it has already been met by the profits derived from the cultivators themselves. When Egyptian finances are sufficiently elastic to bear the strain or experiment of more extended schemes of irrigation, some of these may be adopted.

Cotton is now one of the most valuable crops of Lower Egypt, which, besides, raises maize and wheat; in Upper Egypt dates and various gums are the principal products.

The British Occupation.

Under British control, Egypt has in part recovered from the paralysis she suffered under Turkish mismanagement, and the condition of the Fellahín has been vastly improved; the *kourbash* and all kinds of abuses have been abolished, and something like financial stability established. The commerce of the country is practically in the hands of Europeans, whose principal trade-centre is at Alexandria, and who only await more settled political conditions in order to greatly extend their operations. Should those conditions assume any degree of permanence, and be guaranteed by some sort of European control, the future prosperity of Egypt would be assured; but international rivalries, even at the present day, retard the true development of the country. From its geographical position, as, in a manner, commanding the route to the East, Egypt naturally assumes in the eyes of Europe an importance it would not otherwise possess; but there are critics who point out, with some degree of justice, that the value of the Suez Canal as a route to the East is not so great as is generally assumed, since the possession of territory or islands—such as our island fortress of Perim—at the southern end of the Red Sea, must largely, if not entirely, counterbalance political domination over the Isthmus of Suez. The inter-nationalisation of the Canal would, therefore, appear to be a desirable step in the common interests of the European Powers.

Reference has been made in a former chapter to trade-

routes in Egypt and to their relative value and chief centres **Trade-routes.**
of distribution. But trade-routes are a variable quantity to
reckon with. The revolution that is caused by a change of
conditions or altered circumstances in the routes taken by
commerce is illustrated in a recent report by the British
Consul at Port Said, who demonstrates that that port is
rapidly increasing in importance at the expense of Suez,
because of vessels preferring to touch there for stores and
coal. But though the trade of Suez has also been profoundly
affected in consequence of the disturbances in the Súdan, the
pilgrim traffic is said to have increased to 22,000 annually.
Such fluctuating conditions are bound to attend every important political movement; but, with our modern resources,
it should not be an impossible task to guide any given traffic
in its natural channels.

In the basin of the Upper Nile we encounter lands very **Upper Nile basin.**
unequal in respect of their chief natural productions, but all
of conspicuous value. In the highly fertile country through
which flow the Abyssinian tributaries of the Nile, the alluvial
soil, with the simplest means of irrigation, is capable of producing heavy crops, not only of durrah and maize, but also
of cotton and tobacco: at present, only the two former are
cultivated to any extent. As for Abyssinia, anything could
be grown in the highland regions, according to altitude and
the suitable conditions of climate; yet agriculture is backward, and the industries, where by courtesy they may be
said to exist, are acknowledged to be of no account.

What effect the Italian domination may have on the **Red Sea Littoral, &c.**
commercial development of Abyssinia it is too soon to predict; but doubtless trade, which at present finds its way
direct to Tajura and Berbera, and formerly went through
Shoa, will be deflected more and more to Massawa. In
spite of its loss of trade, Shoa still deals largely in cattle,
hides, coffee, &c. Harar also sends caravans to Berbera.

P

In the depressions between the mountainous regions and the Red Sea the salt-deposits are a valuable commodity; the salt, sold in small blocks, is even used as currency.

Mahdi-land.

Khartúm, which used to be the converging point for caravans and a great commercial centre, has for so long been outside the sphere of European influence that it is difficult to judge what may be its present condition; but it is reasonable to infer that, although it may no longer obtain European goods in exchange for grain, gums, and cotton, its traffic in ivory and ostrich feathers and the trade from the south are still maintained. Immediately south of Khartúm, in Kordofan, the soil is arid and impregnated with iron, and the herds do not thrive very well except in the neighbourhood of springs. Farther south still, in the abandoned Equatorial Province, the country is in every way suited to pastoral pursuits. "Only think," Emin Pacha once wrote, "what a trade could be opened up in ivory, oil of all kinds, skins, corn, ostrich feathers, india-rubber, wax, iron, &c., &c." *

Súdan.

In the border-land between the Sahara and the Súdan a considerable native trade is maintained by caravan, the chief commodities of exchange or barter being slaves, ivory, salt, ostrich feathers, wheat, and cloth. West of Lake Tsad we encounter the prosperous and densely populated Mohammedan States, the natural products of which are very varied. They are thus detailed by Mr. Joseph Thomson: †— "Of minerals, gold is found in the western districts, and silver, lead, antimony, and copper in the eastern. All these valuable articles are more or less worked at present, for the native thoroughly knows their value. Ivory is to be obtained in large quantities to the south of the Benué and around Lake Tsad. Ostrich feathers even now constitute a large trade in the Southern Sahara and north and east of

---

* *Emin Pacha in Central Africa,* p. 431.
† *Scottish Geographical Magazine,* vol. ii. p. 595.

Bornu. In the same parts, valuable gums, musk, and hides are yielded in profusion. Over the entire region enormous quantities of indigo, cotton, shea-butter, palm-oil, ground-nuts, india-rubber, and several valuable medicinal plants are produced. Great herds of cattle are found everywhere, and the trade in hides should be one of much importance. As showing the character of the country, it may be mentioned that the Central Súdan produces capital wheat, rice, onions, dates, limes, pomegranates, bananas, and numerous other fruits, vegetables, and grains." Moreover, horses, camels, and donkeys thrive in the higher-lying regions.

The River Niger and its tributary, the Benué, are the natural highways into this part of Inner Africa. As a channel for commercial operations, the Niger is unrivalled; and the possession of the Deltaic lands is consequently of immense importance. Regular steam-communication is maintained on the river. Vessels of 600 tons can ascend beyond the Benué confluence to Rabba, a total distance of 600 miles, during seven or eight months of the year; whilst the Benué itself is navigable for an equal distance. Within the basin of the Niger there are densely populated districts, under more or less settled and advanced govern-ments, possessing immense natural resources, and capable of yielding an immediate return for any capital expended on their economical development. _{Niger basin.}

That there should be some competition for this trade is natural. The French, from their base in Senegambia, and the Germans, from the Camarons, are making bold bids for commercial supremacy. That, under these circumstances, a certain amount of trade will be deflected from its more natural outlet by the mouths of the Niger is obvious; but it may also lead to healthy competition, which in the end will stimulate European commercial enterprise. The trade of Timbuktu and the Upper Niger, by the recent territo-

Niger basin.

rial arrangement between Great Britain and France, must eventually fall into the hands of the French. Timbuktu of itself has no industries, but from time immemorial it has been a market of great importance, and one of the chief distributing centres. The trade of the Middle Niger, benefiting from the activities of the great Hausa States, is, however, of far greater value, and is entirely in British hands. Kano and other commercial centres offer unlimited possibilities; and the trade of Bornu might easily be tapped by way of the Benué.

Products of West Africa.

The palm-oil industry, which is the most valuable of West Africa, has its centre in the Niger Delta, or, to be more explicit, in what is called the Oil Rivers District. The geographical distribution of the *Elais guineensis*, or oil-palm, may be seen on our map; but although it flourishes over so extensive a region, it is cultivated in certain districts only: on the West Coast, for example, chiefly or exclusively in the vicinity of the villages. Cotton is also grown, and during the American civil war was largely cultivated along the Guinea Coast. Moreover, there are many valuable medicinal plants, and others yielding gum and resin, besides coloured woods (campwood, barwood, redwood), &c., which are rising exports of the West Coast. Kola-nuts are of increasing importance, and take the place of the coffee berry, though coffee, as well as tobacco, could be cultivated much more extensively. A good market for tea should be found in the Mohammedan Sudan.

Labour.

It must also be remembered that, though the ivory of the Ivory Coast is a thing of the past, the gold of the Gold Coast is by no means exhausted. The country is rich in gold, in spite of the numerous companies that have failed to work it profitably. The great drawback in the case of mining, as in all other commercial ventures, is that native labour is so incompetent and unreliable. But if the Kru could be brought to work in larger numbers, surely there would be some prospect of success?

At first sight one might suppose that the basin of the Congo, with its unique system of waterways, was by far the most important field for commercial enterprise in Africa; but for various reasons this view is untenable. The Congo is undoubtedly a region of immense possibilities, but it has not yet been sufficiently exploited or developed to warrant the sanguine views which some take of its present resources. The administration of the State has, unfortunately, not been based on commercial principles: there has been too much "red-tape" and "make-believe" and too little conscientious work. This has been the fault, not of the generous-hearted sovereign who is the nominal head of the State, but of his advisers and officers. *Congo basin.*

The leading commodities of the Congo are ivory, caoutchouc, and gum-copal; but there are, of course, many other sources of wealth. Ivory is the most important article of commerce, though, according to Oscar Baumann,* two-thirds of it is what is known as fossil-ivory. Markets for its periodical disposal have already been opened in Belgium. Beyond the Aruwimi confluence, there appears to be little or no actual commerce; for this is the Arab hunting-ground for slaves. The regions drained by the M'bangi and Kasaï tributary systems of the Congo are equally important, the latter presenting, according to the Rev. George Grenfell, special facilities on account of the "ready-made commerce waiting for an outlet," and because the people are more industrious and their work is of a much higher order than on the Congo proper. At Luluaburg the State has made experiments in raising flocks and herds—it is said, with some success—and in rice-plantations. That the natives themselves have made progress in their methods of cultivating *Trade and commerce.*

* *Handel und Verkehr am Congo.*

the soil has been attested by Wissmann and other explorers who have had the opportunity of judging.

Congo basin. Between the Kasaï and Lomami there is an immense prairie region of great fertility, and in other parts of the Congo basin similar districts occur. Van Gèle points to the Lower M'bangi as one of the most fertile and populous districts he has seen in Africa: woods and plains, maize-fields, sugar-cane and banana plantations alternate without number, and attest the value of the land. That tobacco, coffee, cocoa, vanilla, and other articles of commerce could be extensively cultivated in the basin of the Congo is certain. No doubt, when the railway between the cataracts is finished, greater impulse will be given to its commerce; but, in the meantime, there are numerous initial difficulties to overcome before any immediate return for capital can be expected.

Commercial establishments on the Congo. At the end of 1889 there were some twenty-eight European establishments on the Congo between Stanley Pool and Stanley Falls: seven belonging to the State, two to the French, three to the Roman Catholic missions, six to the Protestant missions; and four Belgian factories, four Dutch, and two French. Some eighteen steamers were at that time said to be plying on its waters: seven belonging to the State, three on the French Congo, five belonging to the Belgian Commercial Company, one to the Dutch Company, and two to the Anglo-American Mission. All these vessels draw only 2 ft. 6 in. of water, or under. Of their inadequacy to cope with any brisk movement of commerce we have had frequent illustrations; but their number will no doubt be duly supplemented. It must be remembered, it was not so long ago, that it took five years or so for European manufactures to reach the Upper Congo from the West Coast, in consequence of their having to run the gauntlet of *honga*, or black-mail, inflicted by the intervening tribes.

The unsuitability of the climate to European settlers, the unstable and ineffective state of the political administration, the difficulty of obtaining steady and efficient labour, and the ravages of the Slave Trade, are among the chief reasons why the Congo basin has not been even more rapidly developed as a field for European enterprise. With more rational administrative measures will come more flourishing times for commerce.

The recent arrangements in regard to the Congo Independent State which have been announced from Brussels, if ultimately given effect to, should go far to remove the disability it has hitherto shown in performing what was originally expected of it at the time of its inauguration. These arrangements include a duty (10 per cent.) on imports—with the ostensible purpose of providing the sinews of war against the slave-traders—and the ultimate reversion of the administration to Belgium. *The future of the Congo.*

The French, on their part, situated between the Congo and the West Coast, have met with much the same initial difficulties in building up their colony, but they have made steady efforts to overcome them. M. de Brazza, speaking of the prospects of the French Congo, in reply to an interviewer, is reported to have said: "From my nine years' experience in the country, I have come to the conclusion that our West African Territories and the basin of the Congo must be left to be developed by the original inhabitants, and not be colonised by emigrants. This new country must be perfectly studied and fully organised before European traders enter it." That there is some truth in this statement, and that it underlies the vital principle of the economical development of all African lands, cannot be doubted. And yet, how very little do we recognise this in practice! *The French Congo Territories.*

The Portuguese colony to the south of the Congo is more prosperous than the sister colony of Mozambique, on *Angóla.*

Angola. the opposite side of the continent. A railway is now open between Loanda and Ambaca, and another has been projected from Mossamedes across the Chella Mountains for 200 miles into the Interior; but only slow progress is made. The cultivation of the ground-nut (*Arachis hypogœa*), which is crushed for oil, besides being a staple nutriment, of coffee, sugar, and cotton, and of other commercial products, though they might be unlimited, is pursued with only relative success. The coffee of Cazengo is of first-rate quality; and elsewhere it is widely grown, as also are india-rubber plants. There can be no doubt that, were adequate transport provided, the trade in rubber and other products could be immensely increased. Though the coastlands are bare, the higher-lying regions are specially suitable for cultivation. Recently the Portuguese Government have been making the experiment of bringing colonists from Madeira, chiefly agriculturists, and establishing them in the Interior, giving each colony a subsidy under a five years' contract. This plan appears to be a step decidedly in the right direction, and to have already met with gratifying success; for there is no doubt that the inland districts of Angola are rich in natural resources.

South-Eastern Africa. Before proceeding to examine the Temperate regions, we may complete our survey of Tropical Africa by passing over to the other side of the continent, to the East Coast. And first as regards the Zambezi basin: though an area of transition, it may at once be said that its commercial relations come chiefly and naturally under Tropical Africa, and it may best be considered in conjunction with the Lakes region, from which it conducts.

Nyassa-land. Nyassa-land has so far been exclusively developed by British missionaries and traders,* in spite of the exacting

---

* The four mission stations on Nyassa and Tanganika cost yearly about £20,000.

and hostile tariffs of the Portuguese. Coffee, which is indigenous and has been successfully cultivated at Blantyre, is said to be a hopeful product, upon which alone, according to Mr. Buchanan,* the success of the country might depend. But Consul Hawes reports (1887) the success of coffee as "doubtful," and speaks of ivory as the chief export. Then there are tea, cinchona-bark, rubber, cloves, medicinal plants, oil-seeds, and indigo. Almost anything could be grown in the highland regions. The country is, moreover, supposed to be rich in minerals. To the west of the Lakes, iron and copper are found in abundance, and silver and gold are not absent. But what is wanting is greater security for life and property. Political embroglios and constant strife with the Portuguese officials have in recent years crippled all the efforts that have been made for the opening-up of the Lakes region. With their final adjustment and the consolidation of British supremacy, we may confidently anticipate the almost immediate success of the commercial operations that have already been started, and which at one time were so hopeful. By her recent Agreement (August 1890) with Portugal, Britain, besides securing the freedom of the Zambezi to the ships of all nations and the recognition of her Protectorate over Nyassa-land and the Shiré Highlands, obtained a reduction of the Portuguese tariff to 3 per cent. ad valorem on transit dues. But this Treaty requires ratification.

Commercial enterprise on the East Coast, between the Zambezi and the Gulf of Aden, has long been paralysed by the blighting influence of the Slave Trade, which has almost entirely destroyed legitimate commerce. The British Indian, or Banyan, traders, whose commercial talents have contributed so much towards the development of the country, are themselves parties to this nefarious Traffic, of which the

* *The Shiré Highlands.*

East Coast. Arabs of Zanzibar and those Arabs of the Interior not engaged in agriculture are the chief instruments. Thus, ivory and slaves have always been the chief commodities of the East Coast. And yet, some of the countries inland behind the dry and unhealthy coastal zone are capable of raising all Tropical products, while the plateaus, besides serving as excellent pasture-grounds, yield good crops of wheat and other cereals. There are splendid prospects for gums alone. The cloves of Zanzibar and Pemba islands are world-famous; and the hides of Somál-land, the gums of the Swahéli Coast, and the ivory of East Central Africa generally, are important articles of export. Among other native products are india-rubber, indigo, copal, orchilla, oil-seeds, copra, myrrh, Indian-corn, wax, &c. Moreover, there are fine agricultural regions, as, for example, in Usambara and around Kilima-njaro, where almost any vegetable product might be raised.

The Arab settlements in the Interior, such as Kavele, on Tanganika, and Tabora, maintain constant communications with the Coast, some of the chief ports of which, as outlets for trade, are Kilwa, Bagamoyo, and Mombaza; whilst Berbera is the chief port on the Gulf of Aden.

The caravan-routes leading to the East Coast are, as we have said, at the same time slave-routes, since the traffic in ivory and that in slaves go hand-in-hand. They are consequently liable to change; but Zanzibar, from its favourable geographical position, is, and always has been, the chief emporium of commerce; it is the "Liverpool" of the East Coast.

In addition to the subversive effects which the Slave Trade has had on the economical development of this part of Africa, there have been other hostile elements; of such are the climatic conditions and the insecure and immoral political administration. Until all these disadvantages are

removed, or mitigated, there can be very little progress for East Coast.
East Africa; and it is therefore gratifying to recognise
a somewhat healthier state of public opinion and international action in these respects.

Easy and safe communication between the coasts and
the Interior being essential for the development of African
lands through the agency of Europeans, it is obvious that
the absence of large rivers debouching on the East Coast,
north of the Zambezi, is another serious disadvantage,
which must be overcome by building railways in their
stead or by constructing highways for wheel-traffic. Since
the coastal lands are now under the domination of European Powers, the construction of such roads or railways
—connecting, as they naturally would, the European
depôts in the most healthy inland regions—is the first
and most effective step to be taken for the "opening-up"
and pacification of the country. From their excellent
harbour of Mombaza, the British East Africa Company
have, with an enterprise that deserves commendation, commenced the construction of a railway to Taveta (which
it is hoped will be reached not later than July 1891),
whence it is to be continued to the Victoria Nyanza,
upon which steamers will be placed. The comparative
absence of suitable harbours on the East Coast is, however, another great drawback.

We now turn to the Temperate regions of South Africa, South Africa.
where we enter what is by far the most valuable commercial
sphere of any we have considered,—and by South Africa
I mean the entire country south of the Zambezi. Apart
from its favourable geographical position and its mineral
riches, the chief reason why South Africa has proved of such
outstanding importance as a sphere of European enterprise
is because it is capable of colonisation by white men, and
is already endowed with fairly adequate political organisa-

South Africa. — tions, so that it is ready to receive any number of skilled immigrants. European influence has, in short, a strong base on the coasts, and none but political obstacles to its further expansion inland.

Exception may be taken to the scanty rain-supply in the north-western region of South Africa; but much may be done to remedy this defect by introducing an adequate system of irrigation, more especially as large areas have an abundant supply of underground waters. Another exception must be made: there is an almost total absence of means of fluvial communication, neither the Orange River nor the Vaal being suitable for navigation; but, even in this case, engineers may be able to effect something, and the construction of railways will accomplish the rest. The rich pasture-lands of the inland plateau and the extraordinary wealth of its mineral resources are elements of future prosperity which nothing but political suicide can destroy.

Minerals. — The discovery of valuable and extensive mineral deposits at once attracts a large population, which has to be supported in some way: consequently an impetus is given to a great many industries. Railways and roads are constructed and ports are opened. For first opening up a new country, therefore, mining is a most effective medium. Now, South Africa is extraordinarily rich in minerals. In the gold-producing regions, moreover, the reef-mining requires steady and skilled labour, and in consequence does not encourage the social evils that are characteristic of alluvial mining. Fortunately, the gold deposits so far occur in reef formations, and the mining towns are consequently filled with industrious and competent workmen. As an extreme example of the rapid growth of such towns, we may instance Johannesburg, the capital of the richest gold-fields, the Witwatersrand, a town which a little over two and a half years ago did not exist, but now possesses handsome public buildings and streets, with a population of over 20,000 souls.

The Transvaal, or South African Republic, has other rich gold-fields, such as the De Kaap, with Barberton, another mushroom town. And there are auriferous regions extending from the northern border of Mashuna-land south-west to Tati and south-east to the R. Sabi and Manica. Kimberley has the most prolific diamond-fields in the world. Copper is found in the north-west, at O'okiep, and coal in the south-east, in the Stormberg Mountains and in Natal. The South African coal-seams may yet prove important and to extend continuously under large areas. *South Africa.*

In addition to its mineral riches, South Africa has vast pasture-lands admirably adapted to stock-raising. Ostrich-farming, which was originated here, has been pursued with success; and wool has for a long time been one of the leading articles of export, coming chiefly from the *karoos*, or inland tablelands of 3000 feet or more in elevation. Wine has of late been produced for export. All kinds of fruits thrive under cultivation, while cereals could be raised over wide regions. Damara-land and Bechuana-land possess some of the best pastures of South Africa, and a practicable route from them to the West Coast is not wanting. *Pasture-lands.*

Several railways have been built or are in course of construction between the ports of the South and South-East Coasts and the chief commercial centres of the Interior; and it is absolutely essential that their extension should proceed rapidly, in order to feed the wants of the growing industries, and to act as outlets for the exports. Kimberley is already thus united with Cape Town and Port Elizabeth; and it is now intended to extend the railway northwards to Vryburg, Mafeking, Shoshong, and Victoria Falls, whilst another line is projected to cross Matabele-land into Mashuna-land. It is further proposed to con- *Railways.*

struct a railway from Colesberg to Bloemfontein, and thence to the Vaal River. The British South Africa Company have taken over the railway to Vryburg, which will be reached in October 1890, and it is hoped the extension to Mafeking will be completed by May 1891. The progress of the line from Delagoa Bay, owing to political machinations, is proceeding very slowly. Great expectations have been formed of this enterprise in building railways; but the relative absence of fine harbours round the coasts of South Africa is undoubtedly a serious drawback to the commercial development of the interior lands.

<small>African islands.</small> Of the islands of Africa very little need be said. Madagascar, though it has little or no commerce, could raise most vegetable growths; and it could also serve as a vast storehouse, which, from its geographical position, should prove of immense value to France, whose Protectorate over the island we have finally acknowledged and recognised. Its soil is fertile and it has mineral riches. Réunion and Mauritius have fine plantations of Tropical produce. The other small islands, especially in the Atlantic, are chiefly valuable to commerce as ports of call and coaling-stations.

<small>Geographical distribution of ivory.</small> So far we have purposely said very little of ivory. Our intention is now to go into the subject in some detail, because of its supreme importance. For not only is ivory the cause, if not the sole cause, of the Slave Trade, which on all hands is considered most detrimental to legitimate commerce, but, like minerals, it affords the prospect of an immediate return for capital in those regions where it is found, and which would not otherwise pay for their initial development. As the elephants are driven farther and farther into the Interior, retreating before the advance of civilised communities, and are gradually becoming rarer, it is essential for us to take effective measures, which are

increasingly difficult, to control the trade in ivory and to preserve the elephant from rapid extinction. By thus protecting a valuable marketable commodity, we should at the same time render more effective service in suppressing the Slave Trade than by causing the combined fleets of Europe to blockade the coasts. Geographical Distribution of Ivory.

Dr. Paul Reichard, in an admirable article in the *Geographische Blätter*,* goes exhaustively into the subject; so that my task is a light one. On the map which accompanies Dr. Reichard's paper, the elephant is shown to range over the greater part of Africa south of the desert zone,—or, say, south of the latitude of Khartúm. In some regions it has been exterminated, and in most regions, but more especially in the south, it has been gradually driven back from the coast-lands into the Interior.

Dr. Reichard distinguishes between what is known in European markets as soft ivory and hard ivory, the former, of a milk-white colour, being the more valuable. A half-hard quality is also recognised, but we need not take that into account. The soft ivory comes from the elephants that feed in the open and dry woodlands and in the savannas covered with short grass; the hard ivory from those which range exclusively through the damp primeval forests and over the savannas covered with long grass. Upon the nourishment of the elephant depend, therefore, the quality and character of its tusks. We may dwell in a few words upon its geographical distribution and frequency. Hard and soft ivory.

Roughly speaking, the elephants that yield hard ivory are confined to the basins of the Niger, Benué, and Congo; while they occur most frequently in the country intervening between the Benué and the Congo and in certain regions of the Upper Congo. Elephants yielding soft

---

* *Das afrikanische Elfenbein und sein Handel.* Band xii. Heft ii. (1889).

ivory are found in two distinct regions: (1.) in the Upper
Nile, Abyssinia, and the country to the south, with greatest
frequency in the Equatorial parts east and west of the
Victoria Nyanza, and (2.) in the South-Central plateaus,
with greatest frequency to the west of Lake Nyassa.

Ivory trade-centres. — The chief focus of the ivory trade in Africa is Zanzibar, whose collecting-ground extends over an immense area, embracing the entire Lakes region, with Tabora as a centre. The East Coast trade is in the hands of the Arabs. On the opposite side of the continent, with the residence of the Muata Yanvo as a collecting-centre, the ivory trade, which is in the hands of the Portuguese, finds its outlets at St. Paul de Loanda and Ambriz, or at Benguela.

Ivory collecting-grounds. — The other collecting-grounds to the north and south of these Central regions, and their outlets on the coasts, may also be mentioned; for not only does the elucidation of this traffic afford a key to the understanding of the Slave Trade, but it also defines approximately the trade-routes.

A certain amount of ivory comes out at the Congo; but to the north, the ports on the Gulf of Guinea receive their supplies from the Interior. The ivory collected in the countries to the south of Timbuktu is taken there for distribution, and is sent across the desert either to Mogador or to Tripoli. The latter port also attracts the ivory gathered round Lake Tsad. The ivory of the Upper Nile region finds its way to Khartúm and Alexandria,—or rather, it did at one time; and that of Abyssinia comes out at Massawa. South of the Zambezi basin, the ivory collected in the plateau regions is carried to Port Natal or Cape Town; whilst that of the entire Zambezi Valley, including Southern Nyassaland, finds its way to Kilimani or Mozambique.

Ivory trade-routes. — These, then, roughly speaking, are the chief trade-routes for ivory and other leading commodities of export from the Interior. It should be noted that to a certain extent they lead through the most unhealthy regions, for the slave-traders seek the back slums, so to speak, for their inhuman traffic, so as to avoid the healthier and more vigorous tribes who might oppose them, *en route*. But they vary from time to time in accordance with political conditions.

Considering the important rôle played by the traffic in ivory, and consequently in slaves, in the economical and political development of Africa, and remembering the enormous sacrifice of human life it entails, the marvel is that the commercial results are so slight; for, according to Westendarp,* the annual value of ivory exported from Africa amounts only to about seven or eight million pounds sterling. Amount of annual exports.

Dr. Reichard is of opinion that, unless some measures be undertaken for the preservation of the elephant, this noble animal will become extinct in Africa in perhaps 150 or 200 years' time. It is estimated that over 65,000 elephants are killed annually. If only a fraction of this working power could be turned to account, how much more valuable it might become! Though we are aware the elephant does not breed in captivity, or even in proximity to civilised communities, some experiments might be made in its employment as a draught animal, or, as in Burma, for work in the forests. It ought to be preserved, too, as in India and Ceylon. It is true we do not yet know whether the African elephant is as tractable as its Asiatic brother. Although the Romans used elephants in Africa for war purposes, it may be assumed they were brought from the East, since, in all the pictures of them, the drivers are represented as carrying in their hand the Indian *ankush*. Preservation of the elephant.

As a *pendant* to the export-trade in ivory, which is so inseparably associated with Arab ascendancy, we may add a few remarks to what has elsewhere been said on the The liquor-traffic.

* *Geographische Blätter*, Band xii. Heft ii. p. 168.

The liquor-traffic. import-trade in spirituous liquors, which goes hand-in-hand with the European domination. North, south, east, and west a flood of the most poisonous spirits is being poured into Africa by European traders. One may judge of its quality by a glance at the price-list. Here are a few examples : *—

Spirits sold at Sierra Leone,	. 4s. 6d.	per doz. bottles.
Superior gin (best quality), Lagos,	2s. 6d.	,, ,,
Hamburg gin, ...	4s. 6d.	,, ,,
Rum (Sierra Leone), . . .	12s. 0d.	,, ,,

From 1883 to the end of 1887 over thirty million gallons of this sort of stuff were imported into Africa. Most of the European Powers participate in this abominable trade. The native chiefs have, in some instances, even begged and prayed for the exclusion of the liquor-traffic from their territories, but in vain. An earnest effort was made at the Berlin Conference (1885) to put a stop to it, but it was thwarted by interested parties.

At the recent Brussels Conference (1889–90), though, as we have seen in a former chapter, certain restrictive measures were adopted, they are wholly inadequate to meet the case. The natives have gone down before the extension of the traffic as under the scourge of a plague,—but what does that matter, so long as a few traders can thereby enrich themselves? The short-sightedness of such a policy is obvious, because the natives are entirely demoralised by drink. Several of the chartered companies have very wisely prohibited or greatly restricted the importation of spirituous liquors into the territories under their control. Similar efforts have been made also in the Congo Independent State,

---

* From a pamphlet issued by the "Native Races and the Liquor Traffic Committee," London. But the prices will be raised, no doubt, when the duty (1½d. per quart) fixed by the recent Brussels Conference comes into operation.

at the Cape, in British Bechuana-land and Zulu-land. But
the traffic still thrives, and will continue to thrive until,
by international agreement, effective measures are undertaken for its total suppression.

Associated with the liquor-traffic is the Labour Problem. <small>The Labour Problem.</small>
This is one of the most important questions for Africa, and
its solution will profoundly affect the ultimate development
of the continent as a field for European enterprise. The
indigenous populations, upon whom we must mainly depend
for supplying the needful labour, are either demoralised
by the liquor-trade or decimated by the Slave Trade; and
of the two processes, many eminent authorities are agreed
that the former, though slower in operation, is ultimately
more effectual in its results: in both cases the natives are
rapidly killed off.

The diversity of opinion in regard to the Labour Problem <small>Divided opinions.</small>
is naturally very great. Some say that Africa should be
for the Africans; but others deny that the native Africans
are capable themselves, or even under European supervision,
of developing their countries.

Emin Pacha, whose experience has been unique and whose
judgment is reliable, says: *—"A few hundred Chinese
established in any suitable place, under the direction of
practical Europeans, will form a better nucleus for the
civilisation of Africa than any number of Indian elephants
and ironclad steamers." And he asks: †—"Would not the
introduction of Chinese settle the Slave Trade once and for
all?" Emin Pacha, therefore, believes in the Chinese as
the best workmen for opening up the country, and that to
employ them would "repay a thousand-fold such undertak-
ing." He does not believe in the regeneration of the Negro
by the Negro. That the Chinese can live under any clime

---

* *Emin Pacha* in *Central Africa*, p. 417.
† *Ibid.*, p. 419.

The Labour Problem.

is undoubted. They thrive in the pestilential swamps of the Malay Peninsula, and have been taken to the West Indies as labourers; they are strong, and make excellent carriers; they are thrifty, expert with their hands, and are excellent artisans. But that they would make better field-labourers than the natives of Africa may be questioned, though doubtless their industry is greater. In the Súdan, along the West Coast, and in South Africa, the natives are capable of labour and willing to supply it; while on the East Coast they have been trained for centuries as carriers. There remains the question: Under what conditions should they be employed?

Consul Johnston bears testimony to the fact that the Portuguese Government apprentices at São Thomé, in the Gulf of Guinea, are well cared for and happy, and that this system of apprenticeship works better and is more justifiable than the coolie-traffic or the Pacific labour-traffic. There is always a danger of the coolie-traffic degenerating into a modified system of slavery; and, in any case, by their temporary engagement, coolies are not the best colonisers, because they do not become permanent settlers.

Under these circumstances, there is a great deal to be said in favour of Dr. Blyden's scheme of bringing from the United States of America those Negroes who are willing to return to the home of their ancestors, and of making them nuclei of native settlements, more or less under the control of Europeans.

It has already been demonstrated that Europeans themselves, except by a very gradual process of acclimatisation, will never be able to colonise Tropical Africa, and can only live with safety in the healthy plateau-regions.

In the earlier part of this chapter it was stated that to open up Africa it is essential to work on commercial principles. From what we have now seen of the value of the various African lands, it is obvious that in most regions it is possible, by enterprise and judicious management, to get a fair return, in the long-run, for the capital expended upon their development.* Consequently, for the rough work of opening up the new countries in Africa, chartered companies are the best agencies. They can advance with boldness where the national flag dare not venture for fear of suffering indignity or repulse. Of course, by entrusting them with governmental powers, the danger is run of establishing monopolies or of sacrificing native interests to the interest of the shareholders. A careful supervision of their administration should, therefore, be the duty of their respective Governments, who should retain the power (as in the charter granted to the British South Africa Company) to control their native and foreign policy. Great Britain, Holland, France, and latterly Germany, have worked with chartered companies: we know with what results. Spain and Portugal have been jealous of crown monopolies: we see with what effect. In the former cases it has been abundantly shown that the adoption of a rational, generous, and continuous policy has always succeeded, though failures have been brought about by unwise governmental interference, or have arisen from non-continuity of policy, neglect, and injustice. The Government, in short, should exercise over the chartered company a wise parental control. Considering the great and dearly-bought experience of Great Britain in dealing with native races, it is astounding to observe the errors into which the Foreign Office, even at the present day, is constantly falling. No excuse for these failures can be advanced except that of sheer ignorance.

Commercial development of Africa.

---

* The total trade of the British Empire with British Africa amounts to about £25,200,000 yearly, exclusive of the annual trade, nine or ten millions Sterling, with Egypt. (H. H. Johnston, *Nineteenth Century*, August 1890.)

By the introduction of new industries into Africa, by teaching the natives to work for themselves and not for others alone, and by giving them freedom and security of life and property, the European Powers will themselves be the gainers. By checking abuses, such as the wholesale traffic in poisonous liquors, and by introducing legitimate commerce, most of the evils under which the Negroes are suffering, of which the Slave Trade is only one, will be more effectually removed than by all the sham philanthropy and mock administrative measures under cover of which Europe is at present advancing into Africa, like a thief in the night.

"Robber-economy." Hitherto, in the Tropical regions of Africa, few serious attempts have been made in the systematic cultivation of products intended for export. The method followed by Europeans is that which has been adopted by the Arab ivory-traders—to destroy what furnishes the product, or what the Germans so happily call "robber-economy."* This will assuredly not pay in the long-run. If we go on reaping where we do not sow, we cannot expect the virgin resources of a country to last very long.

Conclusion. In a word, it is only by adopting sound commercial principles that the African lands, the intrinsic value of which is undoubted, will ever be turned to profitable account; and it is only by the exercise of justice that Europeans will be justified in acquiring those riches for themselves and their posterity. To quote a homely saying: "Honesty is the best policy."

* *Handbook of Commercial Geography* (Chisholm), p. 358.

CHAPTER IX.

THE EUROPEAN DOMINATION.

RELATIVE ABSENCE OF NATIVE POLITICAL RULE—SURVEY OF THE EUROPEAN COLONIES, PROTECTORATES, AND SPHERES OF INFLUENCE—THE POLITICAL SITUATION—COMPARATIVE ABSENCE OF EFFECTIVE OCCUPATION BY THE EUROPEAN POWERS—OBSTACLES TO EUROPEAN POLITICAL SETTLEMENT NOT NECESSARILY INSUPERABLE, BUT LIMITATIONS TO BE OBSERVED.

MAPS.

POLITICAL PARTITION (SHOWING TERRITORIAL BOUNDARIES) . *Plate* XIII.
FORMS OF GOVERNMENT . . . . „ XIV.

THE EUROPEAN DOMINATION.

A GLANCE at the political map of Africa reveals the somewhat remarkable phenomenon that, with relatively few exceptions, the countries—at least along the coasts—are dominated or possessed by European Powers. The only important and unquestionable exceptions are the Native States in the Súdan. There remain others, it is true, such as Morocco, Abyssinia, the South African Republic, and the Orange Free State; but these are all States more or less under the influence of European Powers. Their future destiny cannot fail to be profoundly affected by the expansion of the European Possessions and by the new political conditions growing up in their midst. Liberia may be said to exist by the courtesy and good-will of its neighbours and well-wishers; Dahomé and Ashanti are only political bugbears; and the Congo Independent State should more correctly be classed apart, in the meantime. The remaining portions of the continent, not actually possessed by the European Powers, can scarcely be said to have yet entered the political arena. *Relative absence of native political rule.*

The aspect of our subject now to be considered is the European domination as it exists at the present day in Africa. The partition of the continent, since the Berlin Conference (1885), is of sufficient importance to be discussed apart, in the next chapter.

Commencing with the countries of North-West Africa, lying at the gate of Europe, under the shadow of the mighty Atlas Mountains, we have, existing side by side, the *North-West Africa.*

fanatical Mohammedan State of Morocco, the French colony of Algeria and the French Protectorate of Tunis. These countries are separated from Egypt by the barren coastal strip of territory belonging to Turkey: Tripoli, and the oases of Fezzan. France is undoubtedly the dominant political Power in those regions, though in Morocco she cannot yet compete against British commerce, which monopolises about three-fourths of the trade of that country. The dream of empire in which France indulges nevertheless bids fair to be realised, to a qualified extent, should the present rate of progress be maintained.

North-West Africa.

Mention has already been made of the political conditions in Algeria. In Tunis, which, as we have said, is more of a commercial colony, French policy has been more enlightened and relatively more successful. The Protectorate is not throttled by "red tape." Sir Lambert Playfair, at the Bath meeting (1888) of the British Association, speaking of Tunis, said: "No State assistance of any kind is given, not an immigrant has been imported, not an acre of Arab land has been confiscated; and the whole civil charges borne by France do not exceed £6000 a year.* A very short time ago, the interior of the country was a *terra incognita*; now it is being rapidly opened out to European enterprise." It is evident that, with these encouraging prospects, French dominion in North Africa must continue to expand.

Algeria and Tunis.

The acquisition by France, by the terms of her recent Agreement with Great Britain, of the Saharan regions intervening between Algeria and Tunis in the north and Senegambia and the Niger basin in the south is an event of greater significance than Lord Salisbury seems disposed to

The new French sphere of influence.

---

* On the other hand, Algeria costs France annually, including military expenses, as much as from seventy to eighty million francs, though a proportion of this sum can fairly be reckoned under capital account.

allow. The consolidation of the French Empire in North-West Africa would have been seriously hampered had not this unity of her possessions been recognised by us. As it is, France practically secures the trade of the Upper Niger and dominates the caravan-traffic between the Súdan and North Africa. Even the Sahara Desert itself is not so valueless as is popularly supposed. The projected railway across the Sahara is now being seriously discussed in France; but it appears to me highly problematical whether such a railway could be made to pay, or indeed whether it could be constantly maintained. It would be a difficult matter for France to control the lawless tribes of the Sahara.

Enough has been said of Tripoli, a Turkish dependency, to argue its comparative insignificance as a colonial possession. We may at once pass on to Lower Egypt. And there we enter a land of vast possibilities, a land which might almost be regarded as a British province, but for the very natural jealousies of the European Powers. The present comparatively flourishing state of Egypt is due entirely to the British Occupation, and very little to its own recuperative powers. British arms and statesmanship have restored the Khediv to power, and since 1876 have brought about reforms of a most beneficial and far-reaching character. Abuses under which the Fellahín formally suffered have been gradually abolished, while the irrigation and other public works have produced favourable results in the development of the country. The Egyptian army has been reorganised, and can now boast of excellent materials. Egyptian soldiers can at least be relied upon behind earthworks. It has been stated that our aim in the management of her affairs has been to make Egypt *stand alone*. But, as the Marquis of Salisbury said, at the Lord Mayor's banquet on 9th November 1889: "We have undertaken the guardianship of Egypt for a time, on account of the

<small>Britain in Lower Egypt.</small>

Britain in Lower Egypt. terrible dangers to which, partly through the action of this country (Great Britain) she was exposed. These dangers have not ceased during the present year. . . . The dangers still exist. . . . It is necessary we should remember these things, for there are people who suggest to us that the time has come when, with safety to our honourable pledges, we can evacuate Egypt, which we have undertaken to sustain until she is competent to sustain herself against every enemy, foreign and domestic. We can see that that time has not arrived, . . . but, whether the day comes sooner or later, our policy remains unaltered still, that we shall pursue our task to the end." * That, so far, it has been a thankless and costly task it is evident; and that we shall reap where we have sown is doubtful, owing largely to the jealousy of the Powers. In Egypt, as elsewhere in Africa, it is this international jealousy which stimulates all the subversive elements in the development of the continent. This is a point that will be amply illustrated as we proceed.

Upper Egypt. In Upper Egypt (we continue to use the term from force of habit) a very different set of conditions exists. The political geography of that part of the Nile Valley is inseparably connected with the Red Sea Littoral, and the key to it is undoubtedly Sawákin. But here we open a chapter of history the pages of which—where not obliterated by stains of blood—convey a story of misery on the one hand and of criminal blunders on the other.

Elsewhere we have shown that political administration from Cairo must inevitably stop short of the Nubian Desert,

---

* A well-informed writer in the *Contemporary Review* (September 1889) says:—"As long as the present political position in Egypt undergoes no radical change, it would take a series of untoward events to seriously endanger the stability of Egyptian finance and the solvency of the Egyptian Government." He also states that "Egyptian credit has outpaced all competitors for public favour in the last five years." Yet, when Sir Edgar Vincent went to Egypt (1884), she could not borrow at 7 per cent.

and that Wadi Halfa is the scientific and natural frontier of Lower Egypt. The whole of the Middle Nile region has its most effective base on the Red Sea Littoral. The nomadic tribes of that part of the Súdan, the nature of whose life inculcates habits of independence and the utmost intolerance of restraint or taxation of any kind, can only be controlled—as Sir Samuel Baker assures us—by those who have the power of seizing and occupying the wells: for to these nomads water is the most valuable and essential commodity. General Gordon, writing in 1884,* classified the peoples of the Súdan as follows:—(1.) Bedwin Arabs, living a nomadic life in tribes; (2.) Arabs settled in districts adjoining the river (Nile), who, before Mehemet Ali's conquest, were under their own Sultans, and whose families still exist; (3.) the mercantile classes occupying the towns; (4.) *employés* of the Egyptian Government; and (5.) the adherents of Zebehr (Zibér),—slave-hunters driven out of the Bahr-el-Ghazal.

Middle Nile region.

Eastern Súdan.

Whatever may be the present political situation in the Súdan, the classes 1 and 2 must doubtless still exist. The Mahdi's supporters were recruited from class 5, and included deserters from the Egyptian army. All alike, except class 4, have been haters of the Egyptian Government, though it were wrong to infer that therefore they sympathised with the Mahdists. General Gordon went on to say that "the evacuation of the Súdan by the Cairo Government cannot but array the Súdan in two camps: the one, the Mahdi and his followers; the other, the Bedwin nomad tribes, the Arabs who live by agriculture and who were formerly under separate Sultans, and the mercantile classes. These two camps are united only because they equally hate the Cairo Government. Of the two camps, the one which offers most hope of tranquillity to the Súdan is the latter,

Political situation in the Súdan.

* Published by Mr. Clifford Lloyd in *Nineteenth Century*, November 1889.

and I think that our efforts should be to give over the
country to them. Nothing can be hoped for from the
Mahdi and his party, while we may hope for some degree
of settled government from the native sultans and the
sheikhs of the great tribes. As for the Slave Trade, it will
go on, whether the Mahdi's party gains the ascendant or
whether the two camps remain antagonistic, for both are
equally interested in its continuance." This is the post-
humous verdict of one who fought and died for the Súdan,
and it were difficult to dispute it. The only material point
on which we are inclined to differ from so high an authority
as the late General Gordon is that concerning the continuance
of the Slave Trade. For if, as is confidently and reasonably
asserted, the introduction of legitimate commerce and a
spirited commercial policy were to be the death-blow to the
Slave Trade in other parts of Africa, it is only logical to assume
that the Súdan would prove to be no ultimate exception.

Sawákin.
From whatever point we regard the matter, Sawákin
presents the most effective base of operations, whether for
commercial enterprise, the suppression of the Slave Trade,
or as a political centre. In spite of its unhealthiness—the
causes of which might be partially removed—Sawákin is
also an admirable site for a great naval or coaling station.

Massawa.
Farther south, at Massawa, we enter a new sphere of political action. The dominating Power there is Italy, our ancient
Italy on the Red Sea.
ally, whose policy in Africa would appear to be identical
with our own. But even old friends sometimes quarrel;
and it were well to realise in good time the preponderating
influence which Italy will be able to exercise in the Súdan
when the moment for action arrives.* The route from
Massawa *viâ* Kassala to Khartúm is practically in the hands

---

* This passage was written several months ago; at the present moment
(17th October 1890), Britain and Italy, after discussing their relative interests
in that part of Africa, have failed to arrive at an understanding.

of Italy, and is one of the best and healthiest highways into the Súdan. Indeed, had it been selected by the British expeditionary force in preference to the desert routes, Khartúm might to-day have been in European hands. But sheer contrariness at the time defeated the adoption of this route. It is still open to us, or at least to Italy. The Italian Possessions on the Red Sea Littoral—now united under the name of Eritrea, and placed under the administration of a military Governor—have been steadily expanding. But that is not all: an Italian Protectorate has been proclaimed over Abyssinia and Shoa, and some intervening districts have been occupied. The present Negus of Abyssinia, Menelek, is the "creature of Italy." He owes his position to Italy in the same way as King Johannes partly owed his crown to Great Britain.

Italy on the Red Sea.

From these few indications we are able to estimate the immense influence which Italy has secured for herself on the Red Sea, and, by implication, in the Súdan also. The French and British stations on the Gulf of Aden are of relative insignificance as a base for operations in the interior parts of Africa, though, as halting-places on the route to the East, they may continue to prove invaluable.

As for Egypt—whose dominion before its downfall was gradually creeping south—at the present day she has absolutely no hold whatever upon the Súdan, though a stronger Power behind her, Great Britain, is endeavouring to save some of the *flotsam* and *jetsam* from the wreck. The Súdan is a closed book to us; but when it is re-opened, there should be stirring incidents to chronicle in its pages.

The loss of the Sudan.

Of the course of events in the Upper Nile territories since the fall of Khartúm very little trustworthy news has transpired. The original Mahdi, whose followers braved British bayonets, is dead, and of his successor we know little. The revolutionary—or, should we say, patriotic?—

The Mahdi's dominions.

The Mahdi's dominions.

party must, however, as an essential condition of its existence, be doing something. We have heard of the invasion of Wadai, which met with temporary success, and we know —only too well—that Emin's Province has at last fallen. But no man can foretell what will be the outcome of these events. Only this much seems certain: the reconquest of the territories in the Súdan were a task fitter to be undertaken by the pacific means of commerce than by force of arms. The bases of operations in the future will in all likelihood be on the Red Sea Littoral and the East Coast. From these points of vantage our first messengers into the Súdan should be, not trains of war, but caravans and trains of commerce.

Of the Central Súdan States sufficient has already been said, to indicate their vast power and resources.

West Coast.

Before proceeding farther south in our survey of the European domination over African lands, we may turn to the West Coast. No other part of Africa is divided amongst such a great number of different European Powers. The great bend of the West Coast north of the Equator is occupied at various points by all the European Powers possessing territories in Africa, except Italy; while several Native States have at the same time managed to uphold their integrity.

Britain and France on the West Coast.

This portion of the West Coast has from the earliest times been the chosen field of British and French enterprise, and they have only recently been disturbed by the entrance of a powerful competitor,—Germany. We have seen how, for centuries past, Great Britain and France have been endeavouring to monopolise the trade of the Niger; but Timbuktu, the original objective point, is no longer the sole goal of their ambitions: the field of action has been enlarged. The French in Senegambia and the British chartered Company on the Niger are pursuing an

energetic and enlightened policy, with the aim not only of
attracting the trade of the Interior, but also of developing
their possessions on the Coast. The British Possessions
between Senegambia and Liberia have never been sufficiently
supported by the Home Government to be able to compete
against the French; they appear to have remained stationary,
or in a state of coma. Much the same may be said in
respect of the British colony on the Gold Coast. But in
the Niger Territories a vigorous commercial company have
proved equal to their responsibilities, and have boldly seized
every opportunity. Their only serious competitor, except on Germany
on the
West
Coast.
the Upper Niger, is, as we have said, Germany; and the
German colony of Camarons, from whence to the Benué a
route has recently been opened up, bids fair soon to become
a thriving province.

The chief British Possessions in this part of Africa are British
Possess-
ions on
the West
Coast.
undoubtedly those on the Niger. Between the colony of
Lagos and the Camarons frontier, the coastal lands fall
under two political divisions: (1.) the Oil Rivers District,[*]
comprising the intricate network of channels in the Deltaic
lands, and beyond; and (2.) the territories of the Royal
Niger Company. The Niger itself, being an international
highway, is open to the flags of all nations. For a definite
distance up the valleys of the Niger and Benué, and over
the intervening countries of Sokoto and Gandu, the Royal
Niger Company possess certain rights of sovereignty and Royal
Niger
Company.
extra-territorial jurisdiction. The Company may thus be
regarded as the chief political power in those regions.
It is true they occupy the anomalous position of being
traders and administrators at one and the same time. The
machinery of government is expensive, and the cost has to
be met by imposts, by far the greater part of which is re-
mitted by themselves as traders. This is like taking money

---

[*] So called from the nature of its staple export.

Royal Niger Company. out of one pocket to put into another. Though the Company invite traders to enter their territories, imposing a fee of £50 for the license, it is natural that they themselves should monopolise the commerce of the entire region. In consequence of this exercise of a monopoly, the German traders have sought protection from their Government; but the position they have taken up is an unreasonable one: because it should be remembered that the Company bought up the British and French trading concerns before they received their Royal Charter, and from 1882, as the National African Company, they have themselves been the principal traders. It seems impossible to prevent a monopoly of trade falling to the Company, constituted as it now is. Only by conferring on them purely administrative functions, and thus destroying their dual position, could this monopoly be broken down. Disputes have also occurred between the Company and the Liverpool merchants in the Oil Rivers District, over which there is now a British Protectorate.

The Royal Niger Company are pursuing an intelligent policy in restricting or prohibiting the importation of ardent spirits into the territories under their control. Though they do not publish trade-returns, it may be inferred from the value of their stock that they are able to pay their way. The affairs of the Company are controlled from London, and the administrative staff on the Niger is fairly effective. Owing to the unhealthiness of the Lower Niger, innumerable difficulties occur in the way of settlement, and therefore of administration; but these have been met so far in an enlightened way. The Company are very proud of their small military force (400 or 500 strong), and have occasionally undertaken punitive expeditions. They possess also a small fleet for maintaining order and upholding the machinery of government in the Deltaic water-ways. That the Company have a great future before

them, provided their somewhat equivocal position be relieved
by the Home Government, cannot be doubted. Whatever
may be their actual rights over Sokoto and Gandu, the
countries of the Súdan, as has been demonstrated, should
provide a valuable market for British manufactures, quite
apart from the virgin resources of the intervening regions.
At present the Oil Rivers District would appear to be even
more valuable; but trade with the Súdan can scarcely yet
be said to have been created.

The position of the British colonies at Lagos and on the British Colonies on the West Coast.
Gold Coast is complicated, not only by the presence of
the French but also of the Native States of Ashanti and
Dahomé. Hereditary feuds have been among our chief
legacies in those parts. Lagos itself is a busy port, and,
now that it has a constitution of its own, the colony may
be regarded as a valuable possession. The history of these
colonies is so inseparably associated with the Slave Trade,
foreign intrigue, and native troubles, that, apart from the
inimical climate, their administration has been hampered by
endless difficulties. The Home Government has at no time
retained a strong hold over them, and has always shirked
its responsibilities and discouraged enterprise. Much the
same political conditions obtain in Sierra Leone, where
there is a thriving port, and on the Gambia. The action
of the French all along the line is tending to shut out
British trade from the Interior, though at places their
political moves have been checked. Though the British
West African colonies pay their way fairly well,* their
want of enterprise leaves them in a state of stagnation.

We have repeatedly alluded to the progress of the French The French in West Africa.
in Senegambia. Not only have they now connected their

---

* Consul Johnston estimates the entire trade of Great Britain with the
British Possessions in West Africa, during the year ending 1st December
1888, to have amounted to over £5,000,000,—almost equally divided between
imports and exports.

French Possessions on the West Coast.

possessions on the Senegal with the Upper Niger, on which they have founded stations, and Lake Tsad, but they have also cut off the British and Portuguese colonies from the Interior by entirely surrounding them, and, in defiance of the " Hinterland " doctrine, have extended their sphere to the coast on the other side of them. A glance at the map will elucidate this anomalous situation. A French Protectorate has been proclaimed over the Futa Jallon highlands, and the French sphere of influence has been advanced southwards to the Gulf of Guinea. The consolidation of the French territories on the West Coast may be confidently anticipated in the near future. Possibly the Portuguese may consent to be bought out, since their domination is a mere shadow; and we ourselves have practically relinquished our equivocal position on the Gambia.

Portuguese Possessions.

The islands held by Portugal in the Gulf of Guinea, Principé and São Thomé, are the only valuable possessions she has on or off the West Coast north of the Equator, if we except Madeira and the Cape Verde Islands. Of these, São Thomé is the most prosperous.

Spanish Possessions.

Spain holds the islands of Fernando Po and Annobon in the Gulf of Guinea, and the Canary Islands in the Atlantic. The latter may prove to be valuable as a coaling-station.

Western Sahara.

Opposite the Canaries, at Cape Juby, on the African mainland, a British Company have acquired certain political and trading rights, and are endeavouring to promote intercourse with the Interior. To the south of their sphere Spain also has an extensive establishment on the Coast.

Liberia.

The experiment of creating in Liberia an independent Negro State on the basis of the United States constitution has proved, so far, most disappointing. The Negroes are said to have relapsed into semi-barbarism, and their form of government is regarded as a caricature of its prototype. The Republic, which was founded by the American Colonisation

Society (1822–23), continues to receive support from its friends in the United States, whence detachments of Negroes are sent out as emigrants. It became an Independent State in 1847. The exact colour of affairs in Liberia is, probably, not so black as it is commonly painted; but Dr. Blyden and his friends will have a difficult task in obtaining the necessary support to carry out their scheme of introducing into Liberia a steady flow of American Negro immigrants. The Republic is, however, still young; and the hope of eventually moulding it into a strong Negro community should not be altogether abandoned. Even a measure of success should justify every effort being made to make Liberia the nucleus of a civilised Negro State, the influence of which upon Pagan Africa might be of the most beneficial character.

Between the Niger and the Congo the German colony of Camarons and the French Congo Territories occupy positions favourable to the rapid development of the interior lands. In no other part of Africa does Germany possess a more valuable field for colonial enterprise. Situated at a convenient part of the West Coast, with a healthy sanatorium on Mount Camarons, and not too remote from the threshold of the Súdan, the Colony has every chance in its favour. At the present time trade is at its most primitive stage, being carried on mainly by barter. Until quite recently the interior lands were a blank upon the map. Repeated expeditions have now partly explored the country; stations, both scientific and commercial, have been founded and plantations established. From the reports that have been published it is clear that German action in the Camarons has been undertaken in an intelligent spirit, and has met so far with encouraging results. *Germany in the Camarons.*

The French Possessions on the Congo and Gabún, now united for administrative purposes, having reached their interior limit, are creeping up the right bank of the M'bangi. *The French Congo Territories.*

Steady progress appears to have been made in developing their resources; but, being restricted to the coast, France is disposed to regard her Congo Possessions as a *cul-de-sac*.*
Not that this is, by any means, the case: on the contrary, the products of the country (caoutchouc, ivory, metals, &c.) should defray initial expenses and encourage the further introduction of capital.

Belgium and the Congo Independent State.

In regard to the founding of the Congo Independent State, we have seen that its origin was due in the first instance to the discoveries and enterprise of Mr. H. M. Stanley, and in the second instance to the philanthropy and munificence of its sovereign, the King of the Belgians. The subsequent development of the State has been primarily due to his Majesty, who, out of his private means, is said to have provided an annual subsidy of two million francs. But, by a recent deed of gift, the King has transferred all acquired rights to Belgium, into whose hands the administration of the State will thus ultimately fall. Financial aid by its legatees will consequently be given without delay.

The recognition of the independence of the Congo State by the Berlin Conference (1885) invested it with a nominal entity, but officials of nearly every European nationality were at first employed in its organisation. Latterly, Belgian subjects have been almost exclusively entrusted with its administration. The results have been freely spoken of as unsatisfactory. The Congo officials have at times been sharply criticised and charged with incompetence, negligence, or malpractices, whilst the machinery of the State is commonly regarded as either incomplete or bad. But critics of the State too easily forget that in other parts of Africa European administration is bad, or at least imperfect and ineffectual. To exercise effective control over such an immense area as the Congo basin is, of course, quite impos-

* *La France Coloniale*, 1886, p. 262 (M. Alfred Rambaud).

sible for the present staff of officers: many more would be
required to carry out adequately the orders from Brussels.
For this reason it seems evident that, if any progress is to
be made, some radical changes must first be effected in the
political organisation of the State. Owing to its geographical position and its natural resources, the basin of the Congo
offers a unique field for European enterprise in Africa. Its
resources may have been overrated, as, undoubtedly, they
are in many quarters; but no one can dispute the value of
the Congo river and its magnificent tributary systems as
highways into the Interior, which will at once be thrown
open to the commercial enterprise of Europe as soon as the
railway past the rapids has been completed.

No firm hold can be kept on the Upper Congo while *Tippu Tib and the Upper Congo.*
Tippu Tib and his Arab colleagues and supporters reign
supreme. This African Bismarck, as he is sometimes called,
is perfectly well aware that the Congo State is at present
unable to oust him from his slave-preserves and plantations, or in any way to exercise any effective control over
his actions. He himself, with his own eyes, has seen the
weakness as well as the strength of the State. His astute
diplomacy has, it is true, given him some temporary security,
and has even invested him with the cares of office as
Governor of the Falls Station. Perhaps during his lifetime the political situation will undergo no radical change,
but after his death his mantle may not fall on equally
robust shoulders. It must be plain to him, as it is to us,
that it were quite impossible for the European domination
and Arab rule, under their present relations, to exist per-
manently side by side. For they are as oil and water
together: legitimate trade on the one hand, and the Slave
Trade on the other. These inimical conditions may or may
not bring about a precipitate conflict: that will depend
upon events: in either case, they are quite irreconcilable

with European notions in regard to the development of Africa.

Administration of the Congo State.
The administration of the Congo State looks fairly satisfactory on paper. Excellent enactments have been drawn up, but they remain for the most part a dead letter, in consequence of the inability of the resident officials to enforce them. The common mistake is also made of endeavouring to control local affairs from Europe, direct from Brussels. The consequence is that no effective action is possible; because, in the time that it takes to receive instructions from home, opportunities are lost, and affairs on the spot naturally undergo rapid changes of front.

Europe and the Congo State.
Under these circumstances, it is highly desirable, in the interest of Africa in general and of the European Powers in particular, that every support should be given to the Congo Independent State. All would benefit from the establishment of a strong and efficient government in the basin of the Congo. The State has for too long been a sort of drill-ground for Belgian officers and officials, who have generally been content to let things take their course. It is, therefore, not too much to say that, until a vigorous commercial policy governs the affairs of the State, very slow progress will be made in the development of the Congo basin.

Portugal in Africa.
The Portuguese Possessions in Lower Guinea have, since 1885, shown a slight tendency towards improvement. The marvel is that, with such resourceful lands, their progress has not been more marked. Portuguese colonies all over the world, taken together, are a very expensive luxury to the mother-country, since their administration involves a heavy annual deficit, and those on the African mainland are no exception. Of them all, Lower Guinea is, however, the most valuable.

The chief reason of this failure to achieve colonial success is ascribed to Portugal's selfish fiscal policy, by which she

herself is the loser. Her position in Africa is that of
the fabled "dog in the manger." Yet, were she to evince
more energy and less ambition, her Possessions might be
made, not only to pay their own way, but also to return
handsome profits to the Lisbon Exchequer. The dream of
empire in Africa in which Portugal indulges is fatal to her
own interests, and no less inimical to the more enterprising
and wealthier European Powers, who are quite prepared to
develop African lands, and much better able to do it. Her
long-cherished ambitious claims to the territories intervening
between Angola and Mozambique could never have been
substantiated, and appeared ridiculous in the light of Portuguese action in Africa. Her resources and energies would
be better applied, and indeed entirely absorbed, in the work
of developing those lands to which she has incontestable
right; and, until this obvious fact be recognised by Portugal,
nothing but disaster to herself and inconvenience to others
are likely to ensue. At the same time, it is necessary to
accept Portugal as a helpmate to Europe in Africa. We
should not forget how much is due to the earlier enterprise
of the Portuguese. Poverty is said to induce pride; and the
poverty of her resources renders Portugal the more tena-
cious of her African Possessions, even though they may be
"white elephants." A proud people like the Portuguese
are not to be coerced by high-handed proceedings, and very
properly resent injustice of any kind.

The German Protectorate in South-West Africa occupies Germany in South-West Africa.
a curious position. Although it was the first of German
colonial acquisitions, it is, at the present day, by far the
most backward. Troubles with the natives and the rivalry
of individual Englishmen and of Great Britain, though they
may have interfered with the extension of German influence,
are not the causes of the backward state of the colony.
Germany began her colonial campaign in Africa by securing

from Britain the possession of Angra Pequeña; but Walvisch Bay remains British and the key to the political situation. All the best routes into the Interior diverge from Walvisch Bay, which is also by far the best harbour on that coast. Indeed, with the exception of Angra Pequeña, there is no other serviceable harbour between the Kunéné and Orange Rivers. The desert character of the coastal lands—arid soil and little rain—renders their possession of slight value, although the climate is fairly healthy. Grazing-grounds there may be, but, except in the north, there are no agricultural prospects. At the same time, as we have pointed out in another place, the higher lands of the Interior may possibly prove to be of value.

Walvisch Bay. It is difficult to see the intrinsic value of Walvisch Bay to Britain except as a thorn in the side of the Germans; and it were therefore desirable to effect an exchange between it and some German possession of equal worth elsewhere in Africa. The opposition of the Cape Colony to such exchange might surely be overcome. To Germany Walvisch Bay is absolutely essential, if it be her intention to remain in South-West Africa.

Political situation in South Africa. The political situation in South Africa is of so intricate a nature that we must permit ourselves the use of only very general terms in attempting to define its fundamental conditions. South of the Zambezi, in the plateau-countries between German South-West Africa and the Portuguese Possessions on the East Coast, there are British Colonies and protected Native Territories, British Protectorates and a Sphere of Influence, existing side by side with Dutch Republics; and the ensuing inter-relations are of the most complicated character. The recent foundation of a powerful chartered Company, to take over what has been called "Zambezia," introduces a new factor of the highest political significance; for the vigorous programme of the

Company, by providing for the construction of railways, and thereby quickening the development of the region, must necessarily affect the economical conditions of all the countries of South Africa. This will become clearer to us as we proceed.

Within this sphere of British enterprise we have the old colonies of the Cape and Natal, to which must now be added the crown colonies of Basuto-land and British Bechuana-land. Zulu-land is practically a crown colony. There is also a British Protectorate in Northern Bechuana-land, and over Pondo-land and Tonga-land. The Transvaal, or South African Republic, and the Orange Free State form *enclaves* between these British possessions and Portuguese East Africa. Between them and the Zambezi River in the north lies the British sphere of influence.

In Cape Colony the political situation may be said to be based on the numerical predominance of the Dutch or Boers over the British, and of the native races over both in conjunction. We are in a minority almost everywhere except in Natal, which prides itself on being the most " English " portion of South Africa. In Kafraria there is a strong contingent of Germans, the nucleus of which was formed by the so-called " Legionaries." {*Political situation in Cape Colony.*}

The Afrikanders, or Dutch-speaking colonists, exercise a dominant influence, which no political combination can wholly destroy. The Afrikander Bund, as Sir Charles Dilke points out,* should not be regarded as essentially inimical to British ascendancy; on the contrary, it would appear to be a patriotic league, of which loyal Englishmen are themselves members, and to promote an intelligent policy. This policy may in the main be described as advocating an united South Africa under the British flag; although it is natural that, in the bitterness of party spirit, it may {*Afrikander Bund.*}

* *Problems of Greater Britain*, vol. i. pp. 474-76.

at times be otherwise affected. The ill feeling between the British and the Boers, aggravated as it has been by actual conflicts, is easily understood; but the aim of far-seeing statesmen on either side should be to establish a *modus vivendi*, since the community of interests in several vital respects is obvious. The Dutch party, which eventually may be absorbed, is at present too strong to be either neglected or coerced. A conciliatory policy towards the Boers, and one providing for co-operation as against divergence, would therefore be the most statesmanlike attitude for Great Britain to maintain, since we are apparently unprepared to carry out a vigorous Imperial programme in South Africa. The pursuance of such a policy need not necessarily imply concession, but only consistency.

South Africa: Wanted a programme.

The Boer Republics themselves are not in accord with regard to their mutual interests or in their foreign relations. The Transvaal assumes a bullying attitude towards the Orange Free State. The latter, which is protected by a kind of British suzerainty, is prepared to entertain British proposals, but the former will have little or nothing to do with them. This divergence of feeling is the outcome of political events, for which we ourselves are in the main responsible. Our policy in South Africa, if it can be called a policy, has, notoriously, been characterised by being "too late;" but, in the case of the Transvaal, it was too precipitate. Had it been otherwise, the Transvaal at the present day might have been in the same position as its sister Republic, if not an actual British dependency. We have been consistent only in shirking responsibility, or acting in a half-hearted manner—in short, neglecting to perform our accepted duties towards the natives and the colonies themselves. But the position is not necessarily irretrievable. Indeed, one of the healthiest signs of the inauguration of a new era for South Africa is the recent

The Boer Republics.

appointment of Mr. Cecil Rhodes, an " Elizabethan "
Englishman, to the Premiership of Cape Colony.

In the Transvaal (South African Republic) there is growing up a British contingent, which, attracted in the first instance by gold-mining interests, now out-numbers the Boers in several large districts: it is a pacific British invasion, in fact. The time is not far distant, therefore, when this alien population of British subjects will demand, with justice, what is practically denied them at present— a share in the government of the country. <small>The Transvaal.</small>

The rapid development of the country is daily becoming more rapid. The conflict of customs' dues and freights has superseded the conflict between armed forces, and fiscal revolutions are producing a profound effect on the political situation. The universal cry appears to be: " Save us from Downing Street ! " It is therefore obvious that political action of some kind cannot be long delayed. A railway war is now raging in the Transvaal and surrounding regions, and races to reach the most coveted districts are taking place on all sides. <small>Tariffs.</small>

The charter granted to the British South Africa Company is, fortunately or unfortunately, very vague in its definition of territorial boundaries. But the Company stands in the van of progress in South Africa, and is not likely to let the grass grow under its feet. Its ideal aim, as is well known, is to effect a connection between the spheres of British influence in the Zambezi Valley and the Lakes region. It will altogether depend on the diplomacy of the Company and the support it receives from the British Government whether these aims be eventually realised. <small>British South Africa Company.</small>

To sum up: we observe, and have repeatedly seen in the course of this book, that the British Possessions in South Africa are by far the most valuable in the whole continent, and that there exist there organised political <small>British South Africa.</small>

forces which, properly utilised, should promote the rapid development of the country and its profitable use as a colony.

Imperial interests in South Africa.

Its future government and ownership are points we need scarcely discuss. Till quite recently events were making for Federation,—an united South Africa to some extent. That this union would be brought about by a *Zollverein* or some political confederation was vaguely felt. But with Mr. Cecil Rhodes at the helm and an awakened feeling of interest and responsibility in African affairs prevailing at the Foreign Office, there is room for hope that, instead of encouraging an independent or semi-independent confederacy we may retain South Africa as one of the most valuable possessions of the British Empire. Whatever may be the ultimate issue, Great Britain, as an Imperial Power, has one duty she cannot afford to neglect. Simons Bay and Table Bay must at all hazards be reserved as naval and military stations: consequently, a certain well-defined portion of the Cape must continue to remain under the direct control of the Home authorities, for the loss of those stations would imperil the safety of our Indian Empire.

Portugal on the East Coast.

Portuguese dominion over the Sofala and Mozambique Coasts is as unsubstantial as a shadow. Not only does it not extend for any distance into the Interior, but it is said to be restricted to the range of her guns at the few fortified places on the East Coast and on the Zambezi. The administration of the colony of Mozambique shows an annually increasing deficit. This deficit, if capitalised at 4 per cent., would represent a sum of over two million pounds sterling. Its foreign commerce is of less value than the turn-over of a small private firm, whilst British trade in the province is itself five times as great. The remarks already made on the administration of Portuguese colonies in general apply with double force to Mozambique. Efforts have been constantly made to cripple the foreign commerce entering by the Zambezi. Portugal, it is true, has been content to sit at the receipt of custom, but she has been too blind to her real interests to foster trade which she herself cannot create, and which might bring in a steady income to her empty coffers. Even by fixing prohibitive dues and interposing every imaginable kind of political obstacle, Portugal has been unable to stem the steady stream of British enterprise, which, entering the Interior by way of the Zambezi and Shiré Rivers, has finally established itself in Nyassa-land.

A British Protectorate having now been proclaimed over a portion of Nyassa-land and in the so-called Shiré Highlands, it remains to be seen what will be made of this region. It is essentially the sphere of the Scottish missions and trading companies, by whom it was originally opened up.* {British Nyassa-land.}

The Portuguese have long held posts on the Zambezi— at Zumbo, Tete, Sena, and in the Deltaic lands. Kilimani, on the Kwakwa, is the chief port; and there is a custom-house at the confluence of the Shiré. The line of communications between the Zambezi and the Lakes, extending more or less effectually to the northern end of Lake Tanganika, is, however, maintained by the British missionary and commercial stations, which are established at the most convenient localities. At various points these communications have of late been temporarily interrupted by Arab hostilities and political plots; but the restoration of order is only a question of time, and will doubtless be effected as soon as international difficulties have been finally adjusted.† {Portugal on the Lower Zambezi.}

The English mission on Lake Tanganika carries on the

---
* Over £400,000 has already been spent towards this end.
† The Anglo-Portuguese Convention (1890) requires formal ratification.

chain of settlements by which this valuable land-and-water route can eventually be controlled.

German East Africa.
On the Zanzibar Coast, for so long the exclusive field of British enterprise and influence, the German East Africa Company established itself in 1885–86, but only, after a brief period of maladministration, to be forcibly ejected by an Arab insurrection. A few months of German misrule resulted not only in the entire overthrow of the administration, but also in the total destruction of commerce and the paralysis of every European enterprise on the Coast and far inland within the German sphere of influence. Retaliations only embittered the natives still more against Europeans in general. The Company, on the verge of ruin, was eventually rescued from extinction through the intervention of the German Imperial Government. A Commissioner (Major Wissmann) was despatched to East Africa at the head of a small force. He at once laid siege to the coast towns held by the insurrectionists. Some degree of order was gradually established along the Coast and for a distance inland, though not without bloodshed. It remains to be seen what effect these military operations will have, and what kind of Phoenix administration will be raised on the ashes of the former one.

The extension of the German sphere of influence towards the Lakes, the western limit of which has now been definitely fixed, was both natural and inevitable. Emin Pacha, shortly after his arrival on the Coast in the train of Mr. Stanley, was promptly impressed into the German service; a hasty peace was patched up with the "rebels," and pacific overtures made to the Arab leaders: the obvious aim of such action being the fresh acquisition of territories in the Interior. We have yet to learn the outcome of this enterprise, the objective point of which would appear to be the shores of the Victoria Nyanza.

The British East Africa Company have been more fortu- British East Africa.
nate and adroit in the government of their territories.
In spite of the unsettled political conditions surrounding
them on all sides, they have up to the present made steady
progress, and have not been hampered by native disaffec-
tion of any kind. On the contrary, they have been well
received everywhere, mainly because their administration is
based on justice and common sense, and has been carried
out with a firm hand. Exploring expeditions are rapidly
opening up the country and founding commercial stations.
The recent extension of the Company's territories westwards
and northwards, by agreement with Germany, places the
trade of the Upper Nile within their sphere of operations.

As was set forth in their first prospectus, the Company,
being in possession of the valuable harbour of Mombaza,
relied on this natural outlet to the trade which gravitates
from the Upper Nile Territories. But unfortunately, owing
to the evacuation of the last Egyptian Equatorial Province
and to the civil war in Uganda, the extension of the Company's sphere inland suffered a severe check. Their ideal aim
would appear to be to build a railway from Mombaza to
the Victoria Nyanza, upon which steamers are to be placed;
but, until the countries bordering on the lake have been
pacified and brought under British influence, even the construction of such a railway would be of little avail, though,
trusting to the future, it has already been commenced.
The lawless and predatory Masai will also have to be
reckoned with. But as the success, if not the very existence, of the Company depends on the possession of the
Upper Nile territories, or at least on the monopoly of trade
in those regions, it is obvious that, unless deserted by the
British Government, the Company must eventually establish
their rule there. Ample scope for extension is left towards
the north.

Britain and Germany in East Africa.

Both the British and German spheres of influence on the East Coast are connected by regular steamship-communication with Europe. The trade of that region requires but little fostering care in order to attain to its former magnitude. The Banyans, if they can be kept from dabbling in the Slave Trade, will continue to prove valuable intermediaries between Europeans and natives. What would appear to be the most serious obstacle to the development of the region is the senseless jealousy between the German and British agents. There is ample scope for the energies of both, and there are well-defined limits to their ambitions, if only they would loyally recognise them; but their activities so far appear to have been directed to outwitting one another. The Germans, with an enterprising Government behind them, have in several cases encroached upon the rights of the British Company, whose support by the Home Government has been not only most uncertain, but also decidedly opportunist in character. Yet, the German and British Governments affect the friendliest mutual feeling, and pretend to recognise an identity of political aims in Africa. Considering all things, it is difficult to justify, or even excuse, German intrigue and diplomacy in East Africa: they have been unworthy of a great Power.

In view of this mutual attitude of hostility, it was with a deep sense of relief and gratitude that all who are concerned in the welfare of Africa heard of the recent Anglo-German Agreement. This equitable arrangement redounds to the credit of its negotiators. By it Great Britain, too, obtains —what few could have ventured to anticipate—a Protectorate over the islands of Zanzibar and Pemba.

The German colony of Vitu was by the same Agreement handed over to the British Company, thus securing to them the unity of their possessions, which is in every respect desirable. The Benadir ports on the Somali Coast, which were originally ceded by the Sultan of Zanzibar to the British East Africa Company, were subsequently placed under Italian protection. *Italy in Somaliland.*

Finally, over the large island of Madagascar France has eventually succeeded in establishing her Protectorate, which has now been recognised by Great Britain. Her first settlement on the island was erected some 250 years ago. *France in Madagascar.*

The European domination in Africa, even from what has so far been said of it, is obviously very unequal in extent and uncertain in kind. Except in the sub-Tropical portions of the continent, the climatic conditions of which are not actually hostile to European colonisation, political settlement has in fact been relatively ineffective. To administer and develop the interior lands of Tropical Africa requires such great sacrifice of life, and such an enormous outlay of capital, that European settlement has consequently been restricted to the coastal lands, except in those regions where local conditions have favoured the expansion of an enterprising colony. The quest for new markets and the somewhat illusory ambitions of empire have in a few cases partly overcome these adverse circumstances. Nevertheless, it is no exaggeration to say that, throughout the whole of Tropical Africa, effective occupation by the European Powers is recognisable only in the coastal lands, and for a relatively short distance up the great river valleys. In the strictly Tropical lands of the Interior effective occupation, if it be judged by the standards of other continents, cannot be said to exist, for the natives have pretty much their own way, and few Governments would be rash enough to guarantee the security of life and property. But it will be found that in most respects our standard of moral obligation in Africa is not a high one. It is, in fact, lower than *Limits to the European domination.*

almost anywhere else. We cannot therefore afford to be very exacting.

The European domination.

It is said, and said with truth, that Portugal has done very little to develop her African possessions, and in some cases has done practically nothing. But if we admit this we must also concede the analogy, that the other European Powers have accomplished very little more in their own possessions, except in the sub-Tropical portions of the continent.

Limitations to the development of African lands.

The inference to be drawn from these considerations is clearly this: Tropical Africa, for certain reasons, is unsuited to European colonisation. These reasons have, I trust, been accurately stated in the earlier chapters of this book; they are mainly of a physical nature. But though hostile physical conditions undoubtedly prevail, it has been contended that in the more favourable regions they are not insuperable: that it must be merely a question of time and of prudence for Europeans to eventually overcome them, in part or altogether. It is only by refusing to recognise the limitations that beset the development and colonisation of African lands that we are likely to be repulsed in the near future. These limitations are, of course, at present insufficiently known, and even when known they are rarely observed: experience has been for the most part the sole guide in Africa. But surely the time has arrived when it were more judicious to use a little foresight and circumspection rather than to go blundering on in the old haphazard style. The Powers of Europe are groping about in the darkness of Africa, and knocking their heads together in the most ridiculous fashion. More light is wanted; even the glimmer of a rushlight, such as this book may afford, were better than nothing, for at least it may make the darkness visible.

CHAPTER X.

POLITICAL PARTITION.

CAUSE AND EFFECT—METHODS—DEFINITIONS—THE BERLIN CONFERENCE OF 1884-85—TERRITORIAL BOUNDARIES IN AFRICA PRIOR TO THE CONFERENCE, AND THOSE SETTLED AT OR IMMEDIATELY AFTER THE CONFERENCE—PROGRESS OF THE PARTITION OF AFRICA—DIPLOMATIC NEGOTIATIONS, TREATIES, CONVENTIONS, ETC.—FIXED BOUNDARIES—UNDEFINED TERRITORIAL LIMITS.

MAP.

POLITICAL PARTITION *Plate* XIII.

POLITICAL PARTITION.

AFTER centuries of neglect, Africa has of recent years become the arena of European rivalries. Most of the European Powers have entered the lists, and are striving earnestly after political ascendancy. The general public have, in consequence, learnt more about that unhappy continent than at any previous time. And yet—and yet the British Premier humbly admitted that the Powers were forsooth dividing among themselves lands that had never been explored or were little known, and fixing boundaries the precise delimitation of which could not, in some cases, be made for many a long day. *The awakening of Africa.*

The moral to be drawn from the consideration of these facts is of a twofold character. In the first place, the value of African lands has been universally acknowledged; and, in the second place, the danger of collision between the Powers who have entered upon commercial campaigns, being at last recognised, has been averted, or is being averted, by defining the limits of their respective spheres of action. All true friends of Africa must have rejoiced on learning the terms of the various agreements and conventions which, during the summer that is past, were concluded between the Powers, more especially as they applied to some of the most valuable and hotly contested regions. The good-will thus shown by them in coming to an understanding between themselves, no less than the tact and ability with which the negotiations were conducted, appear to be among the most hopeful signs of better days for Africa. *The dawn of better days.*

The scramble for African lands.

The breathless scramble for African lands, in which all dignity, even diplomatic usages, have occasionally been laid aside, has resulted in the coinage or current use of at least two terms. It is necessary that we should understand them before entering further upon our theme.

"Sphere of Influence."

The first term is "sphere of influence." This is applied to certain regions set apart for the exclusive political action of the Power to whom they have been awarded, or to whom they have been recognised as belonging by incontestable right. It is as if two doctors were to agree between themselves to divide off a village, wherein no other doctors were practising, into districts for their respective operations. A better term than sphere of influence was that originally employed, and still used in Germany, namely, sphere of *interest*.

"Hinterland."

The other term would appear to be indefinable—I mean "Hinterland." Of the full force of its significance some of the Powers affect a child-like ignorance: according to them, it means "as much as one can get." But its legitimate application can never be misunderstood. "Hinterland" applies to the interior parts of the continent, which, geographically or politically, may be justly regarded as the extension or field of expansion of territorial possessions on the coast. Nevertheless, to illustrate the absurdity with which the Hinterland principle is either advanced or disregarded, we may cite the example of France, who, having entirely surrounded the British possessions on the Gambia at a short distance from the coast, gravely advanced the Hinterland theory as an apology for the extension of her political sway from the Mediterranean to the Niger.

Annexation by paint-brush.

The partition of Africa has proceeded so rapidly in the last few years that no sooner has a map been published than it has been out of date. We seem at last to have arrived at a stage when map-makers may be assured of a little more repose. Annexation by paint-brush marked only the incipient stage of the African fever, and serious politicians no longer regard such acquisitions as legitimate. Claimants have now to produce actual treaties made with the native potentates whose territories they propose to annex or protect. Such documents are, of course, easily obtainable; but they satisfy the public conscience: they afford indisputable evidence that a responsible person has been in the country in question.

Treaties with native chiefs.

In describing the various stages at which the continent of Africa within the last few years has been partitioned off among the European Powers, it is not my intention to define every boundary-line: I must trust to the map (Plate XIII.) showing this in detail. But it may serve a useful purpose to cite chapter and verse for every diplomatic transaction of importance.*

It is absolutely essential to distinguish between acquisitions by treaty† and acquisitions by paint-brush.‡ The vast area of Africa and the relative absence of natural frontiers—except on a very large scale—have in the main, apart from our comparative ignorance of the interior lands, rendered the determination of inland boundaries a matter of no little difficulty and uncertainty.

Inland boundaries.

---

* My data have been derived chiefly from the following sources:—*Le Partage Politique de l'Afrique* (June 1888), by Emile Banning, which gives in a convenient form the texts of the treaties and other international transactions and agreements between the years 1885 and 1888; from the two articles which, previous to the publication of M. Banning's book, were contributed by me to the *Scottish Geographical Magazine* (vol. iv., 1888, pp. 152 and 298) on *The Partition of Central Africa* and *The East Central African Question*; and from British and foreign official sources.

† Treaties vary also in their international significance. A distinction is to be observed between treaties binding the contracting parties alone and treaties binding non-contracting parties whose concurrence has been obtained.

‡ "Acquisition by paint-brush" simply indicates the ambition of territorial extension, and, like the "confidence trick," was only practised by desperate characters.

DEVELOPMENT OF AFRICA.

The partition of Africa.

The partition of Africa may be said to date from the Berlin Conference of 1884–85. Prior to that Conference the question of inland boundaries was scarcely considered: the necessity for such had hardly arisen. But the frontiers between the possessions of European Powers on the coasts had in a majority of cases been defined with some degree of certainty.

Awards at the Berlin Conference, 1884-85.

Outstanding disputes were settled at or shortly after the Conference. Only two instances need be given. Portugal received some recognition of her historical pretensions south of the Lower Congo, and also obtained the *enclave* of Kabinda, to the north. To France was awarded an important accession of territory on the Lower Congo. The basins of the Niger and Congo were declared free to the flags of all nations. And, finally, the International Association, founded by the King of the Belgians, was, under its new title, recognised by the civilised world as a sovereign State, and took possession of the conventional basin of the Congo.

Founding of the Congo Independent State.

The founding of the Congo Independent State was probably the most important result of the Conference, apart from the excellent enactments that were drawn up in regard to the development of Africa as a field for European commercial and philanthropic enterprises. The formal recognition of the Congo Independent State by the Powers, its delimitation and neutralisation, and the creation of an immense free-trade * area, were undoubtedly events of the highest importance; for, in the heart of Africa, there was thus created a neutral "Mediterranean" State, the progress of which was, and always must be, intimately associated with the interests of its neighbours.

The boundaries of the Congo Independent State are

---

* Differential duties are, nevertheless, enforced within this zone. Moreover, the Congo State, by the consent of the Powers at the Brussels Conference (1889-90), will itself impose direct taxation in order to carry out the enactments of the *General Act*.

shown on our map. They were roughly defined at the *Boundaries of the Congo State.* Berlin Conference, but their more accurate delimitation was adjusted by separate treaties concluded with contiguous States. Some uncertainty still exists as to the precise boundaries at certain points, but, when the occasion demands, these uncertainties can easily be cleared up. The title-deeds of the State are clearly and, I believe, accurately given in M. Banning's *Partage Politique de l'Afrique* (pp. 89-152).

Two months after the Conference had concluded its labours, Great Britain and Germany had a serious dispute in regard to their respective spheres of influence on the Gulf of Guinea. *Dispute between Britain and Germany.*

The basin of the Lower Niger had long been under the exclusive influence of Great Britain, who possessed also colonies to the west of it. In the Camarons region British missionaries had for forty years laboured in a promising field, and, incidentally, had sown the seed of British sovereignty. But Germany also shared the ambition of occupying a country which her subjects had assisted in discovering and opening up. Her merchants were said to enjoy the monopoly of trade on the Camarons River. The Imperial German Government, therefore, decided to take possession of the country and to establish a naval station on the Coast. *Argument.*

Prince Bismarck, although not a " colonial man," assumed a resolute attitude. In those days, when Prince Bismarck resolved to pursue a definite course, his object was as good as accomplished. Dr. Nachtigal was dispatched with instructions (dated 19th May 1884) to conclude treaties with the native chiefs between the Niger and Gabún and in the district of Angra Pequeña. Britain, with similar objects in view, also issued instructions (16th May 1884) to Admiral Hewett. But Dr. Nachtigal was the first to arrive on the scene of action. The German flag was hoisted (5th July) at Togo and (14th July) at Camarons. Admiral *Action.*

Hewett arrived on 19th July, in time to register his protest.

"Too late." This is how things were done in the good old days. The hesitation of the British Cabinet, which had been discussing the question from October 1883, was the apparent cause of Admiral Hewett being "too late."

Triumph of Germany. On 13th October 1884, Prince Bismarck notified to the Powers the *fait accompli* of a German Protectorate, not only in the Camarons but also at Togo (Slave Coast) and in South-West Africa, between the Orange River and Cape Frio,—Walvisch Bay excepted.

British reprisals. The British Cabinet bowed to its fate, but endeavoured to retrieve its position. On 19th July Admiral Hewett placed the Mission Station at Victoria under British protection and concluded treaties (July to September) with the native chiefs on the littoral between Victoria and Old Calabar.

Results. This action on the part of Admiral Hewett was displeasing to the Iron Chancellor, who expressed his views very clearly and forcibly in his note of 7th December 1884. To add to the complication of affairs, the natives of the contested regions rose against the German Occupation and attacked the Europeans. The revolt was, however, promptly suppressed (20th to 22nd December) by German gunboats.

Diplomatic negotiations. Diplomatic documents were freely exchanged between London and Berlin during the next few months. The most important were Lord Granville's despatch (29th April 1885) to Count Münster, the German Ambassador at the Court of St. James's, and the reply (7th May) of the latter. These despatches laid the basis of an accord between the two Powers, and were supplemented by the Declarations of 16th May and 2nd June.

A compromise. The compromise thus arrived at placed the Mission Station of Victoria within the German sphere of influence, in consideration of an indemnity (£4000) to be paid to the English Baptists by the Basel Missions.

But the frontier between the two spheres of influence on the Bight of Biafra remained undefined. Despatches were exchanged between Lord Rosebery (27th July 1886), on the part of the British Government, and Count Hatzfeld (2nd August), on behalf of the German Government, which resulted in a line being drawn from the Coast to Yola, on the Benué. *The Anglo-German frontier.*

On the 10th July 1886, the National African Company received a royal charter under its new title of the Royal Niger Company, and was given administrative powers over the territories covered by its treaties. The regions thereby placed under British protection are defined on our map. Apart from the Oil Rivers District, which is directly administered by the Crown, they embrace the coastal lands between Lagos and the northern frontier of German Camarons, the Lower Niger (including the territories of Sokoto and Gandu), and the Benué from Yola to its confluence. *Royal Niger Company.*

Germany, having settled the northern boundary of her Camarons colony, was in the meantime negotiating its southern frontier with the French Congo. Dr. Nachtigal's treaties extended almost to the Equator and overlapped French claims. Prince Bismarck, however, in his despatch of 13th September 1884, showed himself accommodating to French susceptibilities, and was met in an equally diplomatic spirit by Baron de Conrcel (despatch of 29th September). All danger of friction being thereby removed, France and Germany eventually signed the Protocol of 24th December 1885, which defined their respective spheres of influence and action on the Bight of Biafra, and also on the Slave Coast and in Senegambia. *Germany and France.*

This Convention between Germany and France fixed the inland extension of the German sphere of influence (Cama-

A provision of the Franco-German Convention, 1885.

rons) at 15° E. longitude, Greenwich. It is important to remember this, because at present it allows the French Congo Territories to expand along the western bank of the M'bangi,* which is their conterminous boundary with the Congo Independent State, and gives access to the Súdan.

France and Portugal.

France at about the same time was engaged in adjusting certain territorial difficulties with Portugal. A Mixed Commission, having assembled at Paris, held sixteen sittings between 22nd October 1885 and 12th May 1886. The deliberations of the Commission resulted in the Franco-Portuguese Convention of 12th May 1886. France thereby secured the exclusive control of both banks of the Casamanza (in Senegambia), and the Portuguese frontier in the south was advanced approximately to the southern limit of the basin of the Casini. On the Congo, Portugal retained the Massabi district, to which France had laid claim, but both banks of the Loango were left to France.

Mutual accommodation schemes.

An attempt at mutual accommodation was made in regard to certain schemes of aggrandisement which, at the same time, were interesting to third parties. Portugal recognised a French Protectorate over Futa Jallon,† thus consenting to her own possessions in Upper Guinea being surrounded, and admitting France dangerously near to the British "Hinterland" behind Sierra Leone. In return, France was prevailed upon to make a qualified admission of the right of Portugal to exercise her "sovereign influence and civilisation"—whatever those may be—in the countries separating the provinces of Angóla and Mozambique. Such a concession, however, incidentally affected the interests

---

* Provided no other tributary of the M'bangi-Congo is found to the west, in which case, according to the Berlin Treaty of 1884-85, the conventional basin of the Congo would gain an extension.

† By virtue of treaties concluded in 1881 between the French Government and the Almamy.

of Great Britain and the Congo Independent State. But
the modesty of the Lisbon Cabinet was not to be suppressed. In a note of 12th December 1885, Portugal
defined the extent of the Trans-Continental empire to which
she laid claim. A more flagrant instance of "annexation
by paint-brush" never occurred, even in Africa. France,
however, proved herself equal to the occasion, and at the
same time displayed her humour of the situation: she
accepted the limits, as defined, "*à titre d'information*,"
but attached a rider reserving the rights of third parties.
Portugal, nothing daunted by this reservation on the part
of France, which she was unable to overcome, next proceeded to "try it on" with Germany, with results that will
be subsequently mentioned. The negotiations, having the
same object, with her historic ally, Great Britain, were of
an even more animated and interesting character. They
were provisionally settled only in August last,—so that we
may be permitted to refer to them in another place.

While map-makers were busy keeping pace with political changes on the West Coast of Africa, their attention was equally demanded by events on the East Coast. East Coast.

Germany, having entered upon a colonial career, and being fired with the ambition of founding an African empire, gave every encouragement and support to her pioneers. Germans at home argued to themselves that, as their compatriots were spread all over the world, engaged in developing colonies for others, they might just as well, whilst there was time, secure a few colonies for themselves. Consequently, the continent of Africa, being a promising and open field, was simultaneously attacked at three points. Their methods of territorial acquisition were of the most approved modern style, in which flags, chartered companies, and gunboats played conspicuous parts. And it should be added that, whilst German agents received the support of their Govern- The expansion of German Africa.

Binding the British Lion.

ment, British agents were put under restraint and bound fast with "red-tape."

German Argonauts.

In September 1884 there landed at Zanzibar three innocent German excursionists, whose names will long be remembered by their countrymen. They were Dr. Peters (the "Jason" of the expedition), Dr. Jühlke, and Count Pfeil. It was hardly presumed that they had come to Zanzibar for the benefit of their health, for there are healthier places than Zanzibar nearer to Berlin. But being discreet and resolute men, and the pioneers of a Colonisation Company, they kept their own counsel, and, before any one was made aware of their intentions, treaties had been concluded with the chiefs of Useguha, Ukami, Nguru, and Usagara, by which those territories were "acquired" by the Society for German Colonisation.

Zanzibar and Great Britain.

Incidentally it may be mentioned that, prior to 1884, the continental lands facing Zanzibar were almost exclusively under British influence.* The principal traders were British subjects, and the Sultan's Government was administered under the advice of the British Resident. The entire region between the Coast and the Lakes was regarded as being under the nominal suzerainty of the Sultan: the various chiefs acknowledged his claims to a certain extent, and his aid was invariably invoked if any European travellers fell into trouble. Still, Great Britain had no territorial claims on the dominions of the Sultan. Though her influence was felt far and wide, it had been exercised solely in the cause of law and order, and with no ulterior object whatever.

Proclamation of a German Protectorate.

Dr. Peters, then, armed with his treaties, returned to Berlin in February 1885. On the 27th February, the day following the signature of the *General Act* of the Berlin

---

* In spite of the Anglo-French Convention of 10th March 1862, regarding the nominal independence of Zanzibar.

Conference, an Imperial *Schutzbrief*, or Charter of Protection, secured to the Society for German Colonisation the territories which had been acquired for them through Dr. Peters' treaties: in other words, a German Protectorate was proclaimed.

When it became known that Germany had seized upon the Zanzibar mainland, the indignation in colonial circles knew no bounds. The British Foreign Office championed the cause of the Sultan, and his Highness himself made a formal protest. But it was useless to invoke shadows. The iron hand of Germany was exposed; its velvet glove was boldly discarded. A German fleet was promptly despatched to Zanzibar, in order, as a German periodical explained, "to show clearly the meaning of an Imperial *Schutzbrief*." It was the first *Schutzbrief* that had been issued; consequently, it was reasonable to infer that its meaning was not clearly comprehended. *Protests.*

It appeared that an Imperial *Schutzbrief*, unlike some diplomatic documents, really meant what it said. Now the *Schutzbrief* in question had referred to certain regions in East Africa over which a German Protectorate had been proclaimed; and it was obviously absurd—even dangerous —to affect any misunderstanding in the matter. It was, therefore, not to be wondered at that Sir John Kirk received instructions to fall in with the views of his German colleague at Zanzibar, "where the interests of the two countries were identical,"—though, by the light of subsequent events, we shall see how little identical those interests really were. *Meaning of an Imperial Schutzbrief.*

Thus it came to pass that Great Britain, weary of her mission, resigned it in favour of Germany. But, in bequeathing the results of many years' labour, she recommended to the favourable consideration of Germany certain British subjects, capitalists, who had conceived the plan of *British bequests.*

T

creating a British establishment—quite a modest one, of course—in the region situated between the Coast and the lake-reservoirs of the Nile, through which it was hoped to run a railway some fine day.

Apology. In reviewing the political situation at this point of our narrative, I have quite unconsciously fallen into a tone of irony unsuited to the serious character of my task. But, upon my word, the style appears to me to suit the subject, for a more unconventional way of acquiring colonies has never been known to this century.

Submission of the Sultan of Zanzibar. Abandoned by his former protector and threatened by a hostile fleet, the Sultan of Zanzibar bowed to the will of Allah. He recognised (14th August 1885) the German Protectorate over the four inland provinces and over Vitu.

The Anglo-German Convention of 1886. Thereupon, a Delimitation Commission was appointed to apportion the spoil. But it was not until the end of October 1886 that the British and German Governments were in a position to exchange identic notes. This exchange of identic notes, commonly designated as the Anglo-German Convention of 1886, had the following for its main provisions:—(1.) The sovereignty of the Sultan of Zanzibar was recognised over the islands of Zanzibar, Pemba, Lamu, and Mafia; as also, on the mainland, (*a*) over an uninterrupted coastal zone, ten nautical miles in breadth, between— roughly—Tunghi Bay and Kipini, and (*b*) over the stations of Kismayu, Barawa, Merka, Mukhdisho, and Warsheikh, each with a small land-circuit. (2.) The countries within which the provisions of the treaty were regarded as applicable were defined as being situated between the Tana and Rovuma Rivers; and the frontier between the British and German spheres of influence was drawn, as shown on our map, from the Wanga or Umbe River to the Victoria Nyanza. (3.) Great Britain entered into an engagement to make no territorial acquisitions, to accept no Protectorates,

and not to compete with the spread of German influence to
the south of the said line, whilst Germany undertook to
observe a similar abstinence in the territories to the north
of the said line. (4.) Both Powers recognised as belonging
to Vitu the coast stretching from the north of Kipini to the
north end of Manda Bay. And (5.), Germany became a
party to the Protocol signed by Britain and France (10th
March 1862) recognising the independence of Zanzibar.

It is to be observed that in this Agreement no internal
boundaries were fixed, nor was the extension of the Anglo-
German frontier and the German-Portuguese frontier, in
the same or in any direction, even alluded to.

By separate arrangements with the Sultan of Zanzibar, *Lease of customs in Coastal zone.*
Germany secured (20th December 1885) the lease for a
period of fifty years of the customs in the coastal zone
belonging to the Sultan within the German sphere of
influence, whilst Britain obtained (30th April 1886) a
similar concession in her zone.

On 8th December 1886 the Sultan gave in his adhesion *Adhesion of third parties.*
to the General Act of the Berlin Conference, reserving to
himself the principle of commercial liberty. The same day
France recognised the Anglo-German Convention.

The German eagle thus became a full-fledged bird of *The German East Africa Association.*
prey in Africa, and it was instructive to witness the manner
in which it first used its wings. Not contented with a
modest flight into space, it essayed to soar, but, being an
inexperienced colonial bird, it fell heavily to the earth.
This unfortunate mishap may be briefly alluded to.

After receiving the *Schutzbrief*, the Society for German
Colonisation transferred (April 1887) their rights to the
newly-founded German East Africa Association, at whose
head stood Dr. Peters. Expedition after expedition was
despatched by the Association to make fresh acquisitions of
territory. Relations were also opened up with some of the

East Coast.

Somâl tribes; and Dr. Peters himself headed a large expedition into East Africa.

In view of these active operations, German map-makers coloured as German the entire *Hinterland* between the Coast and the confines of the Congo Independent State. Obviously this was going too far, and such unfounded claims were never recognised by responsible persons; but they are mentioned here as an example.

The same precipitate haste characterised the conduct of German agents in taking over the administration of their actual sphere of influence: they wished at once to transform the ancient home of Arabs and Negroes into a German colony. Their high-handed action in this respect led to the inevitable result of a general rising. Massacres and retaliations ensued. The Arab chiefs on the Coast, who resented the action of their suzerain, the Sultan of Zanzibar, in transferring their allegiance to Germany, took up arms against their common enemy, the usurper. In a few months not a German was left in the mainland districts; all had fled to Zanzibar.

Arab revolt.

When affairs had reached this crisis, the Imperial German Government interfered. Gunboats were despatched; and a special Commissioner, Lieutenant (now Major) Wissmann, set out at the head of a small military force. The rebels were driven from their positions and the coast towns were re-occupied. After months of desultory fighting, something like law and order were finally introduced. But in the achievement of this end all trade was paralysed for a time, and the Europeans in the Interior, behind the German sphere, were in imminent danger of their lives.

These details of the miscarriage of German attempts at colonisation are given mainly for the purpose of illustrating the fact that the art of governing native tribes and territories is not learnt in a day. We ourselves, a veteran

colonial power, have experienced reverses of a similar kind.
Had Germany respected native prejudices and customs, and
been less overbearing and less precipitate, her rule might
have been welcomed in East Africa. But when we hear
of German petty officers, "booted and spurred," strutting
into Arab mosques, followed by their dogs, we cannot wonder
at Arab susceptibilities being aroused.

As a contrast to this tragic picture of German East Africa, we may point with satisfaction to the course of events in British East Africa. Although that region lay in the path of the wave of unrest that swept along the Coast, its calm was unbroken by the sound of hostile elements. The British East Africa Company, having taken over the concessions granted by the Sultan of Zanzibar to Sir William Mackinnon, assumed the administration of the territories with the good-will of the natives. The Company was not formally incorporated until 18th April 1888, and on the 3rd of September it received a royal charter. One of its first public acts was to liberate a large number of slaves at a considerable cost. Caravans were despatched into the Interior, and the machinery of local administration was promptly and unostentatiously erected. Being a record of successful effort, we have little to say of the founding of British East Africa. The British East Africa Company.

We shall have occasion to return to East Africa further on in our narrative. In order to preserve as far as possible the chronology of events, we must now refer to the progress of German colonial enterprise in South-West Africa. South West Coast.

Undeterred by the fact that the natural and widely known desire of Cape Colony was to expand northwards to the Zambezi, and that since 1878 Walvisch Bay had with that object been occupied as a British naval station, an enterprising Bremen merchant, Herr Lüderitz, and subse- German action.

quently the German Consul-General, Dr. Nachtigal, concluded a series of political and commercial treaties with native chiefs, whereby a claim was instituted over Angra Pequeña, and over vast districts in the Interior between the Orange River and Cape Frio. It was useless for the Cape colonists to protest: the will of the Iron Chancellor was not to be moved, far less moulded to the desires of Cape politicians. On 7th August 1884 the German flag was hoisted at Angra Pequeña, after the "submission" of the British Foreign Office had been received.

<small>Acquisition of Angra Pequeña.</small>

For the third occasion within a brief space of time Germany had thus dispossessed Great Britain in Africa.

<small>German Protectorate over South-West Africa.</small>

On the 13th October 1884 Germany formally notified to the Powers her Protectorate over South-West Africa. A Mixed Commission met at the Cape (14th March to 4th September 1885) to adjust rival claims. Its duty was not to define territorial limits; but Her Majesty's Government permitted it to be understood that the British Protectorate over Bechuana-land extended in the north to 22° S. latitude, and in the west to 20° E. longitude.

<small>Expansion.</small>

The chief inland boundaries being thereby defined, Germany had no further room for expansion except on the coast between Cape Frio and the mouth of the Kunéné: and this tract of country she promptly seized. On 3rd August 1885 the German Colonial Company for South-West Africa was founded, and, after the lapse of ten days, received the Imperial sanction for its incorporation. But in August 1886 a new Association was formed—the German West Africa Company—and the administration of its territories was placed under an Imperial Commissioner.

<small>Germany and Portugal.</small>

By extending her coast-line in South-West Africa from Cape Frio to the Kunéné, Germany encroached upon Portuguese claims. On the East and West Coasts of Africa Germany had become a neighbour of Portugal; so that a precise delimitation of their frontiers was in any case necessary. Portugal claimed Cape Frio as the southern limit of her province of Angóla, whilst Germany advanced her claims up to the banks of the Kunéné in order to incorporate the whole of Ovampo-land, over which she had secured certain rights. The dispute between the two Powers dragged on for six months.

In the meantime, the Franco-Portuguese Commission was sitting at Paris. On the 27th July 1886, Baron Schmidthals proposed as the Portuguese frontier the River Kunéné, with an extension eastwards to the Zambezi, on the parallel of Humbe.* Then it was that Portugal endeavoured to extract from Germany, what she had partially succeeded in obtaining from France, a recognition of her claims to a Trans-Continental empire. Germany, however, was not prepared to go to the length required of her. She simply declared that the River Rovuma formed the southern boundary of her East African Possessions. Portugal then consented to the Kunéné serving as the southern boundary of her Angóla province, and adopted the latitudinal line previously laid down to the Kubango; its extension eastwards was traced by the course of the latter river up to the neighbourhood of Andara, whence it was projected to, and in the same latitude as, Katima.† *Negotiations.*

Portugal also approved of the River Rovuma, up to the confluence of the M'sinje, forming the German-Portuguese frontier in East Africa, and went so far as to obligingly prolong this boundary-line westwards, on the same latitude, across the Nyassa to the "confines of Angóla." But realising the danger of being thus entrapped, Germany modestly accepted Lake Nyassa as the western limit of the conterminous frontier, thereby gaining from Portugal a slight *German-Portuguese frontier in East Africa.*

* Near which, on the Kunéné, rapids occur.
† On the Zambezi, where there are rapids.

extension of boundary that was not recognised by the Anglo-German Agreement of 1886.

German-Portuguese Convention, 1886. On the basis of this mutual understanding, Germany and Portugal affixed their seals to the Convention signed at Lisbon on 30th December 1886.

Thus we have seen that both Germany and France refused to recognise Portuguese claims to a Trans-Continental empire irrespective of the rights of third parties. The third party in this matter was Great Britain, to whose case we may now refer.

Expansion of British South Africa. The intrusion of Germany into South-West Africa acted as a check upon, no less than a spur to, the extension of British influence northwards to the Zambezi. Another obstacle to this extension arose from the Boer insurrection. The treaty of 3rd August 1881 gave autonomy to the Transvaal, under British sovereignty; but these bonds were slackened by the treaty of 27th February 1884. The Transvaal, with increased independence, then adopted the proud title of South African Republic; although, in regard to its foreign relations—the Orange Free State excepted—and dealings with native tribes, the Republic undertook to submit any treaties or engagements for the approbation of Her Majesty's Government.

Zulu-land, having lost its independence, was partitioned: a third of its territories, over which a republic had been proclaimed, was absorbed (October 1887) by the Transvaal; the remainder was added (14th May 1887) to the British possessions. Amatonga-land was in 1888 also taken under British protection.*

Bechuanaland. By a Convention with the South African Republic, Britain acquired in 1884 the Crown colony of Bechuana-land; and in the early part of 1885 a British Protectorate was proclaimed over the remaining portion of Bechuana-land—the

* Treaty with Zambili, similar in kind to that with Lobengula.

western and provisional northern limits of which have already been defined by us. Sir Charles Warren, after subduing the infant Republics of Stella and Goshen, and placing the country up to the River Molopo under British sovereignty, had established a provisional protectorate over Khama's country. At that time, by an agreement between Britain and Germany (January 1885), it was understood that the 20th degree of east longitude should mark the Anglo-German frontier; but this boundary extended north only to the 22nd degree of south latitude. To the south of this latitudinal boundary lay the British Protectorate; to the north of it all was unsettled. The South African Republic, with the intention of stealing a march upon Great Britain, despatched a mission to Lobengula, King of Matabele-land, &c., but its object was frustrated by the prompt action of Mr. Moffat, who, acting under instructions from the Home Government, concluded a treaty of amity between Britain and Lobengula. Similar treaties having been concluded with Khama, chief of the Bamangwato, and Moremi, a chief of N'gami-land, a British Protectorate was instituted over the country bounded by the Zambezi in the north, the British Possessions in the south, "the Portuguese province of Sofala" in the east, and the 20th degree of east longitude in the west. It was at this juncture that Mr. Cecil Rhodes came forward, and, having obtained certain concessions from Lobengula, founded the British South Africa Company. *Matabeleland, &c.*

Founding of the British South Africa Company.

For some time both before and after the declaration of a British Protectorate south of the Zambezi, Portugal endeavoured to substantiate through every means in her power the shadowy claims she possessed over Mashuna-land, to portions of the Zambezi basin, to Nyassa-land and the Shiré Highlands. Into the validity of these claims we need not enter at any length; it is necessary only to record the fact *The case between Britain and Portugal.*

that they have been disallowed by competent authorities. In no case were they based upon occupation; and Her Majesty's Government protested * against any claims in no degree founded on occupation, and stated that they could not recognise the sovereignty of Portugal in territories where she was represented by no authority capable of exercising the ordinary rights of sovereignty. In similar terms the protest was renewed † by Lord Salisbury on 21st November 1889. His Lordship at the same time recalled the agreement between Great Britain and Lobengula (11th February 1888), which recorded the fact that Lobengula was the ruler of Mashuna-land and Makalaka-land.

British South Africa Company.

On the 29th October 1889 the British South Africa Company was granted a royal charter. It was declared in this charter that "the principal field of the operations of the British South Africa Company shall be the region of South Africa ‡ lying immediately to the north of British Bechuana-land, and to the north and west of the South African Republic, and to the west of the Portuguese dominions."

It will be observed that no northern limit was given, and the other boundaries were only vaguely defined; but they were sufficient to serve the purpose in view. The British South Africa Company entered boldly upon its career, and the most encouraging reports have since been received of its activity and enterprise.

Swaziland.

The position of Swazi-land was definitely settled, after a great deal of public discussion, by the arrangement between Great Britain and the South African Republic, which was accepted by the Volksraad on 8th August 1890. This Con-

* Memorandum from Lord Salisbury to Senhor Barros Gomes, 13th August 1887.
† Despatch from Lord Salisbury addressed to the British Minister at Lisbon.
‡ The "District of Tati" excepted.

vention provides for the continued independence of Swaziland* and a joint-control over the white settlers. The Republic is to be permitted to realise its long-cherished desire of building a railway of its own through Swazi-land to the sea (at or near Kosi Bay), provided that, within a period of six months from the date of the Convention, it enters into the existing customs' union with Cape Colony, the Orange Free State, and Bechuana-land.

Mention has been made of the further claim of Portugal to Nyassa-land and the Shiré Highlands, countries that for over thirty years have been the exclusive sphere of British missionary and commercial enterprise. In a paper published by me in the *Scottish Geographical Magazine* (vol. iv., p. 298), I discussed at some length the question at issue between Great Britain and Portugal. As the problem has now received a more or less definite solution, it seems unnecessary here to revert to it. The discussion of claims on either side dragged on for several years, and was varied by local disturbances and other unpleasant incidents. The British Foreign Office was at first indisposed to back British claims with any material support; but the storm of indignation thereby raised in Scotland, and subsequently in England, induced—if I may permit myself that expression—the Foreign Secretary to reconsider the case. Nothing, however, could have been more loyal, more statesman-like, than the manner in which Lord Salisbury subsequently championed the cause of British enterprise in general, and of the Scottish missions and trading companies in particular. The result, it may be remembered, was that a British Protectorate was proclaimed over Nyassa-land and the Shiré Highlands in 1889-90.†

The course of events in these parts of Africa have so

Nyassa-land and the Shiré Highlands.

---

* As recognised by the Convention of 1884.
† Consul Johnston's Protectorate-treaties, and most of the others, were concluded between August and January 1889-90. But further treaties were

European transactions with natives. far engaged our attention that we have omitted to mention several important engagements made between the European Powers and native chiefs in other parts of the continent.

Italy on the Red Sea Littoral. Italy, enjoying the sympathy and support of Great Britain, has eventually succeeded in extending her sway over what may prove to be a valuable African empire. On 5th July 1882, Italy took formal possession of the bay and territory of Assab. The Italian coast-line on the Red Sea now extends from Ras Kasar (18° 2′ N. lat.) to the southern boundary of Raheita,* towards Obok. During 1889, shortly after the death of King Johannes, Keren and Asmara were occupied by Italian troops. Menelik of Shoa, who succeeded to the throne of Abyssinia, after subjugating all the Abyssinian provinces except Tigré, despatched an embassy to King Humbert, the result of which was that the new Negus acknowledged (29th September 1889) the Protectorate of Italy over Abyssinia, and its sovereignty over the territories of Massawa, Keren, and Asmara.† The Italian possessions on the Red Sea subsequently received the name of "Eritrea."

Italy on the Somál Coast. Italy has also succeeded in establishing herself on the Somál Coast. By treaties concluded (8th February 1889) with the Sultan of Obbia, who belongs to the powerful Mijarten tribe, and (April 7th) with the Sultan of the Mijarten himself, the coastal lands between Cape Warsheikh (about 2° 30′ N. lat.) and Cape Bedwin (8° 3′ N. lat.) —a distance of 450 miles—were placed under Italian protection. Italy subsequently extended (1890) her Protectorate over the Somál Coast to the Jub River, by taking

---

made (1) with all the chiefs of the west, south, and north coasts of Nyassa, (2) along the Stevenson Road, (3) on the south and south-west coasts of Tanganika, and (4) inland, round Bangweolo and Moëro.

* This boundary has not yet been defined.

† The treaty thus concluded was similar in kind to the French treaty with the Hova Government in Madagascar. Frontiers were provisionally settled.

over the ports of Kismayu, Barawa, Merka, Mukhdisho, and Warsheikh, which the British East Africa Company had secured (in addition to Lamu, Manda, and Patta, which the Company retained) through a concession from the Sultan of Zanzibar.*

The British Protectorate on the Somáli Coast facing Aden now extends from the Italian frontier at Ras Hafún to Ras Jibuté (43° 15′ E. long.). The island of Sokotra, which was originally acquired by treaty in 1876, was formally annexed in 1886. Britain on the Somáli Coast.

In regard to the West Coast of Africa, we have still one or two territorial arrangements to notice. The activity of France in her Senegambian province, which, during the last hundred years, has been marked by notable success, has finally resulted in a considerable expansion of her territories. The native chiefs, one after another, have been forced to submit to the French ascendancy. Captain Binger, by the treaties he concluded with native chiefs during 1887–89, advanced the French sphere of influence down to the Ivory Coast. Thus, the French have established a claim over the country intervening between our Gold Coast Colony and Liberia. A more precise delimitation of the frontier between Sierra Leone and Liberia resulted from the treaty signed at Monrovia on 11th November 1887. France on the West Coast.

In 1888 Portugal withdrew all rights over Dahomé, her possessions on the Slave Coast having been restricted to the insignificant post of Ajuda, a factory at Whydah. Portugal and Dahome.

Between Cape Blanco, which is regarded as the northern coastal limit of Senegambia, and Cape Bojador, Spain has been endeavouring since 1885 to secure her hold on the Saharan Coast as a *pied à terre* on the African mainland The Western Sahara: Spanish and British enterprise.

---

* The concession was originally made by Said Barghash and was renewed by Said Khalifa. It was disputed by Germany; but, the case being referred to the arbitration of Baron Lambermont, the British Company was awarded its rights. Subsequent disputes delayed the concession being effected.

for the Canary Islanders; whilst an English company has obtained treaty-rights, by which a claim has been instituted over the remaining coast-line between Cape Bojador and the frontier of Morocco.

<small>Anglo-French Agreement, 1890.</small>

These claims to the Littoral of the Sahara will require some adjustment; for, quite recently, a French sphere of influence has been instituted over the whole of the Saharan regions between Algeria and Senegambia. This proclamation resulted from negotiations with Great Britain. By the recent Anglo-German Agreement—to which we shall presently refer—no account had been taken by the Contracting Powers of the old Anglo-French Agreement (1862) respecting the independence of Zanzibar. Utilising this omission as a lever, France very shrewdly negotiated her interests in other parts of Africa, where the complaisance of Great Britain was necessary. Declarations were exchanged * between the two Governments, with the following results:—(1.) France became a consenting party to the Anglo-German Convention of 1st July 1890. (2.) Great Britain recognised the French Protectorate over the island of Madagascar. This island, which had long been the theatre of colonial rivalry between France and Britain, had been placed under French protection by the treaty of 17th December 1885 (which had practically secured the sovereign rights of France), but it had never been formally recognised by Britain. And (3.) Great Britain recognised "the sphere of influence of France to the south of her Mediterranean possessions, up to a line from Say on the Niger to Barrua on Lake Tsad, drawn in such a manner as to comprise in the sphere of action of the British Niger Company all that fairly belongs to the kingdom of Sokoto; the line to be determined by the commissioners to be appointed."

* The Anglo-French Agreement, signed at London, 5th August 1890. *Parliamentary Paper: Africa*, No. 9, 1890.

France thus obtained the formal recognition of the unity of her empire in North-West Africa, which she has been so long planning to effect by railway schemes; and, when the time comes for partitioning Morocco, she will be in the position of the dominant European Power in that region. But perhaps the horizon of the British Foreign Office does not extend as far as Morocco.

France the dominant Power in North-West Africa.

Of even greater importance than the above arrangement with France was the Anglo-German Agreement of July 1890. This Convention attempted to adjust the outstanding rival claims of Great Britain and Germany in Africa. The arrangement was an equitable one and a diplomatic triumph to its negotiators. The following were the main provisions, which have been given effect to on our map (Plate XIII.):—

Anglo-German Convention, 1890.

(1.) The Anglo-German frontier in East Africa, which, by the Convention of 1886, ended at a point on the eastern shore of the Victoria Nyanza, was continued on the same latitude across the lake to the confines of the Congo Independent State; but, on the western side of the lake, this frontier is, if necessary, to be deflected to the south, in order to include Mount M'fumbiro within the British sphere.* (2.) The southern boundary of the German sphere of influence in East Africa was recognised as that originally drawn † to a point on the eastern shore of Lake Nyassa, whence it was continued by the eastern, northern, and western shores of the lake to the northern bank of the mouth of the River Songwé. From this point the Anglo-German frontier was continued to Lake Tanganika, in such a manner as to leave the Stevenson Road within the British sphere. (3.) The northern frontier of British East Africa was defined by the Jub River and

---

* Treaties in that district were made on behalf of the British East Africa Company by Mr. Stanley, on his return (May 1889) from the relief of Emin Pacha.

† Anglo-German Convention, 1886, and German-Portuguese Convention, 1886.

Anglo-German Convention 1890.
the conterminous boundary of the Italian sphere of influence in Galla-land and Abyssinia up to the confines of Egypt; in the west, by the Congo State and the Congo-Nile watershed. (4.) Germany withdrew, in favour of Britain, her Protectorate over Vitu and her claims to all territories on the mainland to the north of the River Tana, as also over the islands of Patta and Manda. (5.) In South-West Africa, the Anglo-German frontier originally fixed up to 22° south latitude, was confirmed; but from this point the boundary-line was drawn in such a manner eastwards and northwards (see Plate XIII.) as to give Germany free access to the Zambezi by the Chobe River. (6.) The Anglo-German frontier between Togo and Gold Coast Colony was fixed, and that between the Camarons and the British Niger Territories was provisionally adjusted. (7.) The Free-trade zone, defined by the Act of Berlin (1885), was recognised as applicable to the present arrangement between Britain and Germany, and its stipulations as binding upon both parties. Thus "it is specially understood that, in accordance with these provisions, the passage of goods of both Powers will be free from all hindrances and from all transit dues between Lake Nyassa and the Congo State, between Lakes Nyassa and Tanganika, on Lake Tanganika, and between that lake and the northern boundary of the two spheres." (8.) A British Protectorate was recognised over the dominions of the Sultan of Zanzibar within the British coastal zone and over the islands of Zanzibar and Pemba. Britain, however, undertook to use her influence to secure (what have since been acquired) corresponding advantages for Germany within the German coastal zone and over the island of Mafia. Finally (9.), the island of Heligoland, in the North Sea, was ceded by Britain to Germany.

The tact and ability with which conflicting claims were thus adjusted by Lord Salisbury were equally conspicuous in his negotiation of the Anglo-Portuguese Convention of 20th August 1890. We have already alluded to the chief points in dispute between Britain and Portugal. Their adjustment—if, perchance, it may be regarded as final— formed the last of a chain of treaties which, it may be hoped, will bind down the European Powers in Africa to "keep the peace" for some time to come.   *[margin: Anglo-Portuguese Convention, 1890.]*

The boundary-lines laid down by the Anglo-Portuguese Convention are approximately shown on our map: some time must, however, elapse before any precise delimitation of the territories can be made.

The adjustment of rival claims, though on the whole favourable to Portugal, has been very fairly carried out. Portugal has obtained the recognition of some of her historical pretensions, and now has ample scope for any possible expansion of her Eastern and Western possessions. In a few words we may broadly distinguish what Britain and Portugal have gained by their compact.

Great Britain acquired a broad Central sphere of influence for the expansion of her possessions in South Africa northwards to and beyond the Zambezi (which, between the Zumbo District and the Katima Rapids, flows entirely through the British sphere), up to the confines of the Congo Independent State * and German East Africa.

Portugal, on the East Coast, secured the Lower Zambezi from Zumbo, and the Lower Shiré from the Ruo confluence, the entire *Hinterland* of Mozambique up to Lake Nyassa,† and the *Hinterland* of Sofala to the confines of the South

---

* The "confines" of the Congo Independent State require more precise delimitation, since treaties have quite recently (January to June 1890) been concluded between British agents and native chiefs, as follows :—In the Barotsé country, and between Nyassa and the Loangwa ; in the Angoni country (British South Africa Company) ; and in Msiri's kingdom (Katanga) by Mr. Alfred Sharpe, acting under instructions from Consul Johnston.

† As far south as latitude 13° 30′, whence the frontier is deflected south-east to the eastern shores of Lakes Chiuta and Shirwa.

U

African Republic and the Matabele kingdom. On the West
Coast, Portugal received the entire *Hinterland* behind her
provinces in Lower Guinea, up to the confines of the Congo
Independent State* and the upper course of the Zambezi.

<small>Application of the Free-trade principle.</small> Lord Salisbury, in his negotiations with Germany and
Portugal, very wisely upheld the principle of free-trade
which was laid down by the Act of Berlin, 1885, in regard
to the free transit of goods through territories in which two
or more Powers are indirectly interested. Thus, by the
Anglo-German compact, the Contracting Powers reserved
for their respective subjects a "right of way," so to speak,
along the main channels or routes of communication.
Through the application of the same principle in the recent
Anglo-Portuguese Convention, Portugal obtains not only a
"right of way" across the British Zambezi zone, but also
the privilege of constructing railways and telegraphs. She
thereby secures free and uninterrupted connection between
her possessions on the East Coast and those on the West
Coast. A similar concession is made to Britain in the Zambezi basin, within the Portuguese sphere. Finally, the Zambezi itself has been declared free to the flags of all nations.

Britain has stipulated for the right of pre-emption in the
event of Portugal wishing to dispose of territories south
of the Zambezi. The transit-dues over Portuguese territories
and waterways are not to exceed 3 per cent. *ad valorem*—
the same as fixed by the Portuguese Tariff of 1877.

---

* Belgium, however, disputes the claims of Portugal to Lunda, Kasanje,
and other territories to the east of the River Kwango, on the strength of a
treaty concluded on 14th February 1885, between the African Association
and Portugal, which fixed the Kwango as the conterminous frontier, and of
treaties with native chiefs alleged to have been recently made by Belgian
explorers. Portugal, on the other hand, disputes the Belgian interpretation
of the Treaty of 1885 and advances prior claims [see Appendix: "Notes on
the Maps"]. Meantime, on 10th June 1890, the district was incorporated (on
paper) with the Congo State, under the designation of "Western Kwango."
Portugal, however, proposes to extend the railway from Ambrose to Kasanje.

This concludes our review of the political partition of Conclusion.
Africa. As a result, it will be seen that, south of the
Equator, the whole of the continent has been divided
among the European Powers; but north of the Equator
the internal boundaries are nearly all unsettled. In other
words, Pagan Africa is at the present day under the domination of Europe, but Mohammedan Africa remains under
Arab or native rule. This striking contrast, viewed in
the light of what has already been said in regard to the
relative progress of Christianity and Islam in Africa, offers
an instructive and suggestive study. It also lends support to
the hypothesis already advanced by me, that the civilisation
of Africa will come from the south, and proceed along the
main continental axis, which now is dominated by Britain,
Germany, and Italy, but chiefly by Britain.

We are tempted to close this chapter with a moral.
The reader will have observed that, in the partition of
Africa, Jacob has occasionally supplanted Esau, and obtained the blessing he was not entitled to receive. We
need not mention any particular names or cite examples.
Furthermore, by mutual concessions and the exercise of a
little tact, prudence, and forethought, Esau and Jacob have
afterwards got on very well together. Let us hope, therefore, they will continue to work side by side in brotherly
love and mutual confidence; for it is only by co-operation
that they can hope to subdue the hostile elements which for
many years to come must of necessity imperil not only their
success, but their very existence in Africa.

CHAPTER XI.

SUMMARY AND CONCLUSIONS.

GENERAL PRINCIPLES UNDERLYING THE DEVELOPMENT OF AFRICA ALONG NATURAL LINES, DERIVED FROM AN EXAMINATION OF THE VARIOUS ASPECTS UNDER WHICH THE CONTINENT IS KNOWN TO EUROPE AT THE PRESENT DAY.

SUMMARY AND CONCLUSIONS.

HAVING completed our survey of the continent of Africa as a field for European enterprise, it may be convenient to those who have been unable to follow step by step if, in this place, we summarise the general results. The following is a *résumé* of each distinct aspect of our subject and of the conclusions to which we have been led:—

I. Political settlement has coincided with the areas of the oceanic drainage-basins. The inland drainage-basins, being barren and unprofitable, are unsuitable for European settlement.

<small>The consolidation of European political rule.</small>

European political rule in Africa requires, for its consolidation, a sea-board as an effective base, and, for its expansion, easy access into the Interior. It naturally follows the lines of least resistance; and these, in a physical sense, are afforded by the great river-valleys. But, owing to the configuration of the continent and the consequent disposition of its river-systems—all of which are fully developed *behind* the seaward border of the inland plateau—free access by river from the ocean is interrupted by the cataracts and rapids that are formed in the beds of all the streams where, at comparatively short distances from their mouths, they finally break through the rim of the inland plateau in order to reach the sea.

Limits. Hence, European political rule in Africa, after its consolidation in the coastal zone, for the most part in contiguity to the mouths of the large rivers, has not yet succeeded in penetrating for any great distance into the interior lands.

Hostile elements of climate. II. Climatic conditions, however, have in the main exercised the most potent repellent force against the expansion of European political rule and the extension of European settlement.

The climate of the coastal lands, being the most dangerous for Europeans, and the least favourable for their acclimatisation, has generally paralysed or crippled the settlements that have been established thereon.

Natural barriers. The unfavourable climatic phenomena have also raised natural barriers in the way of easy access into the Interior:—(1) in the Nile Valley, where the Nubian Desert occurs; (2) south of the Mediterranean Littoral, where the Sahara and Libyan Deserts occur; and (3) between the Red Sea, parts of the East and West Coasts, and the interior lands, where deserts or steppes intervene.

Natural highways. III. The fluvial highways, on the other hand, being so favourably situated in certain parts of Africa, the initial physical obstacles to the extension of European political rule have been eventually overcome:—(1) in the Niger basin, where access into the Súdan is both practicable and easy; (2) in the Congo basin, which offers an unrivalled system of waterways conducting into the Interior; and (3) in the Zambezi basin, which gives access by the chain of great Lakes to the most valuable land-and-water route across the continent.

Trans-Continental land-and-water routes. IV. Land-and-water routes—of which (1) the Zambezi and the chain of great Lakes is by far the most important—are found elsewhere in Africa:—namely, (2) from the Lower Nile

Valley or from the Red Sea, by at least two practicable routes, and from the East Coast, into the basin of the Upper Nile, where a junction with Route No. 1 can be effected; (3) by the Niger, joining the ordinary caravan-routes (*a*) into the Central Súdan and (*b*) across the Sahara to the Mediterranean sea-board; (4) by the Congo and Stanley's most recent path to the East Coast; and (5) from Cape Colony northwards by land, and ultimately by railway, to the great Lakes. These are only the chief, and for the most part trans-Continental, highways; but other practicable routes into the Interior also occur. *Trans-Continental land-and-water routes.*

As regards the respective merits of these natural high- *Compared.* ways:—(1.) the Sahara caravan-route has been shown to be less valuable than, and not at all able to compete with, the route by the Niger; (2.) the Lower Nile route is not so feasible as that from the Red Sea or East Coast; and (3.) the Congo route is not nearly so good as that by the Zambezi and chain of Lakes. Finally, the best route of any has been demonstrated to be that which starts from Cape Colony and joins the great Lakes.

V. European colonisation of the coastal lands within the Tropics has been proved to be impossible without (1) the institution of sanatary precautions, such as the draining or flooding of marsh-lands, (2.) exceptional attention to health, and (3.) a very gradual process of acclimatisation. European colonisation of the high-plateau countries has, on the other hand, been shown to be fairly practicable. Whilst, also, in Temperate South Africa colonists are able to thrive, only the people of Southern Europe show an increase of the birth-rate over the death-rate in Temperate North Africa. *Obstacles to European colonisation.*

VI. The indigenous populations, in their migratory move- *Migratory movements.* ments, have taken directions the very reverse of European conquest: they have either been (1.) thrust back and dispossessed of their lands, or (2.) assimilated, and so have deteriorated, or (3) annihilated,—rapidly by the sword, slowly by vile intoxicants. Nevertheless, they have evinced a capacity not only for nourishing an original culture, but for taking on and assimilating higher alien forms. What we understand by civilisation, or progress, has scarcely yet been planted in Africa. The Negro race must be developed along natural lines.

<small>Development of the Negro race.</small>

From the comparative absence of political cohesion in Bantu Africa, the European domination has met with slight resistance. It is otherwise in the Mohammedan States of the Central Sûdan, where European conquest has been checked wherever it has deeply penetrated; but, up to the present day, no concerted movements have been made against the strongholds of Islam.*

<small>The European domination.</small>

VII. Islam and Christianity, or Arab and European rule, and their attendant evils—namely, the Slave Trade and the traffic in drink, respectively—have resulted in the adoption of very much the same methods of propagandism and conquest. But, in their effect upon the Pagan populations, Islam and Arab rule have succeeded in places where Christianity and European rule have failed.

<small>Islam and Christianity: methods.</small>

The main reasons of such relative success and failure appear to be:—(1.) because Islam, now so long established as to be virtually an indigenous force, has been able to rapidly assimilate the conquered peoples and raise them up to its standard, whilst Christianity, an alien force, with insufficient material power behind it, demands of the natives an impossible standard; and (2.) because Arab rule is suited to

<small>Reasons of relative success and failure.</small>

---

* It is here understood, and has been repeatedly demonstrated in the various chapters of this book, that the Mediterranean lands may be regarded as practically outside of Continental Africa.

the conditions of life in Tropical Africa, whilst European rule, which has been inconsistent with the teaching of its pioneer missionaries, has introduced social revolutions, followed by moral degradation, of the most far-reaching character.

At the same time it has been shown that, even in the comparatively short time of effective missionary enterprise among the impressionable Bantu, a certain measure of success has been attained. This degree of success would have had permanent and important results but for (1.) European international rivalries in, and the ineffective administration of, the territories in Africa, (2.) the immoral practices of traders, and (3.) above all, the debasing and destructive traffic in cheap spirits. Thus, the efforts of the missionaries at ameliorating the lot of the natives or at inculcating a higher life have been either discounted or entirely thwarted. For it has been shown that, wherever the European domination has obtained some degree of permanence, the natives have deteriorated or died out,—the relatively few exceptions only emphasising this phenomenon. *Comparative success of Christianity in Bantu Africa. Inimical factors.*

It is, therefore, pleaded, in the interests not only of humanity, but of national honour—if for no higher reason—that the European Powers in Africa should immediately stop the indiscriminate trade in intoxicating liquors, by which their "customers" are slowly but surely being driven either into sodden barbarism, which can have no desires for other European manufactures, or into untimely graves, which will be imperishable monuments of European hypocrisy and disgrace. *A plea for the natives.*

VIII. The Slave Trade has been another mischievous factor against the healthy development of Africa, for it has undermined its social fabric and introduced a potent element against legitimate commerce. However, it has been shown that the Slave Trade does not pay in itself, but only in *The Slave Trade.*

conjunction with the ivory-trade—ivory being the most valuable export-commodity. As one proof of this statement, it has been pointed out that all slave-routes are trade-routes.

Suppression of the Slave Trade.

For the suppression of the Traffic in Slaves it is, therefore, essential to adopt, in addition to the ordinary and obvious legislation and police measures, a sound commercial policy, with the object of undermining the Slave Trade by legitimate commerce, and thereby introducing an inimical factor over which the European Powers have complete control.

Value of African lands.

IX. The value of African lands appears to be sufficiently promising to guarantee their profitable development in those regions where mineral resources or ivory are abundant. All such regions are able to offer an immediate return for capital. In the absence of those resources, however, or failing the presence of a strong and effective European government, the initial cost of opening up new lands is not likely to meet with a fair return for capital in the immediate future.

The factor of commerce.

X. Commerce, it is advanced, is the dominant factor in African politics; and commercial supremacy is the underlying motive of European enterprise in Africa.

XI. The commercial exploitation of Africa must therefore determine its political destiny. African lands must, and can, be made to pay eventually. The initial difficulties to be overcome arise mainly from: (1) the Traffic in Slaves, (2) the traffic in alcoholic liquors, and (3) the absence of skilled native labour. Upon the solution of these problems will depend the ultimate development of Africa as a field for European enterprise.

XII. Chartered companies have proved invaluable for tentative or experimental efforts, because (1) commerce is the natural instrument for effecting the true development of Africa, and (2) because they can advance boldly where it is not expedient for the national flag to venture. But chartered companies, for this very reason, and because native interests might be sacrificed to the interests of the shareholders, should have the strict parental supervision of their respective Governments. *[Chartered companies as pioneers.]*

XIII. The progress of discovery and exploration, the greatest achievements in which have occurred within the last hundred years, has been shown to have been inspired by the desire on the part of the participating nations of Europe, first, to reach some desired goal in the Interior, the riches and resources of which have been either fabulous or well founded; secondly, to acquire a commercial monopoly over those favoured regions; thirdly, to open up routes thither; and lastly, to develop the country. Commercial aims have, in fact, inspired the action of most European *entrepreneurs* in Africa. At the same time, scientific travellers of all nationalities—but mainly British, German, French, Portuguese, and Italian—have independently discovered and explored various regions of Africa. The Germans in Northern Equatorial Africa and the British in all the regions south of the Equator have been the leading discoverers and explorers; but the roll of British explorers includes the names of the larger number of the most distinguished and successful men. The great hydrographical discoveries have all been achieved, not by the more natural method of tracing the river-systems from the coasts inland, but by the reverse way. From the fact that the unknown or unexplored regions of Africa at the present day lie behind the European Possessions on the coasts, it is argued that, *[Discovery and exploration.]*

DEVELOPMENT OF AFRICA.

Future direction of exploration.
in consequence of the necessity of the Powers to fix their inland boundaries, and to explore and exploit the Interior regions, the march of exploration in the future will be directed by and precede colonisation and political settlement. Furthermore, it has been shown that there is ample scope left in Africa, not only for the surveyor and explorer, but also for the pioneer discoverer; and that small pacific expeditions, or individual explorers with small personal escorts, having in the past achieved some of the best results, would in the future be better suited than big fighting expeditions for finding out new fields for European enterprise and capital.

Effective European occupation.
XIV. The European domination over African lands is intermittently felt throughout the greater part of the continent; but only in the Temperate regions and at isolated points in the coastal zone has it been followed by effective occupation. Throughout Tropical Africa European political administration is practically restricted to the coastal lands and to the lower portions of the valleys of the great rivers. But whilst it has been shown that the obstacles to European political rule are not necessarily insuperable, it is contended that existing limitations should be judiciously observed, in order that they may eventually be overcome, in part or altogether. In place of haphazard administrative experiments, the European Powers would do better to adopt a systematic programme, based on the best principles that experience and knowledge teach us ought to determine the development of African lands.

Political partition of Africa.
XV. Finally, it has been seen that the partition of African lands among the European Powers, which practically commenced after the Berlin Conference of 1884-85, has proceeded so rapidly that by August 1890 the whole of Africa

SUMMARY AND CONCLUSIONS.

south of the Equator had been appropriated by them, whilst, on the other hand, to the north of the Equator very few internal boundaries are yet fixed. In other words, Pagan Africa is now exclusively dominated by the European Powers, whilst Mohammedan Africa remains for the most part under the rule of Arab and native chiefs. Moreover, it has been pointed out that, from south to north, along the main axis of the continent, by which route it may be expected the civilisation of Europe will chiefly advance, the territories are under the control of Britain, Germany, and Italy, but chiefly of Britain.

Future Path of European civilisation.

Thus, from an inquiry into the past, and from an estimate of the future of Africa, I have endeavoured to arrive at the general principles that underlie the development of the continent along what may be regarded as its natural lines. My arguments are, of course, open to criticism; but it is precisely the discussion of this important subject that is so urgently needed at the present time, and by more competent critics than myself. To challenge criticism has been one of the objects of my task, and I believe I have laid myself open to attack on very nearly all sides.

Concluding Remarks.

Africa is not a continent to be developed by the haphazard means which have been employed up to the present. Its conditions and its necessities are differentiated from those of every other continent. These conditions should be recognised, and the necessities provided for, by all the Powers who have interests in Africa. The desiderata most urgently needed are the recognition by them of a community of interests and the adoption by them of a common programme. For, until these ends are attained, we can scarcely hope that the European domination in Africa—at least, in Tropical Africa—will tend either to the ultimate benefit of the natives or to the credit of Europe.

APPENDIX.

NOTES ON THE MAPS

BY

E. G. RAVENSTEIN, F.R.G.S.

NOTES ON THE MAPS.

IN the fourteen maps which follow, an attempt has been made to give a graphic representation of the outstanding features of the physical and political geography of Africa. The utmost care has been taken to utilise all the available information extant. The maps are necessarily imperfect, owing to the absence of precise *data*, but their error in detail is not so great as to detract from their trustworthiness; they give a correct idea of certain leading features in the geography of Africa which mere verbal descriptions could scarcely convey.

The maps explain themselves, but the following remarks are added in elucidation of certain points that might otherwise remain obscure.

No. I. *Height of Land.*—By referring to Plate XII., illustrating the progress of exploration, it will be seen to what extent this map is hypothetical. It is quite possible, for instance, that the areas of relative depression in the Sahara are of greater extent than that shown on the map. The series of "troughs" in Masai-land, including Lake Rudolf and other lakes, is a very remarkable phenomenon.

No. II. *River-basins and Ocean currents.*—Our delineation of river-basins includes in many instances areas which are actually riverless, but which, nevertheless, as far as the general slope of the country and of its torrent-beds is concerned, belong to the basin to which they are accredited. Much still remains to be known before we can be in a position to divide the Saharan region into catchment-basins.

Nos. III., IV., AND V. *Phenomena of Climate.*—These maps have been designed to illustrate the more remarkable features of the climatology of Africa.

No. III. (Mean Annual Temperatures) is an attempt to represent the *actual* temperature in contradistinction to that prevailing at sea-level. A knowledge of temperatures reduced to sea-level is, of course, indispensable for investigating the laws governing the distribution of temperature over the globe; but that of the actual temperature is more immediately useful when it is desired to obtain a general notion of the climate of any given region. Owing to the few stations at which observations for temperature have been made, our map is almost certain to contain many errors as to detail; but, nevertheless, we believe it to be a trustworthy index to the subject. On examination it will be seen that a mean temperature of over $80°$ Fahr. prevails along the East Coast, from the Red Sea as far south as Sofala, beyond the Zambezi; whilst, on the West Coast, owing to the proximity of the cold waters of the South Atlantic, and of the cold currents flowing south along the Saharan Coast, the domain of $80°$ Fahr. of mean annual temperature is much more restricted. Temperatures uniform with those of Southern Europe prevail over only a small extent of country, and are mainly confined to the Barbary Coast and to extra-Tropical South Africa. This is not to be wondered at. In order to enjoy a mean temperature like that of London ($51°$ Fahr.) in any country the seaboard of which has a mean temperature of $80°$ Fahr., it would be necessary to ascend to as great a height above the sea-level as 10,000 feet. There are no plateaus of that height in Africa, and even mountains of that altitude are rare. Even at Gondar, on the Abyssinian plateau, at an elevation of 6200 feet above the sea, the mean annual temperature is $67°$ Fahr.; whilst at Kakoma, in Unyamwezi, 3700 feet above the sea, it is $72°$, and in Uganda it is $70°$ Fahr.

Turning to Map No. IV. (Mean Annual Range of Temperature), we find that the difference between the coldest and hottest months of the year is very slight. Over a large portion of the Congo basin it does not amount to as much as $5°$ Fahr.; whilst a range of $20°$ Fahr. is observable only in North and South Africa. This restricted annual range of temperature is compensated for, to a qualified extent, by an unusually large diurnal range; but it may be doubted whether the latter phenomenon makes up for the entire absence of a "cool season." The prevalent popular idea that, in order to enjoy a temperature congenial to northern Europeans, we have merely to ascend a mountain-side in a Tropical country, is at all events not supported by an examination of our maps.

The climate of Tropical Africa is all the more trying to Europeans on account of its relative humidity, which, over a great part of the continent, exceeds 70 per cent.

On Map No. V. (Annual Rainfall) many recent observations have been utilised for the first time.

I append a few climatological *data* in illustration of the maps.

	Altitude.	Temperature.		Rain.	Relative Humidity.	
		Mean of Year.	Annual Range.		Year.	Annual Range.
	Feet.	Degrees F.	Degrees F.	Inches	Per Cent.	Per Cent.
London	120	51	26	25	81	20
Vienna	640	49	40	23	72	21
Algiers	70	65	23	31	64	28
Cairo	100	70	30	1	56	28
Elmina (Gold Coast)	60	79	7	31	85	7
Akasa (Niger)	...	78	5	138	91	12
Bismarckburg (Togo Land)	2300	75	10	59	75	42
Kuka (Bornu)	850	83	20	..	63	40
Sibange (Gabón)	...	76	5	89	90	...
Vivi (Congo)	370	76	9	43	75	13
Loanda	190	74	12	13	82	10
S. Salvador (Congo)	1900	73	8	39	...	...
Luluaburg	2000	78	2	58	78	30
Lado (Upper Nile)	1500	81	9	37	71	48
Massawa	...	86	17	4	...	...
Gondar	6200	67	12	34	...	...
Zanzibar	...	80	11	98	82	13
Kakoma	3700	72	16	39	62	48
Uganda	4000	70	3	51	...	...
Tete	250	80	11	34	62	28
Blantyre	3320	66	16	53	68	36
Cape Town	...	63	15	25	74	13
Kimberley	400	65	27	18	58	6

No. VI. *Geology.*—This is a mere sketch, based upon the map in Berghaus' Physical Atlas and supplemented by more recent *data*. Certain parts have been filled in conjecturally, in order to obviate blanks. Perhaps the most striking feature in the geology of Africa is the belt of Archaic and volcanic rocks composing the main axis of the continent and prevailing between the Red Sea and Cape Colony.

No. VII. *Zones of Vegetation*.—The references to colouring sufficiently explain the scope of this map. Forests are indicated only where they cover extensive areas. Elsewhere belts of trees fringe many rivers, and timber is abundant even in some parts of the steppe-countries. A comparison between this map and No. V. (Annual Rainfall) will prove instructive.

No. VIII. *Commercial Products*.—On this map we have shown the continually decreasing area of regions yielding ivory, the distribution of the oil-palm (*Elais guineensis*), the products of which play so important a part in the commercial development of Africa, and the region within which the date-palm is cultivated. The map also shows the principal gold-producing regions that have so far been discovered and exploited, and the available coal-fields.

Railways at present open or in course of construction have also been indicated. It will be observed that only in British South Africa, Algeria, and Egypt have the railway-systems been at all developed. Railway-lines of secondary importance—either built or in course of construction—are to be found in Senegambia (Kayes, on the Senegal, to Bamaku, on the Niger), on the Lower Congo (Matadi to Stanley Pool), in Angola (Loanda to Ambaca), in Mozambique (Delagoa Bay to the Transvaal), in British East Africa (from Mombaza into the Interior), and in the Italian Possessions on the Red Sea Littoral (from Massawa to the foot of the plateau).

The distance to which rivers are navigable from their mouths has been indicated by a bar.

No. IX. *Density of Population*.—Trustworthy *data* in this respect are absolutely wanting for the greater part of Africa. Census reports are available only for Algeria, Egypt, the British Colonies, and the Boer Republics. Elsewhere we are dependent for our information on the accounts of travellers. Even for a country so near to us as Morocco we have the most conflicting estimates. This much, however, appears certain: the most densely populated region of Africa, apart from Lower Egypt, is that of the Lower Niger, including Yoruba. I have estimated the total population of Africa (*vide ante*, pages 86 and 87) to be but little over 127,000,000, which shows a density of 11 to the square mile.

No. X. *Languages.*—Much remains to be done before it were possible to classify the infinite number of African tribes either on the basis of language or in accordance with anthropometric characteristics. Our map is intended simply to illustrate broad features, and has been constructed on strictly linguistic principles. In consequence of this classification, many tribes portraying distinctly Negroid characteristics, but who have adopted the language of their conquerors or co-religionists, have been regarded as Semites. The distribution of the Masai, and the Dinka and their relations, who occupy the border-land between the undoubted Hamites (the Galla and Somal), is shown by a pale blue tint. The Bushmen (Bojesmans) have been separated from the Hottentots; but no account has been taken of the numerous scattered tribes of Pygmies, which are found throughout Africa as far north as the Ogowé, the Wellé, and Southern Abyssinia.

The number of Europeans residing in Africa probably amounts to 1,000,000. Of these, 430,000 are in British South Africa, 172,000 in the Boer Republics, 245,000 in Algeria and Tunis, and 92,000 in Lower Egypt. Actual settlers are found only in South Africa and in Algeria, to a small extent also in Angola.

No. XI. *Religions, and Missionary Stations.*—This map gives the general distribution of Christians, Mohammedans, and Pagans. The colouring, however, is intended to indicate simply the dominant faith in the various regions. Within the Christian sphere, for instance, numerous Pagans and many Mohammedans are to be found; while the populations of the so-called Mohammedan countries include large contingents of Pagans. Ancient Christianity, which at one time was the dominant faith in North Africa and in the Nile Valley, has left a survival in Abyssinia; whilst modern Christianity is being propagated from hundreds of

Missionary stations, only the chief of which have been given on the map.

No. XII. *Progress of Exploration.*—Five periods of progress in the exploration of Africa have been distinguished on our map. Each period is represented by a distinctive colour, whilst those parts of Africa still unexplored have been left blank. The map illustrates the discoveries of European travellers only. No notice has been taken of a number of early travellers, who undoubtedly penetrated far into the Interior, but of whose achievements no detailed record has been handed down. As instances of this kind we may mention the Florentine Benedetti Dei, who visited Timbuktu during the second half of the fifteenth century, the Portuguese João Fernandez, Pero d'Evora, Rodrigo Reinel, João Lourenço, and others who ventured into the Sahara or visited the Negro kingdoms on the Upper Niger. Nor has any notice been taken of the Portuguese traders of more recent times who, long before the days of Livingstone and Cameron, travelled from Bihé to the Upper Zambezi, to Lunda, and even to Urua. The only exceptions noted by us are the journeys of Conceição, Graça, and Silva Porto, who have published intelligible itineraries.

No. XIII. *The Political Partition of Africa.*—The territorial arrangements illustrated by this map have been made, for the most part, without the knowledge or irrespective of the wishes of the native chiefs and rulers whose lands have been thus apportioned among the European Powers. Many parts of Africa designated as European "protectorates" or "spheres of influence" have never even been seen by European travellers. These international arrangements are, moreover, far from complete, as they at present stand: the blanks on our map sufficiently attest this fact. Only a certain number of the territorial boundaries claimed by European Powers has been fixed by international agreement, whilst the possession of several lands is disputed between two or even three Powers.

For instance, Lunda and other territories to the east of the Kwango are claimed both by Portugal and the Congo Independent State. The conterminous frontier between Loanda and the Congo State was, it is true, fixed by the Convention of 14th February 1885. This convention stipulated that the boundary-line in question should follow the parallel of Noki to the Kwango, and from thence follow the course of that river; and it was at first interpreted in the same sense by the contracting parties. Colonel Strauch, in a letter to Dr. R. Kiepert (dated 26th February 1885) stated that the boundary to the east of the Kwango followed the 6th parallel (as defined in the Convention with Germany); and M. E. van Eetvelde, in a circular addressed to the European Powers on 1st August 1885, accepted the same interpretation. Moreover, in all the maps published by M. Wauters in the periodical issues of *Le Mouvement Géographique*, from 5th May 1885 up to and including 6th July 1890, the frontier of the Congo Independent State was thus delimitated. Portugal, on her part, on 12th December 1885, claimed the ancient empire of Lunda as lying within her sphere of influence. It was only in August 1890 that the Congo Independent State, pretending to regard Lunda as No-man's Land, claimed possession of it on the strength of explorations recently carried out within its limits and of treaties concluded with native chiefs by Belgian travellers. On both of these grounds, however, Portugal has undoubtedly anticipated the claims of the Congo State. The dispute, it is understood, is to be definitely settled by arbitration.

Elsewhere, and more especially in regard to the British Possessions, the conterminous boundaries of the Congo State with those of other spheres of influence have not yet been defined by international agreements (*vide ante*, page 305). The northern boundary of the State has been drawn on our map up to the Congo-Nile water-parting, as far west as longitude 17° E.,— an extension formerly claimed but, apparently, subsequently abandoned.

British Possessions are coloured as if the recent Convention with Portugal (20th August 1890) had been ratified. The small *enclave* behind Cape Juby is coloured British, although its acquisition by a private company has not yet been sanctioned by the British Government; the territory, moreover, is claimed by both France and Spain. The territories of the Imperial British East Africa Company ("Ibea") are coloured a dark-red up to latitude 5° N., whilst their probable extension northwards is indicated by a paler tint. The total area thus defined is 1,065,000 square miles, of which 245,000 square miles are included within the territories lying to the south of latitude 5° N.

No. XIV. *Forms of Government.*—Whilst Map No. XIII. exhibits what may be regarded as the aspirations of the European Powers in Africa, Map No. XIV. is intended to show the actual state of affairs. It will be seen that European rule has as yet been established only in Algeria, in a large part of British South Africa, in the Boer States, in some of the Coastal districts, and at a few localities in the Interior, which happen to be occupied by small garrisons capable of enforcing the authority of the nominal "sovereigns" of the country. The greater part of Africa is still ruled by native chiefs and in accordance with native laws, even although many of these chiefs have signed treaties with, or accepted the "protection" of, European Powers.

The few native States with Christian rulers are coloured blue. They include Abyssinia, Uganda, Liberia, Khama's kingdom, and Madagascar. Among Pagan States, that of the Muata Yanvo (Lunda) has recently suffered disintegration, and thus offers an easy prey to its neighbours.

INDEX.

INDEX.

ABYSSINIA, description of, 25; mountains of, 26; inland drainage-area near, 27; geology of, 59; malaria in, 75; area and population of, 86; colour of the people of, 114; Arabs arrive in, 133; Christianity in, 141; Portuguese mission to, 186; exploration in, 194; British expedition against, 194; agriculture in, 225

Acclimatisation, 76

Adamawa plateau, 193

Africa (as a continent), geological antiquity of, 3; coast-line of, 4; geological systems of, 4; its conformity to continental type, 5; characteristic physical features of, 6; coastal zone of, 6; inland plateau of, 6; continental axis of, 7; elevation of the land-masses of, 7; highest summits of, 7; vast size of, 8; embossment of, 8; drainage-areas of, 9; lakes of, 11; rivers of, 11, 18; inland drainage-areas of, 10; absence of harbours in, 37; East Coast of, 43; climate of, 51, 71; mean annual temperature of, 51; prevailing winds in, 53; rainfall of, 55; sources of the river-systems of, 56; rainy seasons in, 57; snow-line in, 57; soils of, 58; distribution of vegetation in, 60; desert zone of, 62; forests of, 65, 67; savannas of, 68; fauna of, 68; faunal regions of, 69; insect pests of, 71; diseases of, 74; malaria in, 74; habitability of, 78; settleable and unsettleable regions of, 78; Cross and Crescent in, 81; essentials towards effective occupation in, 81; distribution of the indigenous populations of, 85; area and population of, 86; languages and dialects of, 85, 90; total European possessions in, 87; classification of the races of, 87; occupations of the natives of, 89; archaeology of, 89; Negro linguistic systems in, 92; Negroes of, 96; representative peoples of, 105; light-coloured peoples of, 116; one effect of missions in, 119; Negro kingdoms of, 120; culture of the natives of, 123; disturbing influences on native culture in, 123; native civilisation of, 124; European dominion in, 125, 311, 314; rival religious forces in, 129; Jews in, 140; Islam in, 132; cohesion of Mohammedan forces in, 136; Pagan tribes of, 136; recent Arab hostilities in, 137; Copts in, 141; phases of Christian missionary enterprise in, 141; spheres of missions in, 143; number of mission-stations, missionaries, and native converts in, 145; results of missionary enterprise in, 145; Slave Trade in, 161; civilisation of, 161; causes of the arrested development of, 161; degradation of, 162; abolition of slavery in, 163, 174, 176; fundamental cause of the Slave Trade in, 165; conditions and extent of the Slave Trade in, 167; methods of slave-hunting in, 172; slave-traders of, 173; suppression of the Slave Trade in, 177; pacific measures against the Slave Trade in, 178; exploration in, 184, 317; ancient geography of, 183; Portuguese pioneers in, 185; systematic scientific exploration of, 185; Jesuits in, 186; distinctive spheres of discovery in, 186; character and extent of explorations in, 187; unexplored regions of, 188, 212; periods of exploratory work in, 188; first European to cross, 199;

practical results of exploration in, 202; chartered companies in, 245, 317; comparative view of European exploration in, 210; character of expeditions in, 212; commercial resources of, 217; value of land in, 218, 316; the factor of commerce in, 218; commercial outlook in, 219; labour in, 243; islands of, 238; geographical distribution of ivory in, 238; liquor-traffic in, 242; commercial development of, 244; European dominion in, 249, 275; political partition of, 279; European spheres of influence in, 280; inland boundaries in, 281; obstacles to the colonisation of, 313; migratory movements in, 313

Africa, East, physical features of, 38; vegetation of, 67; fauna of, 69; climate of, 78; linguistic groups in, 90; Christian missions in, 144; Slave Trade in, 169, 176; explorations in, 187, 200, 204, 209; commercial resources of, 233; European domination in, 270; German Company, 272; British Company, 273

Africa, Equatorial and Central, rainfall in, 55; vegetation of, 65; climate of, 80; linguistic groups in, 90; tribes of, 166; Islam in, 135; Christian missions in, 141; slave-preserves in, 167, 177; early discoveries in, 196; commercial resources of, 226; distribution of ivory in, 238

Africa, North, physical features of, 17; vegetation of, 61; fauna of, 69; climate of, 78; archæology of, 80; linguistic groups in, 90; Islam in, 132; Christian missions in, 145; Slave Trade in, 168; explorations in, 187; commercial resources of, 219; European domination in, 250

Africa, South, physical features of, 37; vegetation of, 67; fauna of, 70; climate of, 78; linguistic groups in, 90; Christian missions in, 144; explorations in, 187, 198, 206; commercial resources of, 235; political situation in, 266; British Company, 269; expansion of British, 296

Africa, West, physical features of, 27; vegetation of, 67; fauna of, 69; climate of, 78; linguistic groups in, 90; tribes of, 118; trade and commerce of, 119, 227;

Christian missions in, 143; Slave Trade in, 169; explorations in, 187, 201; European domination in, 256

African Association, foundation of the London, 185

African Lakes Company, foundation of the, 204

Africander Bund, 267

Ahaggar highlands, drainage of the, 19

Akka, height of the, 96

Albert Edward Nyanza, elevation of the, 23; discovery of the, 210

Albert Nyanza, description of the, 23; Baker's visit to the, 197; Stanley at the, 209

Alexander, explorations by, 198

Alexandria, trade of, 224

Algeria, highlands of, 17; rivers of, 18; vegetation of, 75; malaria in, 75; area and population of, 86; Jews in, 140; conquest of, 192; economical progress of, 219; present state of, 250

Amazons and Congo Rivers compared, 11

Anderssen, explorations by, 206

Angola, rainfall of, 57; descent of the Negroes of, 119; maps of, 196; resources of, 231

Angra Pequeña, Germany obtains, 204

Anti-slavery Conference (1889-90), 156

Arabs, descent of the, 91; in Africa, 132; ivory trade carried on by the, 241; recent revolt of the, on the East Coast, 292

Area of Africa, 86

Arnot, referred to, 40; explorations by, 208

Aruwimi River, Stanley's journey on the, 209

Ashanti, 120

Assuan, cataract near, 26

Atbara River, sediment carried by the, 26, 59

Atlantic Ocean drainage-basin, 27

Atlas Mountains, description of the, 18; influence of the, on the rainfall, 56

Atmospheric pressure over Africa, 53

BARISA, origin of the, 110

Bagirmi, adoption of Islam by the, 134

INDEX. 335

Bahr-el-Ghazal, confluence of, with the Nile, 24
Baikie, explorations by, 192
Baker, journey of, 197
Bakoka, origin of the, 109
Balunda, characteristics of the, 117
Bamangwato, character of the, 107
Bambuk, Colin's work in, 207
Banana, the Congo at, 34
Bangweolo Lake, the source of the Congo, 31; elevation of, 33; discovery of, 200
Bantu, manners and customs of the, 93
Bari, characteristics of the, 115
Baringo Lake, *see* Rudolf Lake
Barka, anciently Cyrenaica, 17; soil of, 62
Barotsé, strength of the, 109
Barrakunda rapids, 28
Barrow, surveys by, 198
Barth, explorations by, 193
Bastian, journeys of, 201
Basuto, character of the, 107
Basuto-land, Great Britain in, 206
Batoka, position of the, 109
Baumann, explorations by, 208
Bays, relative absence of, from the coasts of Africa, 4
Beatrice Gulf, as the source of the Nile, 210
Bechuana-land, plateau of, 37; manners and customs of the natives of, 107; opening-up of, 198; political situation in, 296
Bedwin, Arab descent of the, 92
Behm, Dr., on the vegetation of Africa, 60
Beke, explorations by, 194
Belgian Possessions in Africa, area and population of, 87
Belgium and the Congo State, 262
Benguela, early maps of, 196
Benué River, description of the, 29; discovery of the, 193; as a trade route, 227; *see also* Chadda
Berber, route to the Nile from, 26
Berbera, trade of, 225
Berbers, manners and customs of the, 91
Berlin Conference (1885) and the liquor-traffic, 242; awards of the, 262, 282
Bihé, mixed population of, 119
Binger, explorations by, 207
Blue Nile, at Khartûm, 24; sources of the, 24
Blyden, Dr., referred to, 97, 149, 151

Boer Republics in Africa, 268; area and population of, 87
Böhm, explorations by, 205
Bona, port of, 36
Bonaparte's expedition into Egypt, 194
Border Craig, near the sources of the Zambezi and Congo Rivers, 40
Borelli, explorations by, 209
Bowdich, maps by, 199
British Possessions in Africa, area and population of, 87; explorers in Africa, 211; South Africa Company, 269, 298; East Africa Company, 293; *see also* Great Britain
Bruce, explorations by, 185
Brussels Conference (1889-90) and the liquor-traffic, 242
Buccaneer, soundings by the, 34
Buchan, Dr., referred to, 51
Buchanan, Mr. J. Y., referred to, 27, 35
Burton, explorations by, 197
Bushmen, or Bojesmans, characteristics and customs of the, 94

CAILLAUD, explorations by, 195
Caillié, journey by, 192
Camarons (Cameroons), Germany in the, 261
Cambier, explorations by, 208
Cameron, Lovett, explorations by, 200
Cameroons, *see* Camarons
Cannibalism among the Central tribes, 116
Cape Colony, rivers of, 37; political situation in, 267
Capello, explorations by, 203
Caravan-traffic, 105
Cardozo, explorations by, 204
Carthaginians in North Africa, 60
Chadda River, exploration of the, 192; *see also* Benué
Chartered companies, work of the, 207, 245
Chindé River, a mouth of the River Zambezi, 41, 209
Chinese immigration recommended, 243
Christian missionary enterprise, 141
Christianity and Islam, 129, 314
Clapperton, explorations by, 191
Climate, of Africa, 51; factors of, 71; modifications of, 72; effects of, 79
Climates, comparison between, 72
Coast-line of Africa, 4
Colin, work of, 207
Colonies in Africa, true value of, 218

Colonisation (European), obstacles in the way of, 313; see also Climate and Settlements
Colour of the skin of African peoples, 87
Commercial resources of Africa, 217; development of, 244
Congo compared with the Amazons, 11; physical features between the Niger and the, 29; basin of the, 30; obstructions in the bed of the, 31; bird's-eye view of the basin of the, 31; sources of the, 31; orographical features of the basin of the, 32; northern arm of the, 33; southern arm of the, 33; lower course of the, 34; cataracts of the, 34; estuary of the, 34; submarine cañon of the, 34; sediment carried by the, 34; soundings off mouth of the, 34; width of the, 34; means of communication by the, 35; navigable waters of the, 35; orographical features between the Orange River and the, 36; compared with the River Zambezi, 39; rainfall in the great forest region of the, 56; great forest of the, 65; Tuckey's exploration of the Lower, 190, 196; maps of the Lower, 196; Livingstone on the western tributaries of the, 199; discovery of the headwaters of the, 200; problem of the, solved, 202; explorations in the basin of the, 202, 208; De Brazza on the, 203; Stanley on the, 209; Belgian explorers on the, 211; trade and commerce of the, 229; commercial establishments on the, 230; political future of the, 231; French Possessions on the, 231; Tippu Tib and the Upper, 263
Congo State, founding of the, 202, 282; Belgium and the, 262; administration of the, 264; boundaries of the, 282
Cooley, researches of, 197
Copts in Africa, 141
Crampel, explorations by, 207
Cust, Dr., referred to, 85
Cyrenaica, now Barka, 17; Jewish migration to, 131

D'Abbadie, explorations by the brothers, 194
Dahomé, army of, 120; Portugal in, 301

Damara-land, discoveries in, 198, 205
D'Anville, referred to, 183, 195
De Bellefonds, travels of, 195
De Bissey, maps by, 208
De Brazza, explorations by, 203
Delagoa Bay, 39
Delcommune, explorations by, 208
Denham, discoveries by, 191
Desert regions, rainfall, 56; zone of Africa, 62; climate, 73; Traffic in Slaves, 168
Detritus, effects of, on the coasts of Africa, 4; carried by the Atbara River, 26, 59
Development of Africa: summary and conclusions, 311-320
Dialects of Africa, 85
Diebo Lake, an enlargement of the Niger, 29
Dilolo Lake, passage of the Zambezi through, 40
Diseases of Africa, 74
Drainage-areas of Africa, 9; relation between political settlement and, 12
Draken Berge, height of, 37
Dualla, their capacity for trading, 110
Du Chaillu, discovery of Pygmies by, 96; explorations by, 201
Dutch colonisation of Africa, 186

Edrisi, knowledge of Africa at the time of, 184
Egypt, malaria in, 75; area and population of, 86; exploration of, 185; Bonaparte in, 194; the French in Lower, 211; important geographical position of, 224; British occupation of, 224, 251; commercial resources of Lower, 223; state of Upper, 252; natural frontier of Lower, 253
Ehlers, explorations by, 205
Elephant, preservation of the, 241
Elton, explorations by, 206
Emin Pacha, explorations by, 197; on the Labour Question, 243
Erskine, explorations by, 206
Ethiopian tribes, 112
Europe, area of, compared, 4; influence in Africa of, 125; the Congo State and, 264; dominion in Africa exercised by, 249, 275
European exploration in Africa, 210
Exploration of Africa, 184-213

INDEX.

FAUNA of Africa, 68
Felkin, Dr., referred to, 114
Fellata, see Fulah
Fillani, see Fulah
Fischer, explorations by, 205
Flegel, survey by, 193
Forest, great Congo, 65
Forests, effect of, on rain-supply, 60; primeval, of Africa, 67
Fourneaux, explorations by, 207
Fournel, Marc, quoted, 135
France, area and population of the Possessions of, in Africa, 87; missionary efforts of, 138; and the Slave Trade, 164; enterprise of, 192; and exploration in Africa, 211; in Algeria and Tunis, 210; the dominant political Power in North Africa, 250, 303; on the West Coast, 256, 301; Congo territories of, 261; Germany and, 285; Portugal and, 286; Great Britain and, 302
Fulah, manners and customs of the, 92; characteristics of the, 122
Furtado, maps by, 196
Futa Jallon, highlands of, 28

GABÚN RIVER, estuary of the, 30
Gabún, foundation of the French colony on the, 201; French activity in the territory of, 207
Galla-land, description of, 45; area and population of, 86; tribes of, 111
Galton, explorations by, 205
Gambia River, source of the, 28; discovery of the source of the, 192
Gandu, Joseph Thomson at, 207
Geology of Africa, 4
Germany, area and population of the Possessions of, in Africa, 87; the Slave Trade and, 177; explorers from, in Africa, 193, 211; African Association of, 201; on the West Coast, 257; in the Camarons, 261; in South-West Africa, 265; and Great Britain in East Africa, 274, 303; dispute between Great Britain and, on Bight of Biafra, 283; France and, 285; expansion of, in Africa, 287; East African Association of, 291; Portugal and, 294
Gessi, explorations by, 197
Ghadames, Richardson at, 192
Giraud, journey of, 205
Gold, in the Súdan, search for, 194; in South Africa, 236

Gordon, General, work of, 197
Grant, explorations by, 197
Great Britain, in Lower Egypt, 138, 251; on the West Coast, 256; Germany and, in East Africa, 274; dispute between Germany and, on Bight of Biafra, 283; Portugal and, 297, 305; in Somal-land, 301; see also British
Great Karoo plateau, 39
Great Lakes, total area of the, 87
Grenfell, explorations by, 203, 208
Griqua-land, discovery of diamonds in, 206
Guardafui, Cape, 44
Guinea Coast, Upper, described, 28; diseases of, 76
Gulf of Aden, modifications undergone by the, 27
Gulf of Guinea, description of, 27
Gulfs, absence of, from the coasts of Africa, 4

HAIR of African peoples, 87
Harar, trade of, 225
Hausa, language and characteristics of the, 121
Hawash River, 27
Henry, Prince, the Navigator, 129
Herodotus, knowledge of Africa at the time of, 183
Hikwa, Lake, Captain Storms on, 33; discovery of, 204
Hinterland defined, 280
Höhnel, discoveries by 209
Hornemann, explorations by, 190
Hottentots, position of the, 93; manners and customs of the, 93; dispersal of the, 95
Houghton, expedition under, 189
Humidity and soil, 75
Huxley, Professor, referred to, 125

ICHARGHAR River, dry bed of the, 21
Independent Africa, area and population of, 87
Indian Ocean drainage-basin, 38
Islam in Africa, 121, 314; Christianity and, 129, 150; progress of, 131; southern limit of, 135; outposts of, 136; strongholds of, 138; verdicts for and against, 147, 148; the Slave Trade and, 165
Islands of Africa, area and population, 86; resources, 238
Italy, ascendancy on Red Sea Lit-

Y

toral of, 80, 254 ; area and population of the Possessions of, in Africa, 87 ; explorers from, in Africa, 211 ; on the Red Sea Littoral, 254, 300 ; on the Somâli Coast, 300
Ituri River, *see* Aruwimi
Ivens, explorations by, 203
Ivory, geographical distribution of, 238 ; trade in, 240

JAMES, explorations by, 205
Jarabub, oasis of, 135
Jeppe, journeys of, 206
Jesuits in Africa, 185
Jews in Africa, 131, 140
Johnston, H. H., explorations by, 205
Johnston, Keith, junior, expedition by, 204
Jolof, characteristics of the, 120
Junker, Dr., referred to, 114 ; explorations by, 197
Jur, characteristics of the, 115

KAFIR tribes, 105
Kafraria, Britain in, 206
Kaiser, explorations by, 205
Kalahari Desert, winds of the, 56 ; description of the, 64 ; climate of the, 73 ; exploration of the, 198
Kalunda, *see* Balunda
Kanem, Islam at, 133
Kano, Islam at, 134
Kasai River, obstructions in the beds of tributaries of the, 31 ; advantages of the, 229
Katsena, Islam adopted by the, 134
Keane, Professor, quoted, 86
Kénia, Mount, height of, 7 ; snow on, 57 ; discovery of, 197
Khartûm, the Nile at, 24 ; cataracts between, and Assuan, 26 ; Copts in, 141 ; foundation of, 195 ; trade of, 226
Kibo (Kilima-njaro), height of, 205
Kikibbi River, *see* Semliki
Kilimani River, *see* Kwakwa
Kilima-njaro, height of, 7, 205 ; snow on, 57 ; discovery of, 197 ; exploration of, 205
Kirk, referred to, 199, 280
Kordofan, Arab influence in, 134
Krapf, discovery of Kénia by, 197
Krú, characteristics of the, 120
Kund, explorations by, 203, 208
Kwakwa River, commercial importance of the, 41

Kwamouth, the Congo at, 32
Kwanza River, navigable waters of the, 37

LABOUR Problem, the, 243
Lagos, number of Mohammedans at, 136 ; price of gin at, 242 ; port of, 259
Laing, explorations by, 189
Lakes of Africa, 11 ; total area of, 87 ; *see also various designations*
Lakes Region, Dr. Livingstone in the, 199 ; occupation and survey of the, 203 ; *see also various designations*
Land-breezes, 54
Lander, explorations by the brothers, 190, 191
Languages of Africa, 85, 91
Ledyard, expedition by, 189
Lenz, Dr., referred to, 133
Leopold Lake, discovery of, 203
Liambai, *see* Zambezi
Liberia, present state of, 260
Libyan Desert, described, 63
Limpopo River, description of the, 39 ; discoveries on the, 206
Liquor-traffic, 125, 129, 156, 241, 315
Livingstone, Dr., on Negro character, 98 ; on slavery, 173 ; explorations by, 198, 199 ; death of, 200
Livingstone Mountains, average height of the, 43
Loangwa River, a tributary of the Zambezi, 40
Lomami River, value of the, 36
Lualaba River, affluents of the, 31
Luapula River, 31 ; problem of the, 199
Lucas, expedition by, 189
Lujenda River, 44
Lunda, 306 ; *see also* Balunda
Lupton, explorations by, 197

MADAGASCAR, 8 ; rainfall of North-West, 50 ; malaria in, 75 ; linguistic group in, 90 ; mission stations in, 145 ; value of, 238 ; France in, 275, 302
Madi people, characteristics of the, 115
Madredane Channel (Zambezi), 41
Magyar, explorations by, 201
Maladi, dominions of the, 255
Makololo, character of the, 107, 109

Malarial fevers, 74
Malayo-Polynesians of Madagascar, 93
Mambunda, strength of the, 109
Mandingo, characteristics of the, 121; religious faith of the, 136
Manganya, characteristics of the, 109
Manners and customs of the Central African tribes, 116; see also various tribal names
Mantumba, Lake, discovery of, 203
Manumission of slaves, 175
Maples, explorations by, 204
Maps, Notes on the, by E. G. Ravenstein, F.R.G.S., 323-330
Maravi, Lake, see Nyassa
Masai-land, people of, 111; exploration of, 205
Mashuna, oppression of the, 111
Mashuna-land, gold in, 237; partition of, 297, 305
Mason, explorations by, 197
Massawa (Massowah), trade of, 225; political situation at, 254
Matabele, government of the, 100; manners and customs of the, 111
Matabele-land, discovery of gold in, 206; opening-up of, 237; partition of, 297
Matadi, cataracts between, and Stanley Pool, 34; shipping facilities at, 36
Mauch, explorations by, 206
M'bangi River, 32; navigable waters of the, 35
Mediné, rapids near, 28
Mediterranean Littoral, commercial outlook on the, 219; see also various countries
Mejerda Valley, 221
Mendes, maps by, 196
Merensky, explorations by, 206
Meyer, expedition by, 205
Military organisation of certain tribes, 113, 100, 120
Minerals of South Africa, 236
Missions, Christian, results of, 119, 145
Moero Lake, description of, 31; elevation of, 33; discovery of, 200
Mohammedans, distribution of, 136; see also Islam
Mollien, discovery by, 192
Mombaza, harbour of, 273
Monbuttu, characteristics of the, 88; cannibalism of the, 116
Monsoons of Africa, 55

Moors, characteristics of the, 92; treatment of slaves by the, 120
Morocco, 18; vegetation of, 61; malaria in, 76; area and population of, 86; races of, 91; Jews in, 140; commercial resources of, 221, 250
Mountains, see various designations
"Mountains of the Moon," 183, 195
Mozambique, 270
Muata Yanvo, former kingdom of the, 117
Murchison cataracts, 42
Murray, journey of, 198
Murray, Dr. John, on the discharge of rivers, 11
Murzuk, Hornemann at, 190; trade-centre at, 222

NACHTIGAL, on Wadai, 135; explorations by, 193
Naivasha, Lake, elevation of, 45
Namaqua, characteristics of the, 95
Namaqua-land, discoveries in, 198; acquisition of, by Germany, 265, 294
Negroes, linguistic systems in Africa, 92; characteristics of, 96; domestic life of, 100; character and morals of the, 98; labour by the, 98; government of the, 100; war customs of the, 101; weapons of the, 101; dwellings of the, 102; dress of the, 103; practices of the, 103; religious ideas of the, 104; superstitions of the, 104; trade carried on by the, 104; social development of the, 97, 314
New, journey of, 205
N'gami, Lake, fluctuations of, 12; description of, 38; discovery of, 198
Niam-Niam, cannibals, 88; colour and characteristics of the, 114, 116
Niger, River, description of the, 29; problem of the, 189; Mungo Park and the, 190; final solution of the problem of the, 191; the Landers' discoveries on the, 191; incentives to the exploration of the, 192; Baikie on the, 192; Binger's exploration in the basin of the, 207; German activity in the basin of the, 208; commercial resources of the basin of the, 227; British chartered company on the, 257, 285; routes by the, 313

Nile, length of the, 11, 23; valley of the, 23; sources and lake-reservoirs of the, 23, 210; hydrographic system of the, 24; tributaries of the, 25; means of communication by the, 26; cataracts of the, 26; vegetation of its basin, 62; Ptolemy's knowledge of the source-region of the, 183; Bruce's explorations on the, 185; hydrographical problem of the, 194; discovery of the true source of the, 197; commercial resources of the valley of the, 222; rise and fall of the, 222; basin of the Upper, 225; routes by the, 313
North, W., on malaria, 75
Nubia, malaria in, 75
Nubian Desert, 27, 78
Nner, characteristics of the, 115
Nyassa, Lake, elevation of, 33; description of, 43; Livingstone rediscovers, 199; survey of, 204
Nyassa-land, resources of, 232; British, 271; political situation in, 299

Ocean, influence of the, on temperature, 53
Ogowé River, description of the, 30
Olifant River, exploration of the, 206
O'Neill, explorations by, 204; observations by, 209
Oppel, referred to, 140
Orange River, orographical features between the Congo and the, 36; description of the, 37; communications by the, 38
Oswell, journey of, 198
Oudney, explorations by, 191
Ovaherero, characteristics of the, 108
Ovampo, manners and customs of the, 108
Ovampo-land, exploration of, 205
Overweg, explorations by, 193

Pagan tribes of Africa, 136, 307
Park, Mungo, explorations by, 190
Partition, political, of Africa, 279–307
Pasture-lands of South Africa, 237
Peddie, explorations by, 190
Peters, in East Africa, 288
Petherick, journey of, 196
Pinto, Serpa, explorations by, 203, 204

Playfair, Lambert, on North Africa, 220; quoted, 250
Political partition of Africa, 279–307
Population of Africa, 86
Porto, Silva, explorations by, 201
Port Said, increase in the importance of, 225
Portugal, area and population of the Possessions of, in Africa, 87; explorers from, in Africa, 133, 184, 185, 211; the Slave Trade and, 177; Possessions of, in Africa, 260, 264, 270; France and, 286; Germany and, 294; Great Britain and, 297, 305
Products of Africa, *see* Commercial resources
Ptolemy, knowledge of Africa at the time of, 183, 193
Pygmy tribes, 95; occupations of the, 96

Races of Africa, classification of the, 87
Railways, projected or in course of construction, in the Congo State, 208, 230; in Algeria, 219; in Angola, 232; in East Africa, 235; in South Africa, 237
Rainfall of Africa, 55
Rainy seasons in Africa, 57
Rankin, explorations by, 41, 209
Ratzel, Dr., referred to, 96, 99, 105, 120
Ravenstein, E. G., on the area and population of Africa, 86; *see also* Maps
Rebmann, discovery of Kilima-njaro by, 197
Red Sea, drainage-area of the, 27; Arabs cross the, 133; Slave Trade on the, 168; Italy on the Littoral, 254, 300
Reichard, expedition of, 205; on the distribution of the African elephant, 241
Richardson, expeditions by, 192
Rivers, lengths of various, 11; discharge of, 11; of the Cape, 39; sources of African, 56; *see also* rivers of Africa, under their various names
Rohlfs, explorations by, 193
Romans in Africa, 60; use of elephants by the, 241
Ronvier, explorations by, 208
Rovuma River, description of the, 44; Dr. Livingstone on the, 200

INDEX.

Rudolf Lake, mapping of, 209
Ruwenzori Mountains, probable height of the, 7; snow on the, 57; discovery of the, 210

SAHARA, difficulties presented by the, 12; description of the, 18, 63; water supply of the, 21; salt deposits of the, 21; want of means of communication through the, 22; rainfall of the, 56; fauna of the, 69; climate of the, 73; malaria in the, 76; area and population of the, 86; people of the, 91; wild tribes of the, 92; Islam in the, 131, 133, 135, 138; the Slave Trade in the, 168; exploration of the, 191; overland journeys across the, 192; German travellers in the, 211; commercial resources of the, 222, 226; state of the Western, 260; British and Spanish settlements in the, 301
Saldana Bay, a natural harbour, 38
Salisbury, Marquis of, on Egypt, 251; on the Anglo-Portuguese controversy, 298; as negotiator of treaties with Germany and Portugal, 306
Samburru, Lake, see Rudolf Lake
Sankuru River, 31, 33
San Salvador, early Christian missions at, 142; results of Bastian's visit to, 201
São Thomé, position of labourers at, 244
Savannas of Africa, 68
Sawâkin, proposed railway at, 26; climate of, 79; as a base, 254
Schweinfurth, referred to, 88, 217; explorations by, 197
Sea-breezes, 54
Semliki River, description of the, 24; exploration of the, 210
Senegal River, description of the, 28; discovery of the source of the, 192
Senegambia, exploration of, 185; France in, 259
Senusi, power and propagandism of the, 134
Settlements, and drainage-areas compared, 12; European, 78, 80, 180
Shari River, description of the, 22
Shark Point, the Congo at, 34
Shillûk, characteristics of the, 115
Shindé River, see Chindé

Shiré Highlands, political situation in the, 299
Shiré River, description of the, 41
Shirwa, Lake, description of, 43; referred to, 44; discovery of, 199
Shoa, trade of, 225; Italy and, 300
Shuli, characteristics of the, 115
Sierra Leone, rainfall of, 56; the population of, 118; number of Mohammedans in, 136; price of spirits at, 242
Siut, Copts at, 141
Siwah, oasis of, 135
Slavery, on the West Coast, 119; in Africa and elsewhere, 163; abolition of, and Act of Emancipation, 163; predisposing causes of, 171; the legal status of, 175
Slaves, demand for and supply of, 165; Red Sea Traffic in, 168; the Great Desert Traffic in, 168; West Coast Traffic in, 169; the East Coast Traffic in, 169; methods of obtaining, 172; measures against the Traffic in, 174; manumission of, 175; conclusions concerning the Traffic in, 174-180, 315
Slave Trade, public opinion on the, 161; in Africa, 162; Europe and the, 164; Islam and the, 165; causes of the, 165; adjuncts of the, 166; measures against the, 167; condition and extent of the, 167; total annual number of victims to the, 170; incentives to the, 171; resources of the, 173; measures against the, 174; suppression of the, 176; the Congo State and the, 177; pacific measures against the, 178; police measures against the, 179
Snow-line in Africa, 57
Sobat River, description of the, 24
Soils of Africa, 58; humidity and, 75
Sokoto, Clapperton's journey to, 191; Thomson at, 207; resources of, 227; Britain and, 259, 285, 302
Somâli-land, description of, 45; area and population of, 86; people of, 111; traditions concerning the Arabs in, 133; discoveries in, 205; Italy and Great Britain in, 275, 300;
"Sphere of influence," defined, 282;
Spain, area and population of the Possessions of, in Africa, 87; Great Britain and, 260, 301
Speke, explorations by, 197

Spirits, trade in, 125, 129, 156, 162, 241, 315
Stairs, Lieutenant, on Mount Ruwenzori, 210
Stanley, referred to, 36, 139; on the Great Congo forest, 65; discovery of Pygmies by, 96; search for Dr. Livingstone by, 200; explorations by, 197, 202, 209
Stanley Falls, 31
Stanley Pool, cataracts between, and Matadi, 34
Stevenson Road, length of the, 42; awarded to Britain, 303
Stewart, surveys by, 204
Storms, Captain, on Lake Hikwa, 33
Suakin, *see* Sawákin
Súdan, malaria in the, 75; access to the Central, 80; area and population of the, 86; Islam and Arab influence in the, 134, 138; education in the, 138; search for gold in the Eastern, 194; German travellers in the, 211; trade of the, 226; political situation in the, 253; loss of the, 255; *see also various countries*
Suez Canal, 4; and Europe, 224
Swazi-land, political situation in, 298

TANA RIVER, description of the, 45; navigation of the, 205
Tanganika, Lake, overflow waters of, 31; description of, 33; Burton at, 197; Livingstone at, 200; Cameron at, 200; Thomson at, 204; English mission on, 271
Tappenbeck, explorations by, 203, 208
Tariffs in South Africa, 269
Tattooing, custom of, 103
Teleki, discoveries by, 209
Thomson, referred to, 18, 132, 226; treaties made by, 138, 207; explorations by, 204
Tibesti Mountains, height of the, 19
Timbuktu, the Niger at, 29; history of, 133; a goal of early exploration, 186; first reached by Laing, 190; French efforts to reach, 192; trade of, 222
Tippu Tib, referred to, 167; influence of, 263
Tizi-n-Tamjurt (Atlas Mountains), height of, 18
Trade-routes, 166, 225, 240
Trade-winds, 54

Transvaal, progress of discovery in the, 206; discovery of gold in the, 206; mining in the, 236; political situation in the, 269
Treaties, with native chiefs, 281, 300; between European Powers in Africa, 282–306
Tripoli, vegetation of, 62; malaria in, 75; area and population of, 86; Slave Trade in, 109; commercial resources of, 221
Trivier, overland journey by, 211
Tsad, Lake, 10, 12; basin of, 21; discovery of, 191
Tsana, Lake, 24
Tuareg, the, 91, 121; at Timbuktu, 133
Tuat, area and population of, 86
Tuckey, explorations by, 190, 196
Tunis, highlands of, 17; flora of, 62; area and population of, 86; Jews in, 140; commerce of, 219; political situation in, 250
Turkey, area and population of the Possessions of, in Africa, 87

UGANDA, a modern battlefield, 139; *see also* Waganda
Ujiji, meeting of Livingstone and Stanley at, 200
Unyoro, *see* Wanyoro

VAAL RIVER, discovery of diamonds at the, 206; proposed railway to the, 238
Van Gèle, explorations by, 203
Vegetation of Africa, 61; climate and, 72
Victoria Falls, description of the, 42; discovery of the, 199; projected railway to the, 237
Victoria Nyanza, the source-reservoir of the Nile, 23, 197; Speke and Grant at the, 197; Stanley at the, 202, 210; projected railway to, 235, 273
Vitu, Great Britain and, 274, 304; Germany and, 291
Vogel, explorations by, 193
Volta River, drainage by the, 207
Von der Decken, explorations by, 200
Von François, explorations by, 203, 208
Vryburg, projected railway to, 237

INDEX. 343

WADAI, power of the Mahdists in, 135; area and population of, 135; Nachtigal's journey to, 193
Wadi Halfa, the natural frontier of Lower Egypt, 253
Waganda, characteristics of the, 113; *see also* Uganda
Walvisch Bay, 37, 206, 266, 284, 293
Wa-Nyassa, characteristics of the, 109
Wanyoro, characteristics of the, 113
War customs of the Negroes, 101
Warren, Sir Charles, referred to, 297
Weapons of the Negroes, 101
Weissenborn, explorations by, 208
Wellé River, discovery of the, 197
Westendarp, on ivory, 241
Wissmann, referred to, 177, 230, 272, 292; explorations by, 203
Witwatersrand, rapid growth of, 236
Wolf, explorations by, 203, 208
Wollo-Galla, characteristics of the, 111
Wolof, the, 136

ZAMBEZI, compared with the Congo, 39; as a commercial highway, 39, 42; catchment-basin of the, 40; delta of the, 40; Rankin's discovery on the, 41, 209; means of communication by the, 42; ethnography of the valley of the, 108; tribes of the, 109; discovery of the, 198; problem of the, 199; Great Britain, Portugal, and the, 233, 271; ivory trade in the basin of the, 240; freedom of navigation to all nations on the, 306; value of the routes by the, 312
Zanzibar, mainland and island of, 45; disturbances on the Coast, 209; commercial resources of, 233; Slave Trade of, 234; products of, 234; Great Britain and Germany on, 272, 289; German acquisition of, 290; Anglo-French Agreement concerning, 302
Zintgraff, explorations by, 208
Zöller, explorations by, 208
Zoutspansberg, Boers at, 206
Zulu, characteristics of the, 106
Zulu-land, partition of, 296
Zumbo, Portuguese district of, 305

THE END.

GEORGE PHILIP AND SON, LONDON AND LIVERPOOL.

AFRICA
HEIGHT OF LAND.

- Over 10,000 feet
- 6000 to 10,000 feet
- 3000 to 6000 feet
- 600 to 3000 feet
- Sea Level to 600 feet
- Below Sea Level

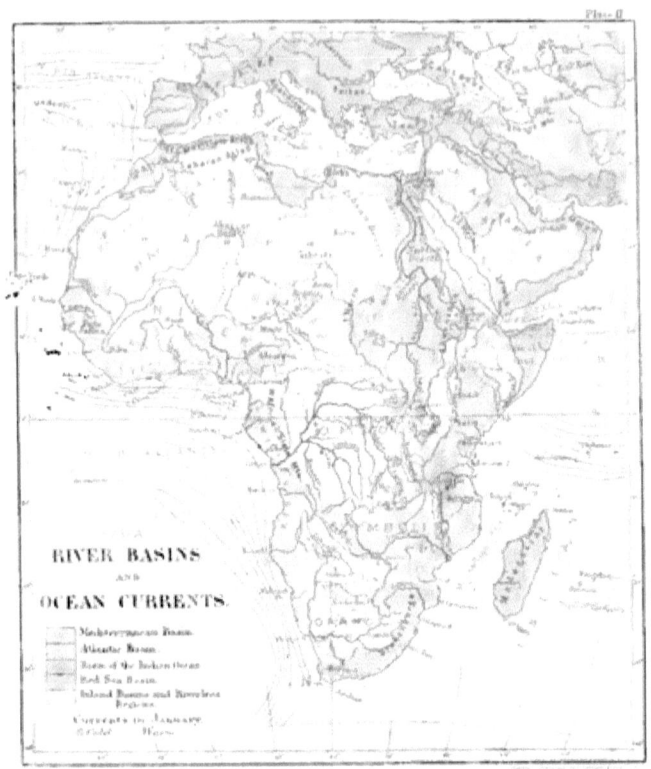

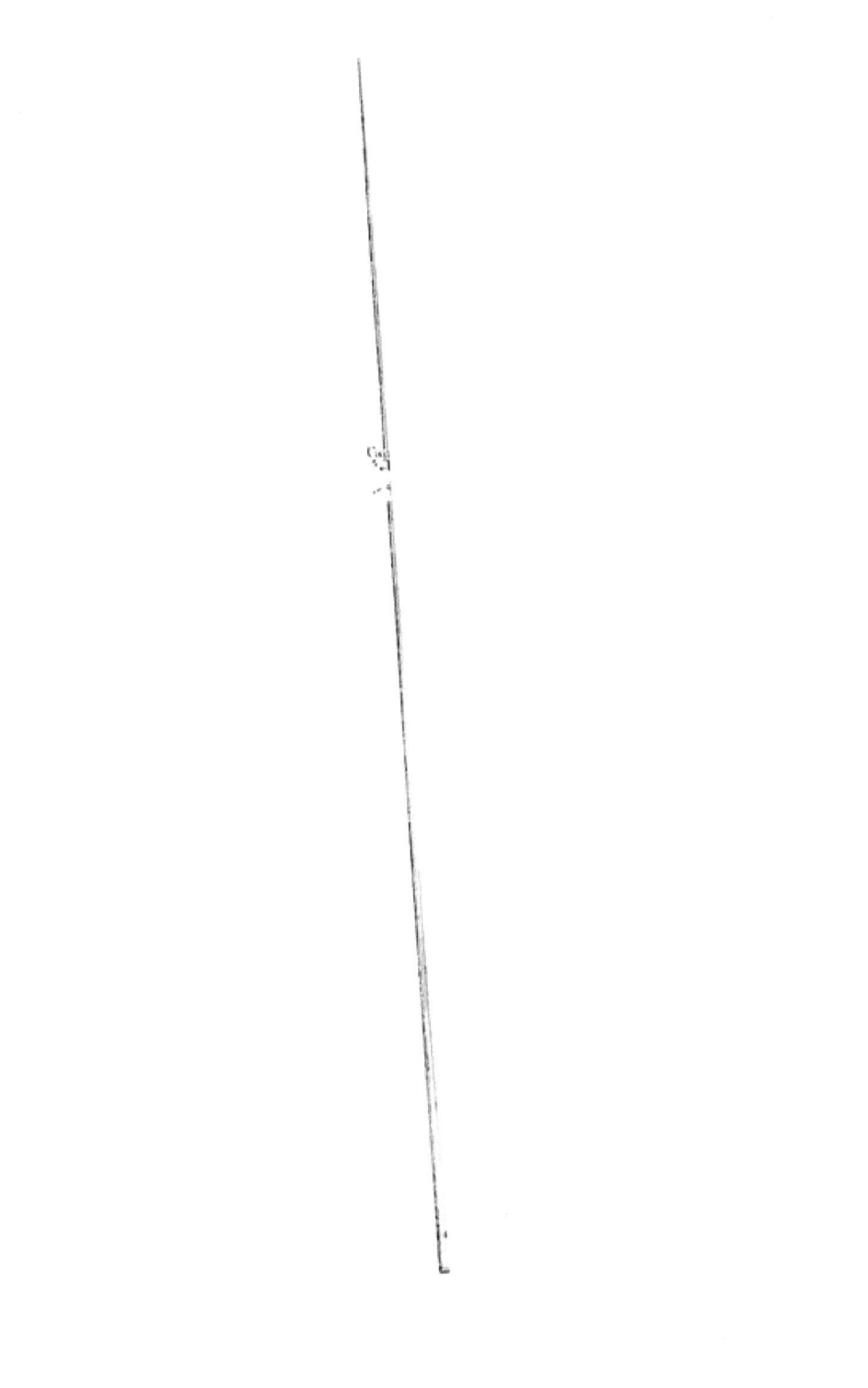

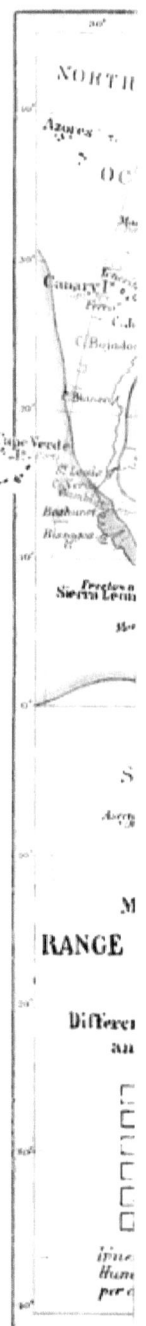

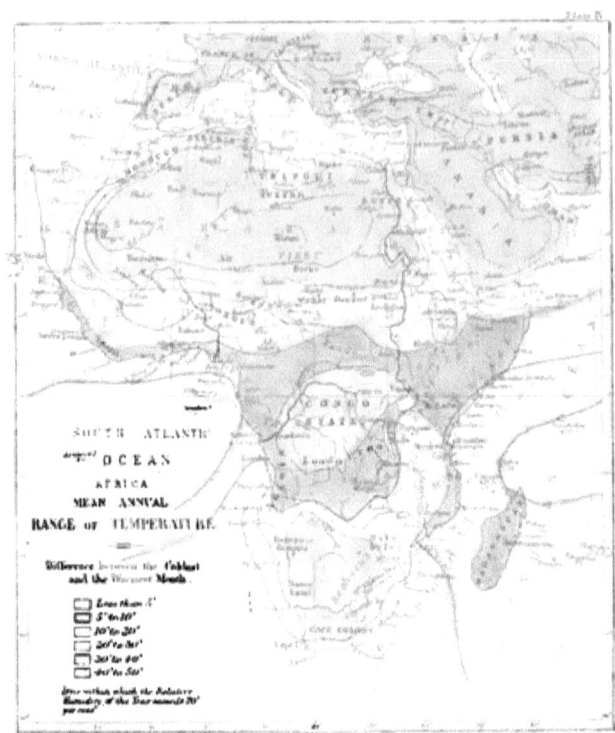

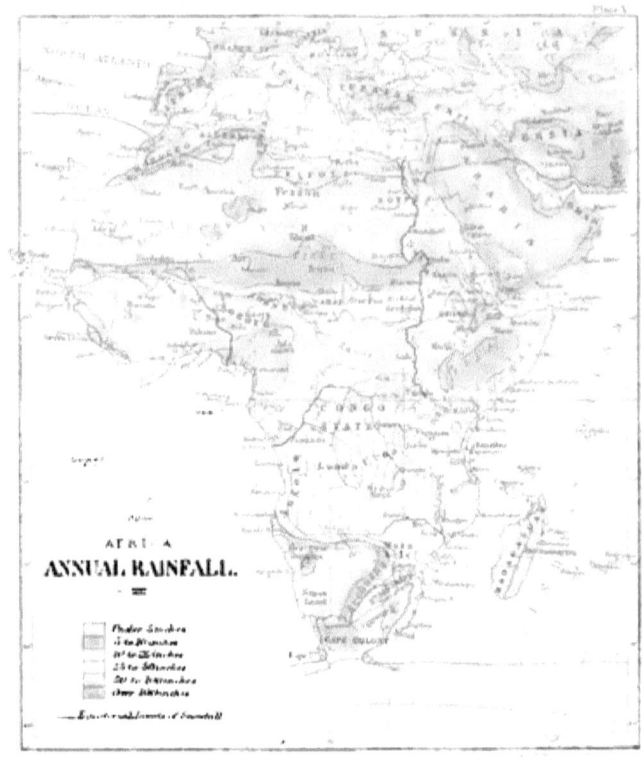

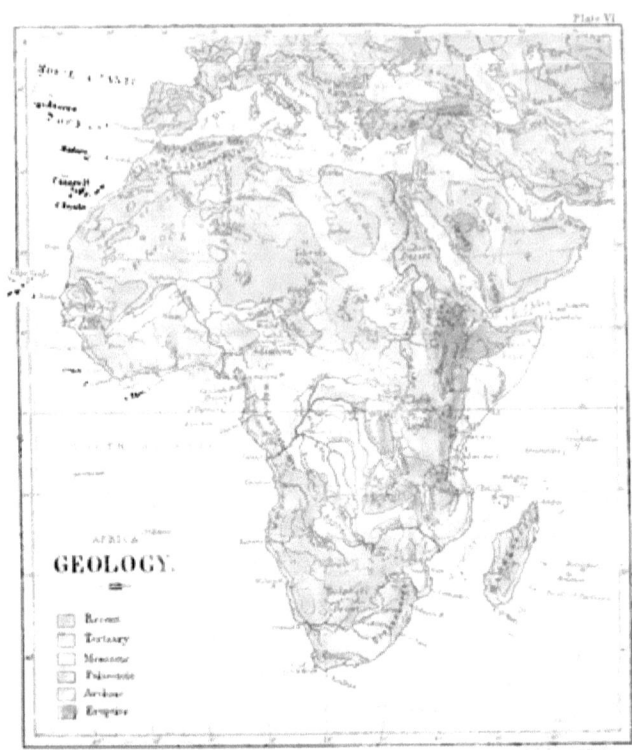

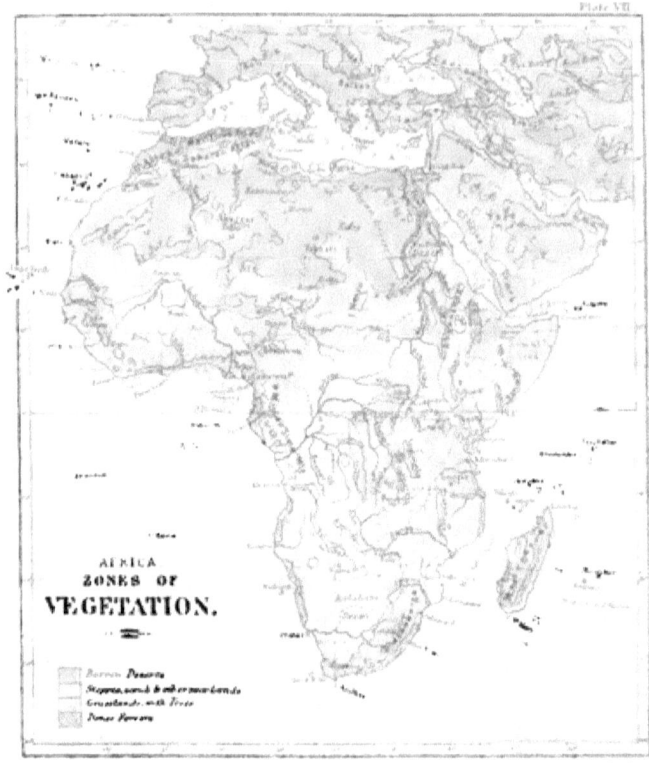

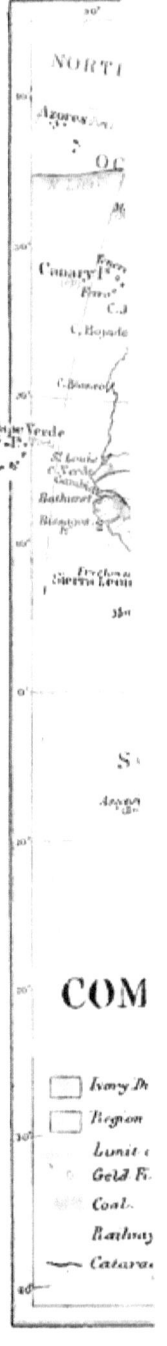

COMMERCIAL.

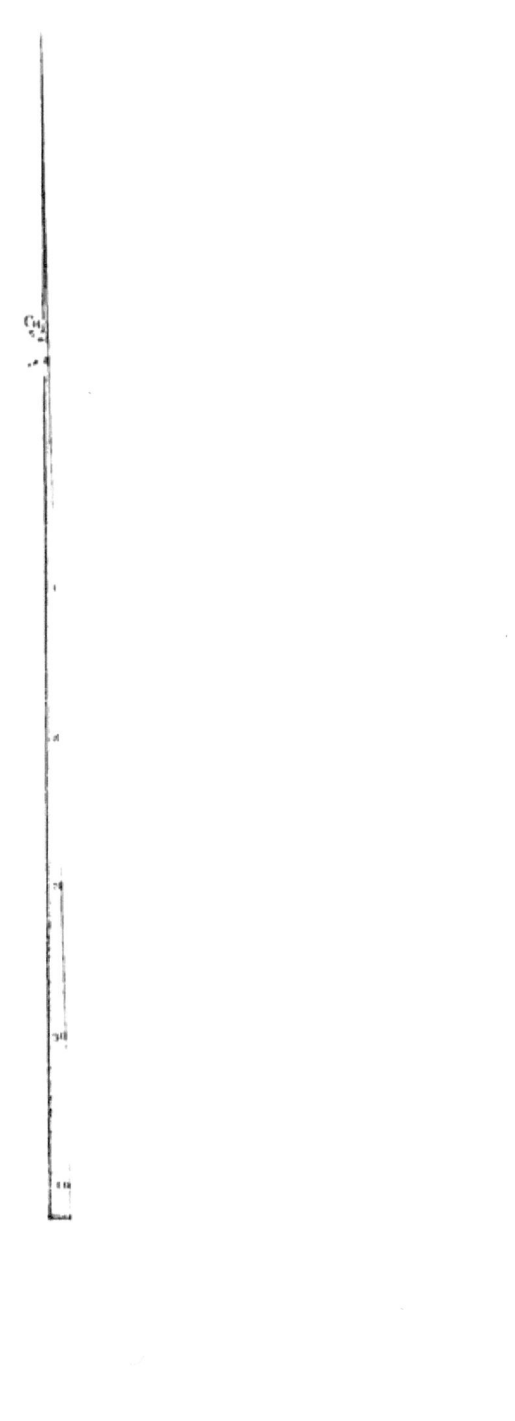

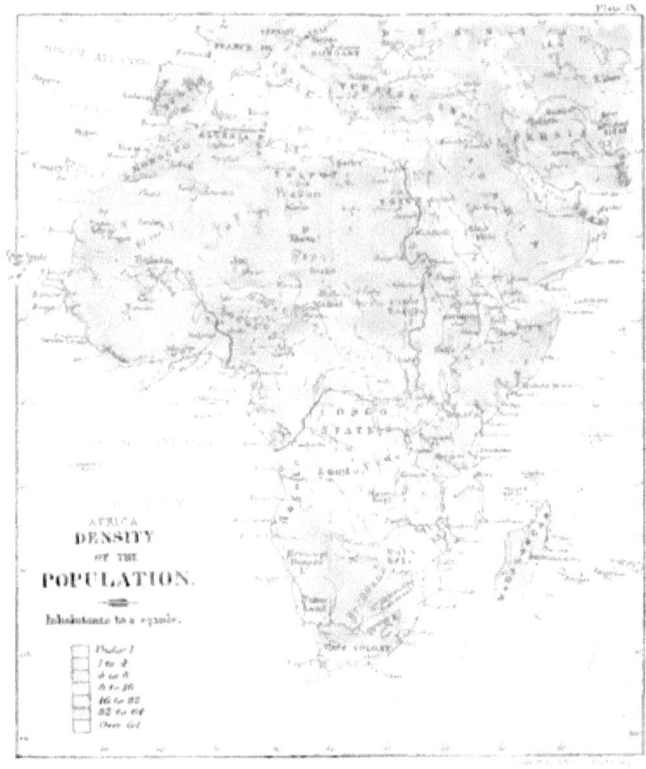

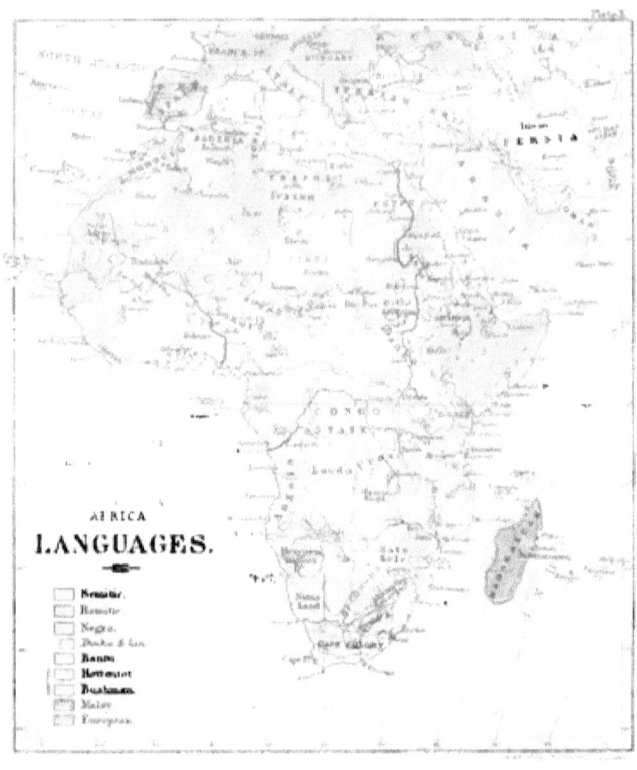

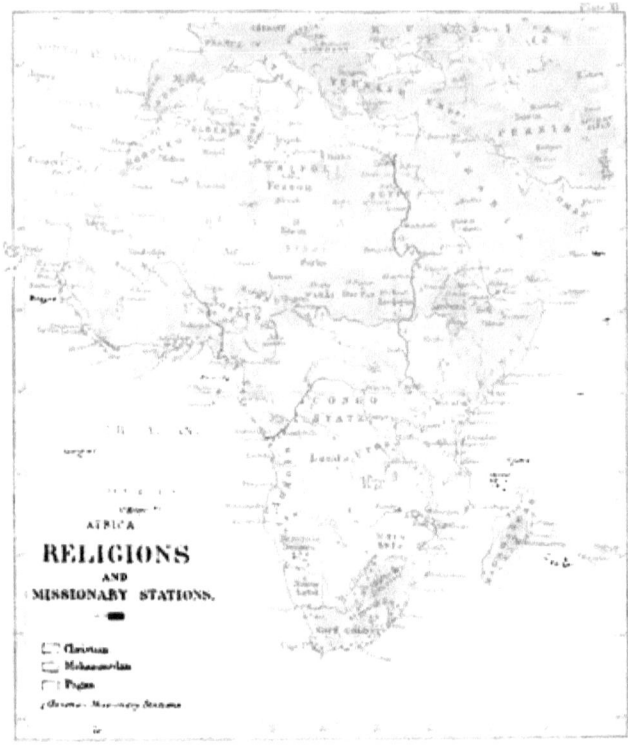

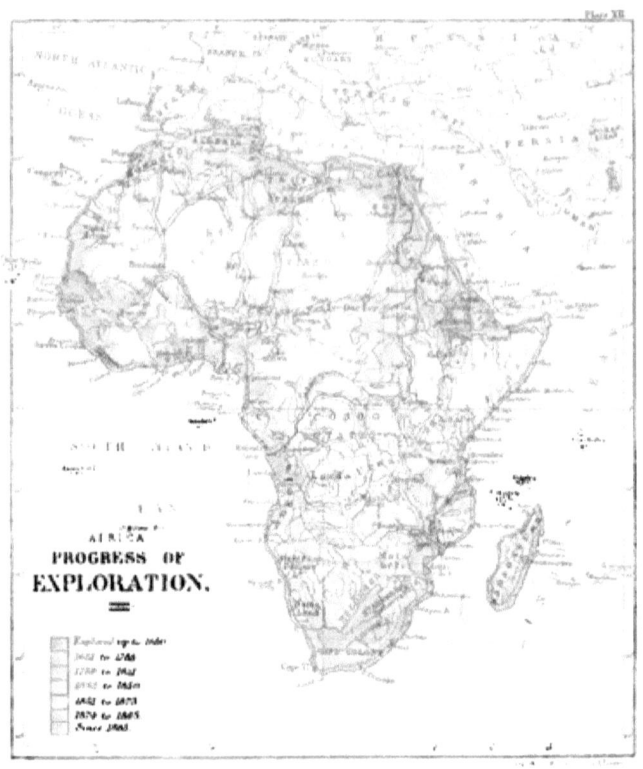

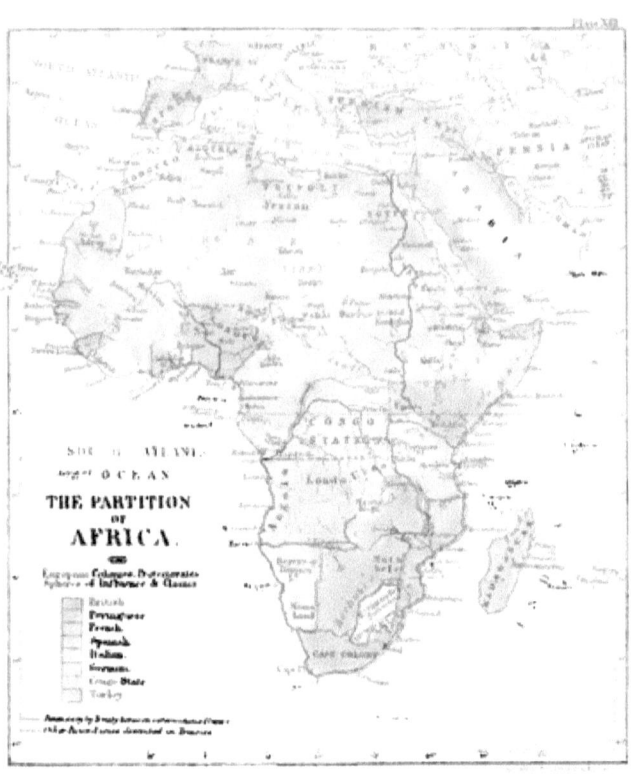

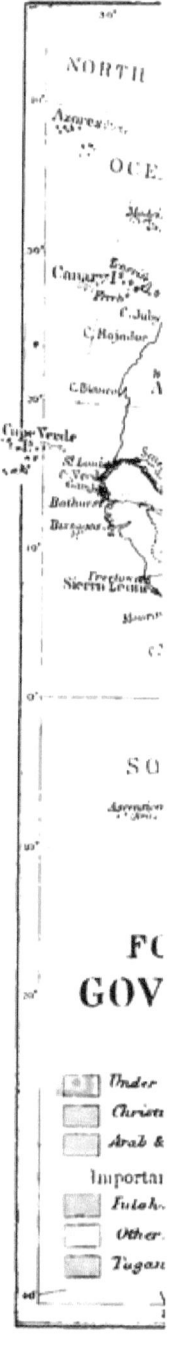

LONDON, 32 FLEET STREET,
NOVEMBER 1890.

GEORGE PHILIP & SON'S LIST

OF

NEW & FORTHCOMING BOOKS OF TRAVEL

AND

GEOGRAPHICAL PUBLICATIONS.

1. **ACROSS EAST AFRICAN GLACIERS,** being an Account of the First Ascent of Mount Kilimanjaro by Dr. HANS MEYER. One volume, super royal 8vo, containing upwards of 40 Illustrations, consisting of Photographs, Heliogravures, and Coloured Frontispiece in *Aquarelle*, accompanied by 2 Coloured Maps. Also a limited Large Paper Edition (not exceeding 50 copies), *sur japon*.
   [*Ready in December.*

2. **THE LIFE OF FERDINAND MAGELLAN,** First Circumnavigator of the Globe. By Dr. F. H. H. GUILLEMARD, Author of the "Cruise of the *Marchesa*," with 20 Illustrations and 18 Maps. Forming Vol. IV. of "The World's Great Explorers and Explorations." Crown 8vo, cloth, 4s. 6d.; or handsomely bound in half polished morocco, marbled edges, price 7s. 6d. [*Just Published.*

3. **HOME LIFE ON AN OSTRICH FARM.** A Brightly-written Account of Life in the Interior of South Africa. By ANNIE MARTIN. With 11 Illustrations. Crown 8vo, antique cover, price 7s. 6d. [*Just Published.*

4. **THE UNKNOWN HORN OF AFRICA.** An Exploration from Berbera to the Leopard River. By the late F. L. JAMES, M.A., Author of "The Wild Tribes of the Soudan." With 27 Illustrations and Map. New and Cheap Edition, containing the Narrative portion and Notes only, to which have been added an Obituary Notice and Portrait. Crown 8vo, price 7s. 6d.

5. **APPLIED GEOGRAPHY.** A Preliminary Sketch by J. SCOTT KELTIE, Librarian of the Royal Geographical Society. With numerous Coloured Maps and Diagrams. Crown 8vo, price 3s. 6d.
   [*Just Published.*

6. **THREE YEARS IN WESTERN CHINA.** A Narrative of Three Journeys in Ssŭ-Ch'uan, Kuei-Chow, and Yun-nan. By ALEXANDER HOSIE, M.A., F.R.G.S., H.B.M. Consular Service, China, with an Introduction by ARCHIBALD LITTLE, F.R.G.S. Eight Full-page Illustrations and a Large Coloured Map, showing the Author's Routes. Demy 8vo, price 14s. [*Just Published.*

"This volume comes at a peculiarly appropriate time. Mr. Hosie, who knows more about it, since the lamented death of Mr. Baber, than any one now living, except, possibly, Mr. Archibald Little, who writes the Introduction to the work, comes forward and answers, in an authoritative way, most of the questions that are being put in relation to Chung-king as a trade centre, and to the trade and productions of the great provinces of Ssŭ-Ch'uan, Kuei-Chow, and Yun-nan." — *Times.*

7. A NATURALIST AMONG THE HEAD-HUNTERS. Being an Account of Three Visits to the Solomon Islands in the years 1886, 1887, and 1888. By CHARLES MORRIS WOODFORD, F.R.G.S., F.Z.S. With 16 Full-page Illustrations and 3 Coloured Maps. Second Edition. Crown 8vo, price 8s. 6d. [*Just Published.*

"Mr. Woodford may be warmly congratulated on what we gather is his first literary venture. He has written in a pleasant and unaffected style a decidedly interesting account of a rarely visited country. We trust the public may again hear from his pen a work which can be as unreservedly recommended as this interesting little book."—*Athenæum.*

THE WORLD'S GREAT EXPLORERS & EXPLORATIONS.

Edited by J. SCOTT KELTIE, H. J. MACKINDER, M.A., and E. G. RAVENSTEIN, F.R.G.S.

The following Volumes are already published, and may now be obtained in three different bindings:— Price per vol.
1. Plain neat cloth cover 4/6
2. Cloth gilt cover, specially designed by Lewis F. Day, gilt edges 5/-
3. Half-bound polished morocco, marbled edges . . . 7/6

1. JOHN DAVIS, Arctic Explorer and Early India Navigator. By CLEMENTS R. MARKHAM, C.B. Crown 8vo. With 24 Illustrations and 4 Coloured Maps.

"If the succeeding volumes attain the high standard of excellence of this 'Life of John Davis,' the series will, when complete, form a biographical history of geographical discovery of the utmost value and interest."—*Academy.*

2. PALESTINE. By Major C. R. CONDER, R.E., Leader of the Palestine Exploring Expeditions. Crown 8vo. With 26 Illustrations and 7 Coloured Maps.

"It is charmingly written, contains much information in a convenient form, and is well illustrated by woodcuts and maps."—*Athenæum.*

3. MUNGO PARK AND THE NIGER. By JOSEPH THOMSON, Author of "Through Masai Land." Crown 8vo. With 24 Illustrations and 7 Coloured Maps.

"Mr. Thomson's book is to be strongly recommended to all who wish to understand the position in Africa to-day, as an intelligent Englishman should do."—*Saturday Review.*

RECENT AFRICAN TRAVEL.

Cheap Edition. Crown 8vo, price 7s. 6d.

TRAVELS IN THE ATLAS AND SOUTHERN MOROCCO. A Narrative of Exploration. By JOSEPH THOMSON, F.R.G.S., Author of "Through Masai Land." With 68 Illustrations from Photographs taken by the Author, and 6 Maps.

"Apart from the distinct value of Mr. Thomson's volume as a contribution to our knowledge of Morocco, it is most attractively written."—*Times.*
"Mr. Thomson's book is a most praiseworthy one; it is not only the best which he has yet written, but one of the most admirable which has ever appeared on Morocco."—*Academy.*

Cheap Edition. Demy 8vo, price 8s. nett.

EMIN PACHA IN CENTRAL AFRICA. Being a Collection of his Letters and Journals. Edited and Annotated by Prof. G. SCHWEINFURTH, Prof. F. RATZEL, Dr. R. W. FELKIN, and Dr. G. HARTLAUB. Forming the only existing Record of his Life and Work in Central Africa.

"A record of the highest type of exploring work. Every page abounds with interest."—*Times.*

GEORGE PHILIP & SON, 32 FLEET STREET, LONDON, E.C.

www.ingramcontent.com/pod-product-compliance
Lightning Source LLC
Chambersburg PA
CBHW032034220426
43664CB00006B/474